ANGLO-SAXON
MILITARY
INSTITUTIONS

Oxford University Press, Amen House, London E.C.4

GLASGOW NEW YORK TORONTO MELBOURNE WELLINGTON
BOMBAY CALCUTTA MADRAS KARACHI LAHORE DACCA
CAPE TOWN SALISBURY NAIROBI IBADAN ACCRA
KUALA LUMPUR HONG KONG

ANGLO-SAXON
MILITARY
INSTITUTIONS

ON THE EVE OF
THE NORMAN CONQUEST

BY

C. WARREN HOLLISTER

OXFORD
AT THE CLARENDON PRESS
1962

PRINTED IN GREAT BRITAIN

TO THE MEMORY OF

DAVID K. BJORK

PREFACE

IT is best to warn the reader immediately that this is a study in institutional history rather than military history. The subject of my investigations has been the organization of the late-Saxon military establishment rather than the art of war. During the warlike age with which this study deals, military organization had economic, social, and political overtones of no small significance. So while the pages that follow may be disappointing to the devotee of military campaigns, battle plans, and vivid combat narratives, they will, it is hoped, prove interesting to students of Old English institutions.

My approach is topical and analytical rather than chronological. Like most institutions, the Anglo-Saxon military system was developing constantly, but rather than to trace its evolution, I have preferred to analyse it as it existed at a particular point in time, or rather at a particular era in English history. I call this era 'late-Saxon England', but I interpret that term rather narrowly to include only the century or so prior to the Norman Conquest. My emphasis, indeed, is upon the reigns of the last two Saxon kings—Edward the Confessor and Harold Godwinson. The problem of development cannot, of course, be ignored, but it is not stressed.

My reason for this approach is the paucity of sources and the general obscurity of the subject. An anonymous scholarly critic wrote in connexion with one of my articles: 'I do not think that whoever advised the author to turn to the Anglo-Saxon army was being very kind. Never was there a more treacherous bog to stray into than this.' There is much truth in these remarks, although I must myself take full responsibility for my intellectual peregrinations.

The Old English military structure is indeed a 'treacherous bog', and I would not have attempted to explore it without the incomparable Domesday Book as a guide. Unhappily, Domesday carries us back only to the end of the Confessor's reign, and although the Anglo-Saxon records are valuable supplements to the Domesday material, they are in themselves an inadequate foundation on which to build. Accordingly, any attempt to reconstruct the fyrd prior to the eleventh century is bound to be highly speculative, and I have preferred, for that reason, to focus on the later period, using earlier documents only to help clarify the situation as it existed on the eve of the Conquest.

The debt which I owe to previous historians is too great to be expressed adequately in my footnotes. At this point I would like to mention one man in particular, Sir Frank Stenton, whose distinguished scholarship has been a challenge and an inspiration to me and to a whole generation of historians. In the present study I disagree with Professor Stenton on several matters. At times I quote him in support of a position which I later attempt to refute. I do this, not in the spirit of antagonism, but out of respect, for even when his conclusions are echoed by numerous other authorities, they are nowhere else expressed so lucidly and convincingly as in his own writings. One cannot study Anglo-Saxon institutions today without reckoning with the sagacious investigations of this great scholar.

I would like to express my deepest appreciation to Professor David K. Bjork, who has made the Middle Ages come alive for thousands of grateful students and who, during my years as a graduate student, gave generously of his time and his wisdom, guiding me with patience and insight through my first researches in medieval history. I am also indebted to the library of the University of California, Santa Barbara, and to the Library of Congress, the libraries of Harvard, Yale, and Berkeley, and the many others which made materials available to me on inter-library loan. The library of the University of California, Los Angeles, accorded me full faculty privileges without which the present work would have been much delayed. Some of the research for this study was made possible by a Haynes Foundation Fellowship in 1959, and I have also received generous support from the Committee on Research of the University of California, Santa Barbara. Finally, I am profoundly grateful for the help and encouragement of my wife and my parents.

C. W. H.

Santa Barbara, California
September 1960

CONTENTS

ABBREVIATIONS

A.H.R.	*American Historical Review.*
A.S.C.	*Anglo-Saxon Chronicle: Two of the Saxon Chronicles Parallel*, ed. Charles Plummer, 2 vols., Oxford, 1892.
A.S. Chart.	*Anglo-Saxon Charters*, ed. A. J. Robertson, Cambridge, England, 1939.
A.S. Wills	*Anglo-Saxon Wills*, ed. D. Whitelock, Cambridge, England, 1930.
A.S. Writs	*Anglo-Saxon Writs*, ed. F. E. Harmer, Manchester, 1952.
Birch, *C.S.*	*Cartularium Saxonicum*, ed. W. de G. Birch, 3 vols., London, 1885-93.
C.Ch.R.	*Calendar of Charter Rolls*, London, 1903 ff.
Chron. Ab.	*Chronicon Monasterii de Abingdon*, ed. J. Stevenson, Rolls Series, 2 vols., London, 1858.
Chron. Pet.	*Chronicon Petroburgense*, ed. T. Stapleton, Camden Society, London, 1849.
C.P.R.	Calendar of Patent Rolls, London, 1891 ff.
Crawford	*The Crawford Collection of Early Charters and Documents*, ed. A. S. Napier and W. H. Stevenson, Oxford, 1895.
D.B.	Domesday Book, 4 vols., Record Commission, 1783-1816.
E.H.R.	*English Historical Review.*
Feud. Docs.	*Feudal Documents from the Abbey of Bury St. Edmunds*, ed. D. C. Douglas, British Academy Records, VIII, London, 1932.
Fl. Wig.	*Florentii Wigorniensis Monachi Chronicon ex Chronicis*, ed. B. Thorpe, 2 vols., London, 1848-9.
H. of Hunt.	Henry of Huntingdon, *Historia Anglorum*, ed. T. Arnold, Rolls Series, London, 1879.
Kemble, *C.D.*	*Codex Diplomaticus Aevi Saxonici*, ed. J. M. Kemble, 6 vols., London, 1839-48.
Maitland, *D.B.B.*	F. W. Maitland, *Domesday Book and Beyond*, Cambridge, England, 1897.
M.G.H.	*Monumenta Germaniae Historica.*
Ord. Vit.	Ordericus Vitalis, *Historia Ecclesiastica*, ed. A. le Prévost, 5 vols., Paris, 1838-55.
P.R.	*Pipe Rolls*. Record Commission and Pipe Roll Society.
R.B.E.	*The Red Book of the Exchequer*, ed. H. Hall, 3 vols., Rolls Series, 1896.

Round, *F.E.*	J. H. Round, *Feudal England*, London, 1895.
R.R.A.N.	*Regesta Regum Anglo-Normannorum, 1066–1154*: vol. I, *Regesta Willelmi Conquestoris et Willelmi Rufi, 1066–1100*, ed. H. W. C. Davis, Oxford, 1913; vol. II, *Regesta Henrici Primi, 1100–1135*, ed. C. Johnson and H. A. Cronne, Oxford, 1956.
R.S.	Rolls Series, *Rerum Britannicarum Medii Aevi Scriptores*, London, 1858 ff.
Stenton, *A.S.E.*	F. M. Stenton, *Anglo-Saxon England*, 2nd ed., Oxford, 1947.
Stenton, *E.F.*	F. M. Stenton, *The First Century of English Feudalism, 1066–1166*, Oxford, 1932.
T.R.H.S.	*Transactions of the Royal Historical Society.*
V.C.H.	*Victoria History of the Counties of England*, Westminster, 1900 ff.
Wm. Malm.	*Willemli Malmesbiriensis Monachi De Gestis Regum Anglorum*, ed. W. Stubbs, 2 vols., Rolls Series, 1887–9.

INTRODUCTION

I

THE Norman Conquest has always been recognized as one of the great watersheds in English history. To many historians it looms as a stark exception to the evolutionary nature of English growth—a harbinger of radical changes in the organization and orientation of English society. It raises one of the most intriguing and perennial of intellectual problems: the issue of evolution versus revolution as the basis of historical development.

Ever since the appearance in the eighteen-nineties of John Horace Round's perceptive essays on the subject of Anglo-Norman feudalism, historians have tended strongly toward the opinion that the Norman Conquest represented a radical break in continuity, at least as regards the English military structure.[1] Since Round's time, much has been written on the subject of the military organization of post-Conquest England,[2] and most of the work done on this subject has tended to confirm Round's thesis that Anglo-Norman feudalism was fundamentally Norman rather than English in its origin. Much work remains to be done, however, before the issue can be settled conclusively, and our investigations must go beyond the confines of the Anglo-Norman age itself. For no matter how well we understand the military system of post-Conquest England (and I doubt that we understand it as well as we might), we cannot determine the origins of that system without understanding also the military structures which preceded it, both in Normandy and in Anglo-Saxon England. Charles Homer Haskins's work on Norman military institutions is now being followed up by more detailed studies in the pre-Conquest Norman sources,[3] but the military organization of Anglo-Saxon

---

[1] On this subject, see my article, 'The Norman Conquest and the Genesis of English Feudalism', *A.H.R.* lxvi (1961), 641–63.

[2] One of the best of these studies is Stenton, *E.F.*

[3] See C. H. Haskins, *Norman Institutions* (Cambridge, Mass., 1918).

England on the eve of the Norman Conquest remains a subject of confusion and obscurity. This situation is most unfortunate, for military organization was one of the most basic aspects of Old English society. It was, indeed, a matter of life or death for the Anglo-Saxon state. In the three centuries prior to 1066, England had lived under the ominous threat of Norse invasion, and during the brief reign of Harold Godwinson, the last of the Saxon kings, the Scandinavian menace was coupled with the danger of a Norman attack. Yet existing studies on the subject are, by and large, inadequate and contradictory. The most promising investigation of the pre-Conquest army was undertaken early in the present century by Sir Paul Vinogradoff.[1] His work was scholarly and perceptive, and although only a beginning, it pointed in the right direction. Unfortunately, it was not followed up, either by Vinogradoff himself or by his successors. Instead, his fruitful insights and cautious conclusions have been ignored. As a result, the subject is now in such a state of confusion as to daunt the most indefatigable student. One is told that the Anglo-Saxon thegn owed military service as a result of the military obligation resting upon his land,[2] and again, that his obligation was entirely personal, having nothing to do with his estate.[3] The peasant's military duty was territorial rather than personal,[4] and again, it was personal rather than territorial.[5] The fyrd was a rude assemblage of all able-bodied freemen whose service was based upon the old Germanic concept of the nation in arms,[6] and again, the fyrd was recruited selectively at the rate of one man from five hides of land.[7] Nobody

---

[1] Vinogradoff, *English Society in the Eleventh Century* (Oxford, 1908), pp. 14–38.

[2] e.g. F. M. Stenton, *William the Conqueror* (New York and London, 1908), pp. 445, 448.

[3] e.g. Stenton, *A.S.E.*, p. 575.

[4] e.g. Stenton, *E.F.*, p. 116: '. . . the duty of peasants . . . was a territorial, not a personal obligation. . . .' See also Maitland, *D.B.B.*, p. 157.

[5] e.g. Stenton, *A.S.E.*, p. 575: 'The military service of the peasant, like that of the thegn, was a personal obligation.'

[6] e.g. Stenton, *William the Conqueror*, pp. 444–5.

[7] e.g. J. H. Round, 'Danegeld and the Finance of Domesday', in *Domesday Studies*, ed. P. E. Dove (2 vols., London, 1888–91), i. 120; *F.E.*, pp. 67–69; Stubbs, *Constitutional History of England* (5th ed., 3 vols., Oxford, 1891–6), i. 155–6, 190–2; M. Hollings, 'The Survival of the Five-Hide Unit in the Western Midlands', *E.H.R.* lxiii (1948), 453–87.

seems quite sure what the fyrd was. Was it the body of peasants as distinct from the thegns and mercenaries? Was it the peasants and thegns together? Or was it a synthesis of all three?[1] And the confusion in terminology does not end with the word 'fyrd'. *Here* was originally the term for the Danish army, and a number of scholars insist that this original meaning never changed, yet we find the terms *here* and 'fyrd' used interchangeably in later sources.[2] Historians are almost unanimous on the point that the fyrd was made up entirely of infantry,[3] yet the sources persist in referring to the fyrd soldier as a *miles*, a word which is normally translated in medieval Latin as 'mounted knight'. And many historians would be disturbed by the suggestion that *miles* might have had a broader connotation in pre-Conquest England where there were, presumably, no mounted knights. One can sympathize with Maitland's complaint that 'No matter with which we have to deal is darker than the constitution of the English army on the eve of its defeat'.[4]

Perhaps the scholarly neglect from which this confusion arises is a consequence of the widespread opinion that pre-Conquest English society was decadent and uncreative and

---

[1] Stenton (*E.F.*, p. 116) limits fyrd duty to peasants. Charles Oman (*A History of the Art of War in the Middle Ages*, 2nd ed., 2 vols., London, 1924, i. 110) refers to the fyrd as 'the shaft of the weapon of which the thegnhood formed the iron barb', and elsewhere (ibid. i. 112) refers to 'the united thegnhood of England, backed by the fyrd'. Yet later (ibid. i. 157) he contradicts himself when, in describing the battle of Hastings, he states: 'The fyrd, divided no doubt according to its shires, was ranged on either flank. Presumably the thegns and other fully-armed men formed its front ranks. . . .' Other scholars interpret the term more broadly as 'the army of pre-Conquest England': e.g. R. H. Hodgkin, *A History of the Anglo-Saxons* (2 vols., Oxford, 1935), ii. 594; Frank Barlow, *The Feudal Kingdom of England, 1042–1216* (London, New York, and Toronto, 1955), p. 49; H. M. Chadwick, *The Origin of the English Nation* (Cambridge, England, 1924), pp. 149 ff.

[2] The editors of the *Crawford Charters*, for example, state that the *Anglo-Saxon Chronicle* restricted the term *here* to the Danish invaders: *Crawford*, p. 47. So also writes L. M. Larson, *The King's Household in England before the Norman Conquest* (Madison, 1904), p. 165, citing Bosworth-Toller, *Anglo-Saxon Dictionary*, s.v. *here*. But in fact the *Anglo-Saxon Chronicle* does not bear them out. In the eleventh century, 'fyrd' and *here* are used interchangeably. See *A.S.C.*, A.D. 1006, 1013; C, 1045; E, 1048; C and D, 1054 and 1055; C, 1066 *v*. D, 1066; D, 1066 and E, 1066 refer to a *here* of Englishmen; D, 1067; D, 1068 *v*. E, 1068; E, 1073 *v*. D, 1074; E, 1090; E, 1097.

[3] But not entirely unanimous: see R. Glover, 'English Warfare in 1066', *E.H.R.* lxvii (1952), 1–18.   [4] *D.B.B.*, p. 156.

that its army cannot therefore have amounted to much. It is all too easy to regard the defeat of the Anglo-Saxon army at Hastings as somehow symbolic of the weakness of the English military structure and the failure of the Old English state. Perhaps this is merely an illustration of the old adage that history is written by its survivors, or a result of our unfortunate tendency to regard events of the past as necessary and inevitable. Doubtless also the gloomy picture of pre-Conquest society which one finds in the writings of so many twentieth-century historians represents something of a reaction against the naïve Germanism of some of their predecessors who had discovered in the Anglo-Saxon state the genesis of English constitutionalism, democracy, and, indeed, everything fine and decent. Some kind of reaction against such views was perhaps bound to occur. Professor D. C. Douglas spoke of 'the civilization which the Saxons produced but could no longer defend', and Sir Frank Stenton had earlier found little to admire in the England of 1066 with its 'obsolete army, a financial system out of relation to the facts on which it was nominally based, and a social order lacking the prerequisites of stability and consistency'.[1] Ferdinand Lot, in portraying pre-Conquest England as a barbaric society saved from its own inadequacies by the Norman Conquest, was expressing the general viewpoint of a considerable body of scholars.[2] Pre-Conquest society, they suggest, was basically untenable, and its fundamental weakness was nowhere more evident than in what Stenton refers to as 'the antiquated military system of England'.[3]

This dour view of Anglo-Saxon society has been challenged by several scholars. Perhaps the most pointed rebuttal is to be found in an article by Professor R. R. Darlington, who argues vigorously and convincingly that the Old English state was strong and viable to the end:

The Normans, a vigorous if somewhat crude race, were confronted

---

[1] *The Norman Conquest and British Historians* (Glasgow, 1946), p. 33. Stenton, *William the Conqueror*, p. 18.

[2] Lot, *Les Invasions germaniques* (Payot, 1935), pp. 318–20. Cf. R. R. Darlington, 'The Last Phase of Anglo-Saxon History', *History*, N.S., xxii (1937), 1.

[3] *William the Conqueror*, p. 186.

in England with a highly developed civilisation, older than and in many ways superior to their own. It is clear that the period which closed with the tragic events of 1066 can in no sense be regarded as an age of stagnation and decay for from whatever angle it is viewed, the last phase of Old English history is rich alike in achievement and promise.[1]

Professor Bertie Wilkinson finds both strength and weakness in the late-Saxon state, but prefers to stress its strength: 'At least, we may suggest, this has, in the past, been unduly ignored'; the forces of cohesion were 'stronger and more enduring' than those of disintegration.[2]

In the present study, the military structure of this controversial late-Saxon society will be examined in some detail in an effort to determine whether or not the Old English army was truly obsolete and incapable of defending the society which produced it. If the broad outlines of the Anglo-Saxon military structure can once be grasped, it will then be possible in some future study to develop a sound comparison between the military organizations of pre-Conquest and post-Conquest England. The basis will then exist for an analysis of the points which the Anglo-Saxon and Anglo-Norman systems had in common, and an isolation of the new elements which the Norman Conquest introduced. This study can also lay the foundation for an investigation of the Anglo-Saxon fyrd under the Norman kings, for historians are agreed that the fyrd was retained by the post-Conquest monarchs and played a role in the military history of Norman and Angevin England. But it is hopeless to trace the fyrd into post-Conquest times without understanding what it was, how it was organized, or what classes it represented in the days of its prime, prior to the defeat at Hastings.

In all these respects the present study is open-ended. In providing a coherent and documented picture of the late-Saxon military structure, it can serve as the basis of future studies which may go far toward solving the riddle of the Norman Conquest.

---

[1] Darlington, p. 13; cf. ibid., pp. 1–13.
[2] 'Freeman and the Crisis of 1051', *Bulletin of the John Rylands Library*, xxii (1938), 386–7; 'Northumbrian Separatism in 1065 and 1066', ibid. xxiii (1939), 504.

II

A careful examination of the original sources suggests
that considerable confusion and misunderstanding has resulted from a tendency on the part of historians to interpret
certain key terms in an unduly restricted and narrow sense.
The term *miles*, for example, as it appears in eleventh-
century and early-twelfth-century documents seems clearly
to mean 'soldier'. Only later and gradually is it narrowed to
indicate a particular kind of soldier: the feudal cavalryman.
Yet historians have traditionally maintained that the *milites*
of Domesday were 'fully equipped horsemen'.[1] But the fyrd
soldiers described in Berkshire Domesday, who have never
been regarded as fully equipped horsemen of the Norman
feudal variety, are referred to as *milites*.[2] Moreover, one of
the *milites* in the *Domesday Monachorum* is listed as *Godfrey
balistarius*—an archer.[3] Stenton suggests that the fyrd
soldiers were called *milites* because they rode to battle and
only then dismounted, but this position seems rather far-
fetched and rests upon a reference which probably does not
refer to military service at all.[4] My own conclusion, that
miles in the Anglo-Saxon and early Anglo-Norman documents refers to a soldier of any kind, is supported by a careful
scrutiny of the Domesday Inquest. M. M. Bigelow notes
that of over one hundred Domesday references to *milites*
which he examined, 'there are but two passages in which
there is any clear indication that the tenure was knight
service [i. 10b, 32]. And the first of these may only mean

[1] e.g. V. H. Galbraith, 'An Episcopal Land-Grant of 1085', *E.H.R.* xliv (1929),
362 n.
[2] D.B. i. 56b. F. W. Ragg, who edited the Berkshire Domesday in the *V.C.H.*,
dutifully translated the term *miles* in this T.R.E. passage as 'knight' (*V.C.H.*,
Berks. i. 327), thereby contradicting the theory of the Norman genesis of knight
service set forth by Round, who, as it happens, wrote the introduction to Ragg's
translation (ibid. i. 285–321). The Latin chroniclers normally describe pre-Conquest foot soldiers as *milites*.
[3] *The Domesday Monachorum of Christ Church, Canterbury*, ed. D. C. Douglas
(Royal Historical Society, 1944), pp. 83, 105.
[4] Stenton, *E.F.*, p. 117 n.; 2 Athelstan 16. The passage states simply that there
are to be two mounted men for every plough. The duties of these mounted men
are not stipulated. As will appear later (pp. 134 ff.) some fyrd soldiers rode to
battle, but by no means all of them did so.

that the land was to furnish a soldier'.[1] On the basis of a similarly exhaustive study of Domesday, Henry Ellis concludes,
'The term Miles appears not to have acquired a precise
meaning at the time of the Survey.'[2]

The terms 'fyrd' and *here* have also been defined too
narrowly. In the eleventh century the two terms were
virtually synonymous: both meant 'military force'. The fyrd
was not merely the body of peasant warriors, nor was it the
combined force of peasants and thegns. Indeed, it was not
limited to the Anglo-Saxon army. It could refer to any
military force, whether composed of Anglo-Saxon foot
soldiers or Norman knights. The *Anglo-Saxon Chronicle*
refers to Irish and Welsh fyrds, Norman fyrds (and,
indeed, Norman *heres*), Scottish fyrds, and French fyrds.[3]
We read that on one occasion King Philip of France came to
Normandy with a great *here*, and with this vast fyrd he,
together with Duke Robert Curthose, besieged a castle
which was being defended by the king of England's men.[4]
Yet such distinguished scholars as William A. Morris and
Sir Frank Stenton have blundered on this point, deducing
merely from the appearance of the term 'fyrd' in the *Anglo-
Saxon Chronicle* that the Old English army was active in
certain campaigns in which it may have taken no part at all.[5]
Even the general term 'army' is an inadequate translation,
for there were sea fyrds as well as land fyrds.[6] A fyrd is a
military force of any kind and from any country. However,
for the sake of convenience and in conformity with general
practice, I will use the term henceforth to signify 'the military
force of pre-Conquest England' (which survived, as an
organization, into post-Conquest times), as distinct from

---

[1] *Placita Anglo-Normannica* (Boston, 1879), p. xli.
[2] Ellis, *A General Introduction to Domesday Book* (2 vols., Record Commission,
1833), i. 58.
[3] *A.S.C.*, C, A.D. 1055, D, 1074 [1073], 1077 [1076], E, 1073, 1076, 1079, 1086,
1090, 1091, 1093, 1106, 1117, 1137.
[4] *A.S.C.*, E, A.D. 1090. E, A.D. 1117 refers to a French and Flemish fyrd. E, 1140
[1153] mentions a Norman and Angevin fyrd led by Henry Plantagenet. E, 1013
alludes to a Danish fyrd.
[5] W. Morris, *Constitutional History of England to 1216* (New York, 1930), p. 214;
Stenton, *William the Conqueror*, pp. 323, 341.
[6] e.g. *A.S.C.*, C, A.D. 1065 [1066]; E, 1071; D, 1072 [1071]; E, 1072, 1091. We
also encounter the 'sea *here*': ibid., A.D. 933; C, 1045; D, 1066.

other military forces. This usage is justified, at least in part, by the fact that 'fyrd' is, after all, an Anglo-Saxon word which refers in the majority of cases to the Anglo-Saxon force. Moreover, references to fyrd duty in Old English sources obviously allude to the Anglo-Saxon military obligation rather than to service in some foreign military force. To insist on using the term in its broad and literal sense would be pedantic, but to ignore the fact that it did have this broad connotation would be hazardous and misleading.[1]

[1] Latin terms such as *expeditio* and *exercitus* have also been interpreted too narrowly by some scholars, e.g. S. Painter, *Studies in the History of the English Feudal Barony* (Baltimore, 1943), p. 124; and Stenton, *E.F.*, pp. 176–7. Both terms are near synonyms for 'fyrd' or 'military force', and are not limited, as some have maintained, to feudal knight service or cavalry duty. In sources of the eleventh century, 'fyrd', *here*, *expeditio*, and *exercitus* usually have identical meanings.

I

MERCENARIES AND WAR FINANCE

THE pre-Conquest English army, like the later Anglo-Norman army, relied to a considerable extent on hired soldiers—men who served for wages as distinct from those whose basic military responsibility arose from personal or territorial obligations. As a matter of convenience, the term 'mercenary' will be used to describe those soldiers who served primarily for pay. As we shall see in the following chapters, men who performed military service as a duty might receive wages and subsistence payments during their term of service, but these men will not be considered mercenaries, because they received their pay from their own localities rather than from the lord whom they served, and because the fundamental reason for their service was their obligation to serve rather than the pay which they received. Mercenaries owed no military service except that which they rendered in return for the wages paid them by the king or some important nobleman. Confusion may also arise from the fact that the term 'mercenary' is currently defined as a soldier who serves a foreign power. But in the present chapter the term will be used more broadly to denote a warrior, either English or foreign, whose service is hired.

The mercenaries of Anglo-Saxon times were called by various names: household troops, stipendiaries, members of their lord's retinue or *familia*, housecarles, lithsmen, &c. Some of these terms have specialized meanings, but they all have to do with various forms of the old Germanic *comitatus*, the famous institution of warriors which Tacitus describes, skilled in their craft and intensely loyal to their lord or *comes*. The *comitatus* tradition is common to both Anglo-Saxon and continental societies, as will be readily seen in a comparison between *The Battle of Maldon* and *The Song of*

Roland. The ideal of loyalty and heroism was not, of course, limited to the retainers; it was shared by French and Norman knights and Anglo-Saxon thegns, who drew their support largely from their own lands, but it was usually more intense among the warriors of the lord's household who were supported directly by their lord and who therefore must be termed 'mercenaries'.

But in differentiating between landed warriors and mercenary retainers we at once encounter difficulties, for mercenaries could also be landholders. Royal household troops of the ninth and tenth centuries often possessed estates which could be far removed from the royal court.[1] In the laws of King Edmund, for example, we encounter the following passage:

And I further make known that I will have no one in my household who has been guilty of shedding blood, until he has submitted to divine penance and all that is proper, as the bishop shall instruct him in whose shire it be.[2]

This passage suggests that the members of King Edmund's household resided in different shires, although on the other hand it may indicate nothing more than that they had the opportunity of shedding blood in a number of localities. The former interpretation is strengthened by Asser's statement that the *satellites* of Kind Alfred were divided into three groups, serving in rotation for a month at the royal court and then returning home.[3] How long after Alfred's reign this custom continued we have no way of knowing, but it seems clear that throughout the Anglo-Saxon era household troops could have homes of their own.

The most vivid account of the activities of Anglo-Saxon retainers is to be found in the well-known poem, *The Battle of Maldon*, a poetic account of the defeat of Ealdorman Byrhtnoth of Essex and his army in 991.[4] The ealdorman's retainers are the most prominent troops in the battle. Byrhtnoth himself dismounts and fights among them after

[1] Larson, *King's Household*, pp. 97–103.   [2] ii. 4.
[3] Quoted in Larson, p. 98.
[4] There are several good editions of this poem: *The Battle of Maldon*, ed. E. V. Gordon (London, 1937); E. D. Laborde, *Byrhtnoth and Maldon* (London, 1936), pp. 100 ff.; *English and Norse Documents*, ed. M. Ashdown (Cambridge, England, 1930), pp. 22 ff.

first riding among the shire levies and giving them instructions. The old heroic ideals of the *comitatus* permeate the English force. After Byrhtnoth himself has been slain, the English press forward, eager to avenge their lord or to lose their lives in the attempt. Among these English warriors we find well-armed peasants, landed thegns,[1] and household troops, all motivated by the same ideal, but the warriors of Byrhtnoth's household are clearly the *élite* force, those who need no instructions, who fight alongside their lord and bear the brunt of the Danish attack, and who infuse the whole army with their heroic spirit.

During the reign of Ethelred the Unready (978–1016) Scandinavian mercenaries first begin to play a prominent role in English warfare. *The Saga of Gunnlaug Serpent's Tongue* describes how Gunnlaug, having come to England, sought out King Ethelred in London and read him a poem of adulation. Ethelred expressed his gratitude by giving Gunnlaug a scarlet cloak lined with the best skins and with lace down to the hem, and made him his retainer. Gunnlaug remained with the king for a winter and was held in high esteem.[2] There are also accounts in the saga literature of St. Olaf's activities in England as the leader of a Norwegian force in the pay of King Ethelred. The English king is reported to have summoned to his banner every man who wished to gain a reward in helping him to recover the land. Among the great host that joined him was King Olaf with his Norwegian force.[3] The details of this saga literature are, of course, of doubtful authenticity, but we can be certain of the generalization that during the second great Danish invasion many Scandinavian warriors great and small served for pay under King Ethelred the Unready. In 1012 Ethelred took the Danish warrior Thorkell the Tall into his service with forty-five ships, and Danish seamen continued to serve English kings for several decades thereafter.[4]

---

[1] *Crawford*, p. 123 n.; Stenton, *E.F.*, p. 119.

[2] *Gunnlaugs saga Ormstungu*, c. 9.

[3] *Óláfs saga Helga (Heimskringla)*, cc. 12 ff. See Alistair Campbell's account of St. Olaf's early career in *Encomium Emmae Reginae* (Royal Historical Society, 1949), pp. 76–82.

[4] *A.S.C.*, A.D. 1012. Cf. ibid. ii. 190, and *Óláfs saga Tryggvasonar*, cc. 34 ff. Thorkell was the brother of Jarl Sigvaldi the leader of the Jómsborg Vikings.

II

With the Danish conquest under Swein and Cnut the housecarles first appear in England. The term presents certain difficulties, for it was apparently used by contemporary writers in both a special and a general sense. The term is, of course, Norse in origin, as is the institution which it describes, but from the reign of Cnut onward the word 'housecarle' is generalized to embrace almost any kind of household warrior or retainer. We encounter English as well as Danish housecarles,[1] we find men who are classified alternatively as housecarles and as thegns,[2] and we discover occasional housecarles in post-Conquest England, at a time when the housecarles as an organization had ceased to exist.[3] In addition to the royal housecarles there were housecarles in the retinues of important lords who cannot have differed greatly from the household troops of the previous age.[4]

But the term is also used in a special context to describe a unique, closely knit organization of professional warriors who served the kings of England from Cnut to Harold Godwinson and became the spearhead of the Old English army. Laurence M. Larson was one of the first scholars to grasp the real nature of this organization.[5] Basing his investigation on an analysis of eleventh-century English documents, the Norse poems of the same period, the Norse laws and sagas, and the works of the twelfth-century Danish historians Sveno and Saxo, he concluded that the housecarles constituted a royal guard governed by certain rules of

---

[1] Cf. *A.S.C.*, E, A.D. 1064 [1065], mentioning *hiredmenn* both English and Danish, with *A.S.C.*, C, 1065, which describes these same men as housecarles.

[2] D.B. i. 130*b*, 138; 146*b*, 147; 152*b*, 217.

[3] Domesday mentions a number of housecarles holding T.R.W. (at the time of King William: 1086). These references are listed in Larson, p. 164 n.

[4] e.g. D.B. i. 213; *A.S.C.*, D, A.D. 1054; housecarles of Earl Siward; C, 1065: housecarles of Earl Tostig.

[5] Larson, pp. 152–71. In general, I agree with Larson's interpretation and use his work in the following discussion. His chief weakness is in terminology, as for example his failure to see that the term 'housecarle' was used in a general as well as a specialized sense. See also J. C. H. R. Steenstrup, *Normannerne* (4 vols., Copenhagen, 1876–82), iii. 374 ff.; iv. 146 ff.; and Vinogradoff, *Engl. Soc.*, pp. 19 ff.

conduct and capable of meeting as a deliberative and judicial body which passed judgement on its own members. The guard was patterned in certain ways upon an earlier group of Norse warriors, the Vikings of Jómsborg. These Jóms-vikings were a pirate brotherhood bound by a set of strict rules governing membership, administration, and general conduct.[1] As such, they represent another kind of evolution from the old *comitatus* tradition. The Jómsvikings were said to have been founded by King Harold of Denmark, the father of Swein, the invader of England, and they served King Swein with ruthless effectiveness during the period of his attacks against King Ethelred. Rules similar to those which bound the Jómsvikings also governed the housecarles of the kings of Norway and the Varangian Guard of the Byzantine emperors.[2] Thorkell the Tall, who deserted King Swein to become a mercenary of Ethelred, was apparently a Jómsviking and there were other Jómsvikings among the housecarles of the English kings.

The sources disagree as to the exact time when the corps of housecarles was first established in England. The *Flatey-jarbok* discloses that King Swein introduced them into England, dividing the organization into two groups, one with its headquarters in London, and the other in northern England.[3] But scholars have tended to be sceptical of this account and to accept the testimony of Sveno and Saxo that the housecarles were established in England as an organiza-tion by Cnut, probably around the year 1018.[4] From the time of their inception, they constituted the most highly trained and battle-ready force available to the English

---

[1] *Jómsvikingasaga*, 12; Larson, pp. 154–5; P. Hunter Blair, *Introduction to Anglo-Saxon England* (Cambridge, England, 1956), pp. 93–98.

[2] Sveno, *Lex Castrensis* in *Scriptores rerum Danicarum* (Copenhagen, 1772–1834), iii. 139–64. *Corpus Poeticum Boreale*, ed. Vigfusson and Powell (2 vols., Oxford, 1883), i. 256–7; Larson, pp. 157–8. *Íslenzk fornrit* (Reykjavík, 1933 ff.), vii. 214, 271–6; Snorri Sturluson, *Heimskringla*, ed. F. Jónsson (Copenhagen, 1911), p. 449; T. J. Oleson, *The Witenagemot in the Reign of Edward the Confessor* (London, 1955), pp. 168–9. The Varangians were Norse mercenaries.

[3] *Flateyjarbok* (Christiania, 3 vols., 1860–8), i. 203, 205; ii. 22; *Crawford*, p. 140. The northern headquarters was at Slessvik, a location that is difficult to identify. It was probably not far from York.

[4] *Lex Castrensis*, iii. 144; Larson, pp. 158–9; Steenstrup, *Danelag* (*Normannerne*, iv. 1882), p. 138.

monarchs. Many of the housecarles were landholders,[1] yet
they remained essentially mercenary troops and were referred to by Anglo-Norman chroniclers as *solidarii* and
stipendiarii.[2] They first appear in English sources in a
charter of 1033, and thereafter they are occasionally mentioned in the *Anglo-Saxon Chronicle*, where they are described
as serving as tax collectors as well as soldiers.[3] The exact
nature of their organization is obscure, since we possess no
sources which describe it specifically,[4] but we can gain a
general impression of it from the Norse sources, which
describe similar organizations in the service of Scandinavian
monarchs. Larson has argued convincingly that the English
organization probably did not differ greatly from that of the
Danish housecarles whose laws and regulations are preserved
in Sveno's *Lex Castrensis*. Indeed, these Danish regulations
seem to have been based on those governing the housecarles
of Cnut. They specify that the housecarles received wages
and subsistence from their monarch in peacetime as well
as in time of war. Individual warriors could separate themselves from the organization, but they could do so only on
New Year's Day. Disputes within the organization were
to be settled in the *huskarlesteffne*, the assembly or *gemot* of
the corps, meeting with the king. If a housecarle should be
guilty of the murder of one of his comrades he was to be
executed or banished; treason was to be punished by death
and confiscation.[5]

These regulations, appearing in a Danish source of the
late twelfth century, purport to describe the English organization as it existed in the first half of the eleventh century.
Under the circumstances, they must be viewed with a
certain scepticism, yet their general import is corroborated

---

1 Kemble, *C.D.*, nos. 843, 871, 1318; D.B. i. 17, 36, 56, 95, 99, 129, 130, 130*b*,
136*b*, 138, 138*b*, 140, 140*b*, 146*b*, 147, 149, 152, 152*b*, 164, 167, 195, 202, 213, 216,
217; ii. 59, 441*b*, 442; Steenstrup, *Danelag*, pp. 151–3; Larson, pp. 163–4.

2 *Fl. Wig.* i. 204; Wm. Malm. i. 282.

3 Kemble, *C.D.*, no. 1318. See also ibid., nos. 843, 871. *A.S.C.*, E, A.D. 1036
[1035]; C and D, 1041; D, 1054; C, 1065. See also *Fl. Wig.* i. 195, 223.

4 On the subject of the housecarle organization see Steenstrup, *Danelag*, pp.
127 ff.; Stenton, *A.S.E.*, p. 406, and *E.F.*, pp. 119 ff.; Larson, pp. 153 ff.; Vinogradoff, *Engl. Soc.*, pp. 19–22; Oleson, pp. 103 ff., 168–9; Wilkinson, 'Northumbrian Separatism', pp. 513–14 n.

5 *Lex Castrensis*, 6, 7, 8, 10.

by certain pre-Conquest passages in the *Anglo-Saxon Chronicle* which enable us to conclude that the housecarles of England were indeed organized as a guild with a body of regulations and a *huskarlesteffne* or *gemot*.[1] The *Chronicle* reports that in 1049 Swein, the son of Earl Godwin, who had revolted against the king and had murdered Earl Beorn, was exiled and declared a *nithing* by the king and all the *here*.[2] As we have seen, the term *here*, as used in the mid-eleventh century, does not necessarily refer only to the Danes in the English army and it surely is not a synonym for 'housecarles'. Yet even though the term does not necessarily mean 'housecarles', it can under certain circumstances have that meaning. The housecarles were a part of the *here*, and any given reference to the term *here* could connote the thegns, the peasants, the housecarles, or any combination of them. And there is reason to believe that this particular passage refers exclusively to the housecarles, for so far as we know no other component of the Anglo-Saxon army exercised this judicial function. The use of the term *nithing* is most significant, for according to the regulations governing the Danish corps of housecarles, a member of the guild who murdered one of his fellows 'shall be driven off the king's estates with *nithing's* word, and shall be exiled from every land under Cnut's rule'.[3] It was doubtless this very law, or at least one very similar to it, that the housecarles of King Edward invoked against Swein in 1049. Again, in 1051 the Witan and the king's *here* outlawed Earl Godwin and all his sons, and here again the *here*, sitting in judgement on some of its own members, is exercising a function very similar to that of the Scandinavian *huscarlesteffne*.[4]

[1] On the relevance of these regulations to the English corps of housecarles, see Larson, pp. 160 ff.; Oleson, p. 104.

[2] *A.S.C.*, C, A.D. 1049. Beorn was the son of the famous Danish earl Ulf, who claimed to be descended from a bear. Many modern historians are sceptical of this claim.

[3] *Scriptores rerum Danicarum*, iii. 162; *Lex Castrensis*, 10.

[4] *A.S.C.*, D, A.D. 1052 [1051]. Cf. E, 1048 [1051], reporting that the king met with his witan and summoned the *here*. Larson (p. 166) points out that *A.S.C.*, D, 1052 [1051], calls this meeting a *stefna*, a term reminiscent of the *huscarlesteffne* in the *Lex Castrensis*. Cf. *Fl. Wig.* i. 206 (1051): 'rex in suo concilio, et omnis exercitus unanimi consensu, illum [Godwin] et quinque filios ejus exules fore decreverunt.' See also Oleson, pp. 103 ff.

The problem of mercenaries in pre-Conquest England is further complicated by the appearance in the sources of several other terms evidently referring to warriors who fight for pay. We encounter, for example, the term *hired* or *hiredmenn*, which is used on at least one occasion as a synonym for 'housecarles'. In the account of the Northumbrian revolt of 1065, the D and E manuscripts of the *Anglo-Saxon Chronicle* report that the Northumbrians slew all of Earl Tostig's *hiredmenn* they could catch, whether English or Dane,[1] but the C manuscript refers to these same retainers of Earl Tostig as *hus karlas*.[2] Tostig's housecarles are certainly unconnected with the royal corps of housecarles which have just been discussed; they are men of the earl, not the king, and the passage merely illustrates the fact that the term 'housecarle' was by this time serving as a synonym for 'mercenary' or 'retainer' in addition to its more specialized meaning. Tostig's retainers were both English and Danish; they were doubtless similar in function to the retainers who had surrounded great Anglo-Saxon lords long before the invasions of Swein and Cnut, and to the retinues which soon afterwards would be found attached to the households of important Anglo-Norman barons. The *Anglo-Saxon Chronicle* discloses, for example, that in 1095 King William's army captured many prisoners of the rebellious earl of Northumbria, including almost all of the best of the earl's *hirede*.[3]

Pre-Conquest mercenaries also appear under the name of 'lithsmen' or *lið*. This is an ambiguous term which is thought to mean 'sailor' in Anglo-Saxon, but seems to mean 'warrior' in the Norse literature. Some scholars have assumed that lithsmen are housecarles,[4] but if so they are housecarles only in the general sense of the word. Undoubtedly they are

---

[1] *A.S.C.*, E, A.D. 1064 [1065]; D, 1065; literally, *hired* means household or court; *hiredmenn*, retainers, members of the household.

[2] Ibid., C, A.D. 1065. Cf. *Fl. Wig.* i. 223, where a distinction seems to be made between Tostig's *Danicos huscarlas* and the *viros ex curialibus illius*.

[3] Ibid., E, A.D. 1095.

[4] e.g. J. H. Ramsay, *The Foundations of England* (3 vols., London, 1898), i. 450-1.

mercenaries of some kind, for on occasion they are described specifically as awaiting their pay.¹ Normally they appear in the sources in connexion with maritime duty,² but not always, for the mercenaries who accompanied King Harold Godwinson on his northward march against Harold Hardrada in 1066 are termed 'lithsmen'.³ The term is also used to describe the Danish warriors who came in ships to threaten the Anglo-Norman monarchy in 1069 and 1070.⁴ Probably neither 'sailor' nor 'land warrior' is an adequate translation of the term, for these lithsmen seem to have been warriors who fought in the old Viking tradition and were equally at home on land and at sea. In this respect they cannot have been unlike the other Norse mercenaries of eleventh-century England, and I suspect that the term 'lithsmen' is to be understood in a rather general sense as describing mercenaries who could handle ships but fight on land as well.

Much uncertainty and confusion have resulted from the statements in the *Anglo-Saxon Chronicle* that Edward the Confessor dismissed nine of his fourteen ships of lithsmen in 1050 and that he dismissed the remaining five ships in 1051.⁵ This fact has been taken as proof that lithsmen were not housecarles, for housecarles appear in a later period.⁶ The difficulty is that lithsmen also appear after 1051. They appear in fact in 1052, when King Edward ordered his lithsmen to man forty small ships and to wait in Sandwich for the coming of Earl Godwin.⁷ These lithsmen pursued Godwin, but, unable to capture him, they returned to Sandwich and then homeward to London. The *Chronicle* mentions the lithsmen of the rebel Ælfgar in 1055 and those of King Harold in 1066, where the term seems to imply housecarles.⁸ One must conclude either that the warriors whom Edward dismissed were only a particular sort of lithsmen or else that

---

¹ *A.S.C.*, C, A.D. 1055, referring to the *sciplið* of Ælfgar. See also E, 1047 [1050], C, 1049 [1050], and C, 1050 [1051], referring to the payment of the king's lithsmen.
² Ibid., E, A.D. 1036 [1035]; E, 1047 [1050]; 1052 *bis*; C, 1055; 1066.
³ Ibid., C, A.D. 1066: *lið*.
⁴ Ibid., E, A.D. 1069 and 1070; D, 1071 [1070].
⁵ Ibid., E, A.D. 1047 [1050]; C, 1049 [1050] and 1050 [1051].
⁶ Larson, p. 169. Oleson (p. 169) concludes from this fact that lithsmen cannot have been *butsecarls* who also appear later on.
⁷ *A.S.C.*, C, A.D. 1052: *lið*. ⁸ Ibid., C, A.D. 1055, 1066.

having dismissed them he called them back almost immediately.

One last term which is occasionally used to describe mercenaries is *butsecarls*. This term also has been translated both as 'sailor' and 'warrior',[1] and again it is very likely a combination of the two. Professor Oleson has noted that a group of warriors, which Florence of Worcester describes as *butsecarls*, are called *burhwaru*—garrison—by the *Anglo-Saxon Chronicle*.[2] Nevertheless, as in the case of lithsmen, *butsecarls* are found performing sea duty.[3] Very likely the two terms are nearly identical and refer generally to men who fought for pay and who were equally valuable to their lord in the army or in ships. Lithsmen and *butsecarls* were both *hiredmenn*, and all three were housecarles in the general although not the specific sense of the word. Each term has its own shade of meaning, but none of them refers necessarily to specific or exclusive groups of men. They were all mercenaries, and perhaps it is safest to leave it at that.

To summarize, then, the mercenaries who fought for England on the eve of the Norman Conquest were of several general types. There were bands of foreign warriors under foreign leaders who were hired in groups by the English monarchy, such as the followers of Thorkell the Tall. There were also the retinues or household warriors of important Anglo-Saxon lords, and the highly organized corps of housecarles who served the king as a standing army. And there were other groups, less easily defined—the lithsmen and *butsecarls*—mercenaries who were equally adept in land and maritime warfare. The mercenaries of post-Conquest England were divided into roughly similar groups, yet the Norman Conquest brought with it certain significant changes in mercenary organization. The corps of housecarles seems to perish at Hastings, and warriors of the amphibious lithsman type no longer play an important role. These facts point to a much more fundamental development—the shift

---

[1] See *A.S.C.* ii. 239–40; Stenton, *A.S.E.*, p. 558; Vinogradoff, *Engl. Soc.*, pp. 20–21; Oleson, p. 169.

[2] *Fl. Wig.* i. 228; *A.S.C.*, D, A.D. 1066. The term *butsecarls* also appears in this context in Kemble, *C.D.*, no. 956. See Oleson, p. 169.

[3] e.g. *A.S.C.*, C and D, A.D. 1066. See also ibid., A.D. 1052; *Fl. Wig.* i. 208, 209, 225.

in English diplomatic orientation from Scandinavia to the Continent. Viking tactics such as the lithsmen apparently employed give way after the Conquest to land warfare; Norse warrior guilds recede to Scandinavia and cease to be significant in England; Norse mercenaries are no longer employed; their place is taken by Flemish, Breton, and French mercenaries such as those who fought alongside William the Conqueror at Hastings.

IV

But perhaps the similarities between Anglo-Saxon and Anglo-Norman mercenaries outweigh their differences. The most startling similarity is in the very fact that mercenaries were important to the military structures of both societies in an age when they were relatively rare elsewhere in Europe. The large-scale use of mercenaries by both the pre-Conquest and post-Conquest kings was made possible by the existence of a financial system which, by the standards of the time, was remarkably efficient. The revenues flowing into the Anglo-Saxon treasury were large indeed by comparison with the rest of Europe (there was apparently nowhere else anything quite like the danegeld), and by far the greater proportion of these revenues was devoted to military expenses—chiefly to the hiring of mercenaries. Broadly speaking, there were four separate methods of raising money for general military purposes: (1) the land tax or danegeld (sometimes called the 'heregeld'); (2) special taxes assessed on particular towns for the purpose of paying wages to mercenaries; (3) the *fyrdwite* or fine for non-performance of the fyrd obligation; (4) commutation payments which certain towns were allowed to render in lieu of actual military service. The first two obligations are direct military taxes; the last two are payments rendered in lieu of personal service. *Fyrdwite* and commutation differ in that the former is a fine assessed for failure to serve, whereas the latter represents a legal alternative to military service, not unlike the later scutage. Consequently, commutation is always considerably lower in amount than *fyrdwite*.

The danegeld was undoubtedly the most important of

these taxes. It was a general land tax, sometimes assessed at
2s. a hide.[1] It was first collected in 991 as a tribute payment
to the Danes, and was assessed again for the same purpose
in 994 and seemingly in subsequent years.[2] From the year
1012 onward, the danegeld was used for the support of
mercenaries rather than the payment of tribute,[3] and thus
the practice continued until 1051 when King Edward the
Confessor abolished it.[4] It was assessed again by the Norman
kings after the Conquest, and may even have been re-
instituted in the closing years of Edward the Confessor's
reign, for several passages in Domesday suggest strongly
that it was in effect at the time of his death.[5]

In addition to the danegeld obligation, or, more probably,
in lieu of it, certain towns were assessed a fixed sum of
money which was to be used by the monarchy for the support
of mercenaries. Dorchester (Dorset), which was assessed at ten
hides and would therefore pay 20s. according to the normal

[1] e.g. *Kalendar of Abbot Samson of Bury St. Edmunds*, ed. R. H. C. Davis (Royal
Historical Society, 1954), pp. xv, 61. It was often 1s.: *Leges Henrici Primi*, 15.

[2] *A.S.C.*, A.D. 991, 994; *Fl. Wig.* i. 149, 151–2: 'Tunc rex Ægelredus, procerum
suorum consilio, ad eos legatos misit, promittens tributum et stipendium ea con-
ventione illis se daturum, ut a sua crudelitate omnino desisterent'; cf. ibid. i. 155.

[3] In 1012 the king began paying for the military service of Thorkell the Tall and
his ships' companies: *A.S.C.*, A.D. 1012, 1013; *Fl. Wig.* i. 165–6. Thorkell aided the
English in the defence of London against Swein in 1012: ibid. i. 167. Stenton identifies this payment as the heregeld and believes that the term 'danegeld' is a mis-
nomer (*A.S.E.*, p. 406), but this is by no means certain. A charter of King Cnut, for
example, makes reference to the *census Danis* which Englishmen pay either for
ships or arms: Kemble, *C.D.*, no. 735; and Florence of Worcester (i. 204) describes
the abolition of the tax in 1051 as follows: 'Rex Eadwardus absolvit Anglos a gravi
vectigali, tricesimo octavo anno ex quo pater suus rex Ægelredus primitus id
Danicis solidariis solvi mandarat.' For other references to the danegeld between
1012 and 1051 see *A.S.C.*, A.D. 1018, 1040; *Fl. Wig.* i. 166, 182. In 1040 the assessment was unusually heavy, 8 marks being paid to every rower in the fleet, and 12 to
each steersman: ibid. i. 194.

[4] *Fl. Wig.* i. 204 (see preceding note). *A.S.C.*, D, A.D. 1052 (1051). On the general
subject, see also *Die Gesetze der Angelsachsen*, ed. F. Liebermann (3 vols., Halle,
1903–16), ii. 344–5 (on the question of whether or not the tax was assessed yearly);
Stenton, *A.S.E.*, p. 106; *Kalendar of Abbot Samson*, pp. xv ff. Several sources state
explicitly that the money was used for the support of mercenaries; e.g. *Fl. Wig.* i.
204; *A.S.C.*, A.D. 1012, 1040; *Leges Henrici Primi*, 15: 'Denagildum quod aliquando
þingemannis dabatur', the term 'thingemanni' being a normal Norse equivalent
for 'housecarles'; Kemble, *C.D.*, no. 735.

[5] There are a number of Domesday references to the danegeld obligation T.R.E.
(on the day that King Edward was alive and dead); e.g. i. 336b, where the borough
of Stamford is reported to have paid danegeld at the rate of 12½ hundreds or 150
carucates.

danegeld rate of 2*s.* on the hide, owed instead 1 mark of silver in support of the king's housecarles (*ad opus Huscarlium*). Bridport (five hides) paid half a mark, Wareham (ten hides) paid a mark, and Shaftesbury (twenty hides) paid 2 marks, all for the same purpose.[1] The Domesday passage relating to the town of Exeter suggests that these sums were to be paid as an alternative to the danegeld obligation rather than a supplement to it, for the Exeter passage separates the hidage assessment from the military financial obligation. Exeter contributed *men* to the army on the basis of a five-hide assessment, but it contributed *money* to the army at a fixed rate; i.e. Exeter paid the king half a mark of silver for the use of soldiers.[2] In other words, Exeter was assessed at five hides only with respect to actual military service, and we are left to conclude that it did not pay danegeld on those five hides, but instead paid the specific sum of half a mark.[3] The passage also makes it clear that although this special military assessment might have been paid in lieu of danegeld, it was not a substitute for actual military service, but rather an additional obligation.

It is interesting to note that all of the towns examined so far are paying at the identical rate of 1 mark for ten hides or 6*s.* 8*d.* for five hides.[4] These towns are all located in the two adjacent coastal shires of Devon and Dorset and were formerly within the kingdom of Wessex. Elsewhere in England we also occasionally find towns paying special military assessments, but they pay them at no fixed rate. The citizens of Lewes, for example, paid 20*s.* toward the support of mercenaries in ships whenever the king sent his men to guard the sea.[5] If the king led a military expedition

---

[1] D.B. i. 75.   [2] Ibid. i. 100.

[3] The supposition that towns which owed a fixed sum for the support of mercenaries were exempt from the normal danegeld assessment is confirmed by a passage in the *A.S.C.* (A.D. 1018) which separates the military tax paid by London in 1018 from that collected elsewhere in England.

[4] On this general subject, see E. B. Demarest, 'The Firma Unius Noctis', *E.H.R.* xxxv (1920), 85.

[5] D.B. i. 26: 'Si rex ad mare custodiendum sine se mittere suos voluisset de omnibus hominibus cujuscunque terrae fuissent colligebant xx solidos et hos habebant qui in navibus arma custodiebant.' See below, pp. 89, 121, and *V.C.H., Sussex*, i. 382, where the obligation is interpreted in terms of the Malmesbury arrangements (below, p. 23).

overseas, the burghers of Leicester contributed four horses to carry arms and supplies as far as London. Every house in Colchester that was able to do so paid 6*d*. a year which the king might apply either to the maintenance of his standing army in peacetime or to the expense of a military campaign. The total sum came to £15. 5*s*. 3*d*. a year in the days of Edward the Confessor.[1]

Another source of military revenue was *fyrdwite*, the fine for default of the military obligation. Numerous references to *fyrdwite* occur in the Anglo-Saxon documents, and it was clearly a general rule that men who were expected to serve but failed to do so had to make heavy financial amends to the royal treasury. The fine was scarcely ever less than 40*s*. and was often considerably more.[2] Since the subject of *fyrdwite* will be recurring throughout this study, it will suffice at this point merely to make note of the practice and to compare it with the fourth and final source of military income—commutation. The distinction between *fyrdwite* and commutation is illustrated by a Domesday passage relating to the borough of Warwick, which states that when the king went on a military campaign by land, the town was to send ten of its burghers to serve on the expedition. If one of the ten selected to serve failed to do so, he owed the king 100*s*. in *fyrdwite*. But if the king went by sea against his enemies, the town sent him either four boatswains or four pounds.[3] In both the land campaign and the maritime campaign the burghers might either provide warriors or pay a sum of money, but in the first instance the payment is clearly a fine whereas in the second it is merely an alternative way of performing the military obligation—the personal military duty could be commuted at the rate of 20*s*. per warrior, a far lower rate than the *fyrdwite* fine of 100*s*. Nor is this the only reference to commutation in Domesday. At Oxford the fyrd quota was satisfied either by the service of twenty burghers or by the payment of twenty pounds,[4] and here also there is no indication whatever that the payment of twenty pounds was construed as a fine. It was a simple

---

[1] D.B. i. 230 (Leicester); ii. 207 (Colchester).
[2] e.g. ibid. i. 132 (40*s*.). The figure of 100*s*. is frequently encountered; e.g. ibid. i. 154*b*.   [3] Ibid. i. 238.   [4] Ibid. i. 154.

alternative, a commutation of personal service at the same low rate of 20s. per warrior which we observed at Warwick. The town of Malmesbury rendered the service of a five-hide estate and as such owed either one warrior or 20s. to maintain the royal mercenaries (*buzecarles*) whenever the king undertook a campaign by land or by sea.[1] Here again, the commutation rate was 20s. per warrior, and the language of this Domesday entry suggests that the Malmesbury obligation may have been a common one, for Malmesbury served as an honour of five hides, and the five-hide unit, as we shall see, was the general and fundamental unit of military assessment throughout much of England. Yet it is doubtful if the typical five-hide unit could contribute 20s. in lieu of its warrior when the fyrd was summoned, for the institution of *fyrdwite* would then be meaningless. Nor is it likely that the king could collect money in lieu of personal service except in certain relatively limited areas such as those which we have examined. In 1094, when King William Rufus wished to extract money from his fyrd soldiers in lieu of their personal military service, he was driven to the cumbersome method of actually having the soldiers summoned and led to the coast, and then demanding that they pay him for the privilege of returning home.[2] He apparently had no intention of using them in his campaign. At that, he was able to collect only 10s. from each soldier instead of 20s., the customary rate of commutation at Warwick, Oxford, and Malmesbury. The Domesday passages relating to commutation fail to make clear whether the option to pay or serve was with the king or the burghers, but in either case the custom, although highly significant, must have been limited in its scope. It is interesting to note that the rate of 20s. per warrior

---

[1] Ibid. i. 64b. See below, pp. 42, 76.

[2] *Fl. Wig.* ii. 35; *A.S.C.*, A.D. 1094; H. of Hunt., p. 217; see below, p. 43. But the practice of commutation was probably not limited in Anglo-Saxon times merely to the towns described above. A writ of William the Conqueror to Archbishop Lanfranc and Bishop Geoffrey of Coutances orders that a dispute between Bishop Wulfstan of Worcester and Abbot Walter of Evesham was to be settled on the basis of the conditions that prevailed in King Edward's time when the geld was last taken for the fleet ('qua novissime, tempore regis Edwardi, geldum acceptum fuit ad navigium faciendum'): *Heming's Cartulary*, ed. Hearne (2 vols., Oxford, 1723), i. 78. Round interprets this somewhat ambiguous passage as implying that service in the fleet could be commuted for money in Edward's reign. *V.C.H., Worcs.* i. 249 n. 3.

represented the exact sum necessary to hire a replacement, for in another Domesday passage we learn that a fyrd soldier was customarily paid 20s. for his term of service.[1] Thus, the burghers of Warwick, Oxford, and Malmesbury were obliged either to produce their quota of warriors for the fyrd or else to pay the monarch the exact sum necessary to hire a like number of substitutes. The income which the monarchy derived from commutation was doubtless insignificant when compared with the danegeld revenues, yet the institution itself was of critical importance as an anticipation of feudal scutage. In the decades following the Conquest, scutage became an immensely lucrative source of royal revenue. Spreading gradually from England to the Continent, it became by the thirteenth century a fundamental and characteristic aspect of the feudal military system. The feudal knight paid scutage in lieu of personal military service, and normally the assessment was levied at the exact rate necessary to hire a qualified mercenary for a term identical to that which the knight had originally owed.[2] The first references to scutage are to be found in the documents of post-Conquest England,[3] yet even before the Conquest the institution existed without the name. In the Anglo-Saxon custom of commutation we are witnessing the genesis of one of the most significant of feudal institutions, an institution which emerged, paradoxically, out of the military structure of a society that is usually described as pre-feudal.

[1] D.B. i. 56b. The fyrd soldier in this passage represents five hides, each of which pays him 4s. whenever he serves on a royal expedition. I know of only one passage in Anglo-Saxon sources indicating a commutation rate other than that of 20s. per man. A charter of King Edgar to Ely states that since olden days the people at Well on the Isle of Ely had given the king 10,000 eels yearly in place of military service; Birch, C.S., nos. 1266, 1267; Kemble, C.D., no. 563; A.S. Chart., no. xlviii.

[2] See my article, 'The Significance of Scutage Rates in Eleventh- and Twelfth-Century England', E.H.R., lxxv (1960), 577–88.

[3] See W. A. Morris, 'A Mention of Scutage in 1100', E.H.R. xxxvi (1921), 45–46.

II

THE NATION IN ARMS

I

ALTHOUGH mercenary soldiers often served as the spearhead of the Old English fyrd, they were numerically only a small part of the total force. They represented, as it were, the *élite* corps of a large army composed predominantly of non-mercenaries. The rank and file of the army was made up of men who served as a result of some customary obligation resting either on their lands or on their persons. These men were bound, under certain circumstances, to perform fyrd service. But what, precisely, were these circumstances? On what basis could an Englishman be summoned for military duty? And what was the exact nature of the fyrd service which he might be called upon to perform? It is from an inability to provide clear answers to these questions that the present state of scholarly confusion arises, and until they are answered, at least tentatively, the military structure of late-Saxon England will remain mysterious and obscure. The answers are not easily discovered, yet the questions demand solution. In the next five chapters, the problems of military organization and military service will be explored carefully, in the hope of shedding light on the recondite dilemma of the Old English fyrd.

Considerable confusion has resulted from the existence of a large body of evidence indicating that all able-bodied freemen owed military service, together with an equally impressive collection of sources which state that only a certain rather small percentage of these men were obliged to serve, the service being assessed in some instances at the rate of one man from five hides. Historians have tended to choose one position or the other, the result being a complete absence of consensus on the subject or even of progress in understanding it. A few historians have attempted to arrive at a compromise between the two positions, with somewhat mixed results. Stenton suggests that the universal obligation gave way just before the Conquest to the more limited one;[1] but the five-hide military unit seems to have existed long before 1066 and the universal military obligation of freemen seems to have persisted beyond the time of Hastings. The only plausible conclusion is that the two obligations existed concurrently.[2] The duty of a particular unit of land to produce a warrior for military campaigns seems to have been the more common one. This was the system which the kings employed to assemble an army of trained or at least partially trained warriors—an army of manageable size—for the normal campaign. But in an emergency every freeman of a particular region might be summoned to defend his homeland against invasion. Only in the darkest days of the Danish attacks in the reigns of Ethelred and Edmund Ironside is there an indication that this general obligation was enforced on anything like a national scale. Ordinarily, an invasion was met by the select five-hide army buttressed by the freemen of the immediate vicinity. Thus, the military obligation of all able-bodied freemen was an exclusively defensive and local one which the king enforced only in cases of extreme emergency. The Anglo-Saxon fyrd consisted ordinarily of representatives from land units of five hides or thereabouts. For purposes of convenience, I shall refer to the army of freemen—the nation in arms—as the *great fyrd* and to the army of five-hide representatives as the *select fyrd*. Since the organization of the select fyrd presents numerous complexities and technical difficulties, I shall turn first to the simpler, cruder, and less significant body, the great fyrd.

---

[1] Stenton, *William the Conqueror*, p. 445.

[2] This is the view of Vinogradoff: *Engl. Soc.*, pp. 23–38, 110–11. See also Clapham, 'The Horsing of the Danes', *E.H.R.* xxv (1910), 292–3. Vinogradoff contends that the five-hide system was clearly inadequate to produce local forces of sufficient size to cope with the huge Danish hosts consisting of many thousands of warriors (op. cit., pp. 27–28). This argument is seriously weakened, however, by the researches of P. H. Sawyer, who concludes that the largest of the Danish armies in England probably did not exceed 200 or 300 men: 'The Density of the Danish Settlement in England', *University of Birmingham Historical Journal*, vi (1957), 16. Cf. ibid., pp. 1–18.

II

The military obligation of all freemen is a custom deeply
imbedded in the Germanic past and one which persisted in
England throughout the Middle Ages. It is illustrated by
the manumission ceremonies in which the former master of
a liberated serf would place in his hands the weapons of
a freeman as a symbol of his new status.[1] The freeman's
military duty and its essentially defensive character is stated
expressly in *Willelmi Articuli Retractati*, where all free men
are commanded to uphold their king's lands and honours
and defend them against enemies and aliens.[2] Although this
is an Anglo-Norman document, it clearly refers back to pre-
Conquest English practice. The principle can also be traced
forward into later documents such as the *Assize of Arms*
(1181) which require all burghers and the whole community of freemen to have gambesons, iron caps, and lances.[3]
In Anglo-Saxon times the freeman who might be summoned
for emergency defence was termed 'fyrdworthy'. The term
occurs in a royal writ in which Edward the Confessor grants
to Ramsey Abbey legal jurisdiction over all men in a certain
district who are foldworthy, mootworthy, and fyrdworthy,
in other words, to all freemen—all who are subject to service
in the great fyrd.[4]

The limited, defensive nature of service in the great fyrd
emerges unmistakably in certain borough charters. All the
burghers of Swansea, for example, are obliged to serve in
the army when summoned, at their own expense, but they

---

[1] *Leges Henrici Primi*, 78: Liebermann, *Gesetze*, i. 594. Cf. ibid. i. 491; A. L.
Poole, *Obligations of Society* (Oxford, 1946), pp. 32–33.

[2] 'Statuimus eciam, ut omnes liberi homines . . . affirment quod intra et extra
universum regnum Angliae, quod olim vocabatur regnum Britanniae, Willelmo
regi domino suo fideles esse volunt, terras et honores illius . . . ubique servare cum
eo et contra inimicos et alienigenas defendere': *The Laws of the Kings of England from
Edmund to Henry I*, ed. A. J. Robertson (Cambridge, England, 1925), p. 244.

[3] Clause 3; *Select Charters*, ed. Stubbs (9th ed., Oxford, 1913), p. 183: 'Item
omnes burgenses et tota communa liberorum hominum habeant wambais et capellet
ferri et lanceam.' Cf. *Close Rolls of the Reign of Henry III, 1237–1242* (London,
1911), pp. 482–3.

[4] *A.S. Writs*, pp. 259, 260 (Anglo-Saxon and Latin versions of the writ). The
writ is seemingly spurious. On the term 'fyrdworthy' see ibid., p. 476.

need not serve beyond the immediate locality of their town.[1] They must be able to return to their homes by nightfall. If the king should lead them farther, he is obligated to pay them wages. In short, if their service goes beyond that of local defence, the burghers of Swansea cease to be members of the great fyrd and become mercenaries. Both of the criteria for service in the great fyrd are present here: the service is local and defensive in nature, and the obligation rests upon all the freemen of the borough rather than a select group of warrior-representatives. The burghers of Pembroke served in the great fyrd on the same terms. All the burghers must serve when summoned, but their service is limited to the immediate locality. Like the burghers of Swansea, they have the right to return home by nightfall.[2] It is interesting to find that the burghers of several towns on the Continent served on precisely the same terms. Indeed, the charter of Tournai displays two separate military obligations which are exact counterparts of the two fyrd obligations in England. The town usually sent 300 armed infantrymen on expeditions, but in the event of an invasion of Artois all the burghers went with the army.[3] The same kind of arrangement, although on a much smaller scale, can be shown to have existed at Exeter in Devonshire. Here, the obligation to the select fyrd seems to have been only one warrior,[4] yet when the Danes besieged the town in A.D. 1001 it was defended vigorously and successfully by large numbers of its citizens.[5] They were less successful two years later, when their town fell into the hands of King Swein.[6] In 1067 the citizens of Exeter again rallied to its defence against William the Conqueror, who reduced the town after a short siege.[7] In all these instances the select-fyrd obligation was hopelessly inadequate and the general obligation of home defence was invoked.

Reflections of the great-fyrd obligation are found in some

---

[1] *British Borough Charters*, ed. A. Ballard (Cambridge, England, 1913), p. 89. For similar limitations on the service of French commoners see E. Boutaric, *Institutions militaires de la France* (Paris, 1863), pp. 143-4, 146-9, 157-8; Guilhiermoz, *Essai sur l'origine de la noblesse*, p. 288 n. 96.

[2] *British Borough Charters*, p. 89.   [3] Ibid., p. cxi.   [4] D.B. i. 100.

[5] *Fl. Wig.* i. 154-5; cf. *A.S.C.*, E, A.D. 1001.

[6] *Fl. Wig.* i. 156; *A.S.C.*, A.D. 1003.   [7] *Fl. Wig.* ii. 2.

of the sergeanty tenures of post-Conquest times, in which military sergeants are required to serve or to lead the local infantry only within a particular shire. If they are obliged to fight outside their shire, they do so at the king's expense.[1] The distinction between these two types of fyrd service is also illustrated by the *fyrdwite*, which is usually assessed at one of two figures: 40*s.* or 100*s.*[2] From the context in which these two figures appear, one gets the impression that the 40*s. fyrdwite* pertains to neglect of service in the great fyrd, whereas the larger *fyrdwite* applies to the more specialized and more valuable select-fyrd obligation. The 40*s. fyrdwite* is especially conspicuous, for example, in connexion with local military service along the Welsh border, where warfare was frequent and the local military obligation of the great fyrd was therefore particularly relevant. The Domesday passages relating to the military service of Shrewsbury and Hereford against the Welsh not only mention the 40*s. fyrdwite* but also suggest strongly that all able-bodied freemen were bound to serve when summoned.[3] Here again the military service was typically that of the great fyrd—it was local and primarily defensive.

It is by no means easy to distinguish between the great fyrd and the select fyrd in the numerous military campaigns mentioned in the narrative sources. It is, in fact, one of the great misfortunes in a study such as this that medieval chroniclers and historians seldom explain the composition of armies. Not infrequently the language of the narrator implies that a particular kind of military force is being used, but there usually remains a degree of uncertainty. In A.D. 916, for example, when the Danes from Northampton and Leicester broke the peace, the *Anglo-Saxon Chronicle* reports that the people of the country (*land leode*) routed them. In 993 the *provinciales* of Lindsey and Northumbria were

---

[1] *Book of Fees*, ed. H. C. Maxwell-Lyte (3 vols., London, 1920–31), ii. 1186, and *passim*.

[2] Vinogradoff, *Engl. Soc.*, pp. 110–11. Another figure which one sometimes encounters is 120*s.*: Ine, 51; 2 Cnut 65.

[3] D.B. i. 252 (Shrewsbury): 'Cum in Walis pergere vellet vicecomes qui ab eo edictus non pergebat xl s. de forisfactura dabat.' Ibid. i. 179 (Hereford): 'Si vicecomes iret in Wales cum exercitu ibant hi homines cum eo. Quod siquis ire iussus non iret emendabat regi xl s.'

hastily assembled to oppose a plundering force of Danes. In 1004 Ealdorman Ulfkytel of East Anglia ordered some of the country people (*provincialibus*) to destroy the ships of a Danish pirate band, but they failed to carry out his orders. Again in 1006 a force of local inhabitants was led into battle against the marauding Danes, and in the same year King Ethelred summoned all the people of Wessex and Mercia on a defensive campaign. Similarly, in 1009 the king ordered that the whole nation be called out to make a stand against the Danes (yet in spite of this the Danes went exactly where they pleased). In May 1010 Ealdorman Ulfkytel fought a desperate but unsuccessful battle against the Danes and suffered heavy losses, including several noblemen of major importance, numerous thegns, and immense numbers of common soldiers (*populusque innumerabilis*).[1] In all of these passages we are given reason to assume that the great fyrd was active, but in none of them can we be absolutely certain. It seems likely that the great fyrd saw service in A.D. 1016, when orders were issued summoning every man fit for military duty on penalty of the full fine in default of service.[2] But 'all the English people' were summoned no less than five times against the Danes in 1016, and there is reason to doubt that all five summonses were directed toward the great fyrd. In the fourth and fifth campaigns of 1016 the entire fyrd seems to be mounted, for in both campaigns it pursues and overtakes a Danish army fleeing on horseback. It is most unlikely that the majority of warriors in the great fyrd would be mounted, and we can perhaps conclude that 'all the English people' is merely loose phraseology and that only the select fyrd was called to duty on these campaigns. But on the other hand, perhaps it was merely a relatively small mounted contingent of the great fyrd that participated in the pursuit. Here as in many other instances definite conclusions are impossible.

One of the primary functions of the great fyrd was to provide a large defensive force, poorly armed yet quickly assembled, against sudden attacks from the sea. The force

---

[1] For these passages see *A.S.C.*, A, A.D. 917 [916]; D, 914; E, 1006 (cf. ibid. 1051, 1052); E, 1009; *Fl. Wig.* i. 151 (993), 157 (1004), 159 (1006), 162 (1010).
[2] *A.S.C.*, A.D. 1016.

could form around a nucleus of relatively well-trained and well-armed warriors who constituted the select fyrd of a particular locality. The select fyrd alone might well be insufficient in number to cope successfully with a large-scale amphibious invasion, and the great fyrd would provide the necessary mass to conduct an adequate defensive operation. Thus, in 1048 a Danish army attacked the coast at Thanet but the inhabitants resisted courageously, refusing to let them land and at length driving them off. In 1052 the exiled Harold Godwinson sailed from Ireland and attacked the English coast, defeating a defensive force of Englishmen from Somerset and Devon and slaying more than thirty thegns.[1] Indeed, the great fyrd played a role at Hastings itself, for the Bayeux Tapestry shows a number of men in King Harold's army who were armed merely with clubs or with stones tied to sticks, fighting alongside the better-armed contingents of the Anglo-Saxon force. Harold's army included both housecarles and elements of the select fyrd from many regions of England, but it also included the great fyrd of Sussex, the large body of ill-armed local freemen who served in accordance with the old traditional obligation of all free subjects to defend their home district against the enemy.[2]

III

Since the mission of the great fyrd was essentially local and defensive, it played a particularly significant role along the borders of Scotland and Wales. In these frontier regions the great-fyrd obligation differed in certain ways from its normal pattern elsewhere, perhaps because nowhere else was it so active as in the Marches. For one thing, the frontier obligation involved a continuity of service extending considerably beyond the duty period of the townsmen who returned home by nightfall. The burghers of Shrewsbury

---

[1] Ibid., E, A.D. 1048; A.D. 1052.
[2] Stenton, overlooking the distinction between the great fyrd and the select fyrd, is obliged to offer the unlikely suggestion that these crudely armed warriors were 'peasants trying to avenge a fortnight's harrying rather than normally recruited members of the national *fyrd*'. *A.S.E.*, p. 575.

were obliged to accompany the sheriff on Welsh expeditions whenever he chose to summon them,[1] and there is nothing to suggest that these expeditions were limited to half a day's march. All the free tenants of the borough of Hereford had to accompany the sheriff on Welsh expeditions which, we are left to assume, were not limited in duration.[2] Elsewhere one encounters allusions to a special service term of fifteen days in connexion with border service against both Wales and Scotland,[3] which contrasts sharply with both the two-month term of select-fyrd service which will be discussed later on, and the brief and flexible term which we have thus far encountered in connexion with the great-fyrd obligation.

Indeed, certain kinds of border duty differ radically from the customary service in the great fyrd. Vinogradoff called attention to the unique characteristics of military service in the Marches of Scotland and Wales, observing that unusual arrangements for Welsh service are often mentioned in the post-Conquest feodaries of Shropshire, Worcestershire, and Herefordshire which almost certainly relate back to pre-Conquest customs.[4] To cite only a single example of this, Roger de la Mare held an estate in Shropshire by sergeantry. His obligation consisted of serving as constable in charge of foot soldiers whenever the king led his army into Wales. The service was to be performed at the king's expense at a wage of a shilling a day.[5] Such references relate to specific obligations of fixed numbers of warriors owed by particular estates long after the Norman Conquest.[6] Although they doubtless are based on pre-Conquest traditions, the obliga-

---

[1] D.B. i. 252.   [2] Ibid. i. 179.

[3] *Bk. of Fees*, i. 100: 'Franci et Wallenses de Urchenesfeld tenent tenementa sua in capite de socagio de domino rege reddendo xxx. l. vij. s. vj. d. Et debent invenire xlix servientes in servicio domini regis in Wallia per xv. dies ad proprium custum.' In 1577 the Council of the North mentioned that certain tenants of Durham were required by custom to serve in expeditions against Scotland for fifteen days at their own expense: *Rolls of the Halmotes of the Prior and Convent of Durham* (Surtees Soc., 1889), p. xxxviii. See also ibid., p. xliii (another reference to the fifteen-day military obligation against Scotland). Maitland maintains that passages such as this probably refer back to pre-Conquest obligations: 'Northumbrian Tenures', *E.H.R.* v (1890), 631–2.

[4] Vinogradoff, *Engl. Soc.*, pp. 32–33.

[5] *Bk. of Fees*, i. 145, 347, 383.

[6] Several Anglo-Norman sergeanty tenures relate specifically to Welsh service, e.g. *R.R.A.N.* ii. 569, 1945.

tions must have evolved considerably in the intervening years. Their similarity to the great-fyrd obligation lies solely in their local, defensive character. In so far as they are tenurial obligations they are alien to the spirit of the great fyrd.

But these fixed, tenurial obligations are overshadowed by another sort of border service which was particularly common along the Scottish frontier and which harmonizes much more satisfactorily with the Anglo-Saxon great-fyrd obligation. Throughout much of Northumbria, border service seems to have been required of all men holding their lands by particular kinds of tenure. For example, all the cornage tenants in Cumberland were obligated to join the king's army in Scotland, serving as the vanguard when the army was advancing and as the rearguard when it returned.[1] Postponing for the moment an analysis and definition of cornage tenure, we will observe simply that by far the greater part of Cumberland was held by cornage[2] and that consequently a general military obligation incumbent upon all cornage tenants in Cumberland is very nearly identical with the military duty of all freemen which characterizes the great fyrd elsewhere.

The obligation to lead the army when it advances and to bring up the rear as it withdraws may have been a widespread custom, for we find it also in connexion with the Welsh border service of the inhabitants of Archenfield in Hereford: 'When the army advances against the enemy, they customarily form the vanguard, and on the return, the rearguard.'[3] It is natural that the king should want men familiar with border conditions to lead his army into Scotland or Wales and to protect it from surprise attacks as it withdrew, and this seems to have been the special duty of English landholders along the Scottish and Welsh frontiers.

---

[1] *Bk. of Fees*, i. 199, 351.   [2] J. Wilson, in *V.C.H.*, *Cumb*. i. 313.

[3] D.B. i. 179. By the thirteenth century the Archenfield obligation has become tenurialized at the rate of forty-nine or fifty men who served for fifteen days annually on Welsh campaigns. *Bk. of Fees*, i. 100; ii. 810–11, 1273; see above, p. 32 n. 3. See also *Calendar of Inquisitions Post Mortem* (4 vols., London, 1898–1913), ii. no. 51, where the service of a sergeanty connected with the manor of East Garston, Berks., consists of leading the vanguard of the royal army when it advances into West Wales and the rearguard when it returns. Cf. ibid. ii, no. 477, and *Bk. of Fees*, ii. 863.

D

The exact basis of this frontier military obligation is by no means clear. It seems to have been shared by tenants in thegnage, drengage, and cornage, three ancient and obscure types of land tenure which are exceptionally difficult to distinguish from one another. Indeed, it seems likely that drengage tenure and cornage tenure were essentially the same thing—that drengage tenants held by cornage and cornage tenants held by drengage.[1] And the thegnage tenants mentioned in these Northumbrian sources seem far removed from the normal pre-Conquest thegn. Thegnage tenants, like drengage tenants, frequently held by cornage,[2] and there are numerous confusions in the documents between tenants of thegnage and tenants in drengage.[3] A survey of the early thirteenth century, for example, lists a number of Lancashire tenants who hold by thegnage and drengage, without attempting to distinguish between the two tenures in any way.[4] And the ambiguity of the sources results in considerable confusion among modern scholars. They agree that these tenures are restricted largely to Northumbria and pertain generally to service against the Scots, but they agree on little else. A great deal of the confusion arises from the fact that most of our information regarding these ancient tenures is to be found in post-Conquest documents, many of them dating from the thirteenth century, when such terms as thegnage, drengage, and cornage were becoming increasingly ambiguous and anachronistic. Vinogradoff writes, 'thanes are of English origin, drengs of Scandinavian, but in both cases we have to do with the armed sergeants of the king who held land endowments from him'.[5] Rachel Reid, on the other hand, distinguishes between the barons who held by thegnage or fee-farm and those who held by drengage or sergeanty.[6] But even this distinction is doubtful, since tenants owing nearly identical duties are described as drengs in certain

---

[1] G. T. Lapsley, 'Cornage and Drengage', *A.H.R.* ix (1904), 670–95. Cf. N. Neilson, *Customary Rents* (Oxford Studies, ii, 1910), pp. 120 ff.; and Wilson, op. cit., i. 313 n. 2.
[2] Maitland, 'Northumbrian Tenures', p. 629.
[3] Ibid.; Vinogradoff, *Engl. Soc.*, p. 65.
[4] *R.B.E.* ii. 572.   [5] *Engl. Soc.*, p. 66.
[6] Reid, 'Baronage and Thanage', *E.H.R.* xxxv (1920), 191.

regions of Lancashire, and as thegns or *homines* in other
regions of the same county.[1]

The obligations normally incumbent upon these tenures
are not primarily military, but fiscal and agricultural. They
involve the payment of money rents, the performance of
judicial and administrative services, the carting of timber
(truncage), the carrying of messages and supplies, and
numerous other duties of a miscellaneous sort such as feed-
ing animals and assisting on hunts.[2] Cornage itself is primarily a money payment of some sort.[3] Miss Reid called it
a food rent, while Lapsley believed that it originated in
a payment given by vills to their lords for right of pasture,
later becoming attached to certain specific tenements.[4] This
view is supported by passages from *Boldon Buke* which disclose that certain vills did not pay cornage because of a lack
of pasture.[5] Yet these passages also support the view of
Miss Neilson that cornage originated as a form of geld
which in the pastoral localities of northern England was
levied on the number of animals which a tenant or a vill
possessed rather than on the assessment of land.[6] Thus,
whoever was obliged to pay the normal geld was obliged also
to serve on frontier military campaigns. But whatever the
origin of the cornage payment may have been, it was usually
only one of several duties which the cornage tenant normally
performed. *Boldon Buke* provides an admirable summary of

---

[1] D.B. i. 269b, 270. See Vinogradoff, *Engl. Soc.*, pp. 64–65, and Maitland, op. cit.,
p. 629.

[2] Ibid., pp. 629–30, 632; *Boldon Buke*, ed. Greenwell (Surtees Soc., 1852), p. 36
and *passim*. On the general subject of Northumbrian thegnage, see Maitland, op.
cit., pp. 625 ff.; Vinogradoff, *Engl. Soc.*, pp. 64 ff. On drengage, in addition to the
above references see *Placita Anglo-Normannica*, p. 2; Ellis, i. 56–58; Reid, p. 189 and
passim; Lapsley, op. cit., p. 685 and *passim*; Neilson, p. 120. On cornage, in addition
to the works cited under thegnage and drengage, see Round, *The Commune of
London* (Westminster, 1899), pp. 278 ff.; G. T. Lapsley, in *V.C.H., Durham*, i.
273 ff.; Wilson, op. cit., i. 313 ff.; J. E. A. Jolliffe, 'Northumbrian Institutions',
E.H.R. xli (1926), 1–42.

[3] *Boldon Buke*, pp. 4, 5, 6, 8, 10, 11, and *passim*, where cornage obligations are
always expressed in monetary terms. See also Seebohm, *The English Village Community* (London, 1883), p. 71, and *Sir Christopher Hatton's Book of Seals*, ed. L. C.
Loyd and D. M. Stenton (Oxford, 1950), no. 465 (A.D. 1209–15). Cornage may
earlier have been rendered in kind: Wilson, op. cit., i. 315 ff.

[4] Reid, p. 187; Lapsley, *V.C.H., Durham*, i. 273 ff.

[5] *Boldon Buke*, pp. 12, 13, 14 *bis*.

[6] Neilson, pp. 120 ff.

these obligations:[1] a tenant named William holds the vill of Oxenhall and performs the service of one-quarter of a drengage, i.e. he ploughs four acres and sows it with his lord's seed; he harrows it and performs other specified services in connexion with the harvest, in certain of which he is aided by his men; he keeps a dog and a horse for three months; he carts wine with four oxen; and he renders *utware* whenever it is assessed on the bishopric of Durham.[2] Obviously, none of these duties is remotely military except possibly the last.[3] Yet the military obligations of these tenants were far from insignificant. Some scholars have associated their duties with Anglo-Saxon fyrd service, although in the absence of any clear recognition of the distinction between the great fyrd and the select fyrd such assumptions are necessarily highly speculative.[4] In addition to the passages already discussed which show that cornage tenants in Cumberland joined royal military campaigns against the Scots, we find thegnage tenures being converted without apparent difficulty into knight's fees, cornage tenants who are bound specifically to perform military service and construction work on castles, and thegnage and drengage tenants who pay fines in lieu of their military obligation, or who are bound to serve on Scottish expeditions.[5] Evidently the military duties of these tenants are connected with their obligation to render *utware*. It seems clear that *utware*, like the more common forinsec service, is 'outward' service—service to the king as distinct from service to the immediate lord. As such, it included the pay-

---

[1] *Boldon Buke*, pp. 17–18. Cf. ibid., p. 20.

[2] '. . . et facit utware quando positum fuerit in Episcopatu.'

[3] Elsewhere in *Boldon Buke*, however, drengs are listed as owing castlemen: pp. 36, 37.

[4] See Maitland, op. cit., pp. 629–32 and *passim*; Lapsley, 'Cornage and Drengage', p. 685: 'In many cases the dreng is required to perform *utware* (probably a survival of the ancient obligation of the fyrd) when it is appointed in the bishopric.' Reid, pp. 187–9: after raising the possibility that *utware* was a survival of the fyrd obligation, Reid concludes that it 'was not just the general service in the fyrd required of all freemen, but was the special service in the king's "utware" required of all drengs'.

[5] Cf. *Bk. of Fees*, pp. 554, 598 (Hepple), and *Rotuli Chartarum*, ed. Hardy (Record Commission, 1837), p. 51; Maitland, op. cit., pp. 628–9; *Newminster Cartulary*, ed. Fowler (Surtees Soc., 1878), p. 269; T. Madox, *History of the Exchequer* (2nd ed., 2 vols., London, 1769), i. 659; *Bracton's Note Book*, ed. Maitland (3 vols., London, 1887), pl. 1270.

ment of royal gelds,[1] but it also included the obligation of border service against the Scots. In Cumberland and Westmorland a special term, *endemot*, is used to describe the military part of the *utware* obligation. *Endemot* refers to the forinsec military service due from cornage tenants in these districts—a service which retained its military character in later years to such an extent that under King John tenants had to explain that they did not owe scutage for it.[2] But the *endemot* tenant owed military service only against the Scots, and was exempt from other military obligations.[3]

To summarize, the tenants in thegnage, drengage, and cornage who are found in such profusion in the districts bordering Scotland and whose tenures, although of ancient origin, survive into the later Middle Ages, owe services that are primarily non-military. But they normally have the additional obligation of rendering forinsec service or *utware*. This 'outward' service to the king is itself only partly military, for it includes gelds and other royal services. But it also includes royal military service, which in these districts signifies a special duty of aiding the king's army on frontier campaigns, usually in the van of the advancing army and in the rear of the retiring force. This same special obligation appears in the Domesday survey in connexion with military service along the Welsh frontier. There, all the inhabitants of certain border districts are obliged to serve, and in Northumbria the tenures owing frontier military service were so widespread that the obligation can be said to have applied to the great majority of freemen. It was general in application and local in scope, and must therefore be regarded as an interesting variant of the great-fyrd duty. And it is also a vivid reminder that the history of the great fyrd by no means ends with the coming of the Normans.

[1] See *Transcripts of Charters Relating to Gilbertine Houses*, ed. F. M. Stenton (Lincoln Record Society, xviii, 1922), p. xxxiv; and *Danelaw Charters*, ed. Stenton (London, 1920), pp. cxxvii–cxxxv, where it is shown that forinsec service later came to include feudal military service. On the subject of *utware*, see also Vinogradoff, *Growth of the Manor* (London, 1911), pp. 239, 284; F. M. Stenton, *Types of Manorial Structure in the Northern Danelaw* (Oxford Studies, ii, 1910), pp. 30–31.

[2] *P.R. 3 John*; Reid, p. 187; Wilson, op. cit., i. 321–8.

[3] *Rotuli Litterarum Clausarum* (Record Commission, 2 vols., 1833–44), i. 614; Maitland, op. cit., p. 629; Wilson, op. cit. i. 319–21.

III

THE SELECT FYRD AND THE
FIVE-HIDE UNIT

I

THE most complete description of the select-fyrd obligation is to be found in a Domesday passage relating to Berkshire: 'If the king sent an army anywhere, only one soldier went from five hides, and four shillings were given him from each hide as subsistence and wages for two months. This money, indeed, was not sent to the king but was given to the soldiers.'[1] We find here a military obligation which differs fundamentally from service in the great fyrd. The Berkshire passage relates not to the duty of all able-bodied freemen, but rather to the obligation of a select group of warrior-representatives serving in behalf of a unit of land assessment and supported financially by the men from the hides which they represent. The warrior-representative might, in fact, be the sole possessor of his five hides, in which case he would collect his 20s. (4s. from each of five hides) from his own subordinates or, perhaps, from his own income. On the other hand, he might possess no land at all, in which case he would collect his 20s. from the men of the five-hide unit who did hold land. Finally, he might be a small landholder within a five-hide unit, supplying part of the 20s. sum from his own income and receiving the remainder from his fellow landholders within the unit. Thus, if he held two hides, he would be responsible personally for 8s. of his pay, and would collect an additional 12s. from the holders of the remaining three hides of the unit. If he held four hides, he would collect 4s. from his

---

[1] D.B. i. 56b: 'Si rex mittebat alicubi exercitum de quinque hidis tantum unus miles ibat, et ad eius victum vel stipendium de unaquaque hida dabantur et iiii solidi ad duos menses. Hos vero denarios regi non mittebantur, sed militibus dabantur.'

neighbours and be responsible himself for the remainder, &c.[1]

The Berkshire passage does not tell us how the warrior-representative was selected. Vinogradoff and others have suggested the possibility of some system of rotation,[2] but there is good reason to believe that the same man usually served on every campaign. If one man held the entire five hides, he was normally expected to serve personally, although he might, if necessary, provide a substitute.[3] Several Domesday passages report that when the hide unit was divided among a number of holders, one of them was designated as the normal representative and was expected to respond personally to the military summons, although if for some reason he was unable to serve, his obligation might be met by the service of one of his neighbouring landholders.[4] This system harmonizes with our general concept of the select fyrd as an army of relatively well-trained and well-equipped warriors; it would surely produce a considerably more seasoned force than could possibly be provided by any system of rotation, and one can easily understand why the Anglo-Saxons might prefer to hold one particular man responsible for the military duty of his five-hide unit.

Thus the Berkshire entry in Domesday Book discloses a military recruitment system of considerable sophistication based on the unit of five hides. The system is at once simple and effective, and provides us with an excellent point of departure in our study of the select fyrd. But it also raises a crucial problem: does the five-hide recruitment system described in this passage relate to England as a whole or merely to Berkshire? One cannot help but be impressed with the bewildering diversity of custom in Anglo-Saxon England, and it would be hazardous indeed to assume without further investigation that the Berkshire practice represented a nation-wide system. For one thing, the nature

---

[1] See Vinogradoff, *Engl. Soc.*, pp. 33–34.
[2] Ibid.
[3] D.B. i. 56b, 172.
[4] This is illustrated by certain Domesday passages relating to parage tenures, e.g. i. 67, 375. Some historians would question my belief that these passages refer to the same sort of service as that described in the Berkshire passage. I discuss this issue in Chapter IV.

of landholding differed drastically in various regions of England, ranging from the numerous independent holdings of East Anglia through the Kentish hamlets and the carucate system of the Danelaw to the open fields and nucleated villages of the Midlands. Bracton, writing in the thirteenth century, was describing a situation which had long existed when he observed:

There are numerous and diverse customs in England according to the diversity of places. For the English hold many things by custom which they do not hold by law, as in various shires, cities, towns, and villages where it must always be asked what the custom of that place is and in what way those who claim the custom apply it.[1]

Surely the five-hide system cannot have existed in the Danelaw where the land was assessed in carucates rather than in hides, and indeed there is nothing in the Domesday passage itself which would justify us in extending the custom beyond the borders of Berkshire. Sir Frank Stenton maintains that the Berkshire recruitment system was almost certainly a local phenomenon, since the Berkshire hide was unusually small, probably forty acres, whereas a hide of 120 acres was common in many other regions.[2] He also points out that Berkshire was far from the coast and was in fact one of the regions of England least exposed to attack. These considerations lead Stenton to the conclusion that outside of Berkshire and perhaps one or two neighbouring shires the fyrd obligation was assessed at a far heavier rate than one man from five hides.

Yet despite these arguments I am convinced that the five-hide rule governed the system of military recruitment throughout most of Anglo-Saxon England outside the carucated region of the Danelaw. In the first place, the hide was normally regarded as a standard unit of assessment regardless of its size. It was a fiscal and military unit rather than an areal unit. Danegeld was customarily levied at the rate of 2s. per hide irrespective of the number of acres which the hide might contain. The same holds for the assessment

---

[1] *De Legibus et Consuetudinibus Angliae*, ed. G. G. Woodbine (New Haven, 1915–22), ii. 19.

[2] *E.F.*, pp. 116–17; *A.S.E.*, p. 575.

of ship service in Anglo-Saxon England. The *Anglo-Saxon Chronicle* reports that in A.D. 1008 the king demanded that ships be built throughout the whole of England; every 300 hides should provide a large warship, every ten hides should produce a cutter, and every eight hides should produce a helmet and a coat of mail.[1] No allowance is made for variation in the acreage of hides; the assessment is standard throughout England. The hide serves also as a standard assessment unit for Anglo-Norman aids.[2] Indeed, whenever we find the hide used as a unit of assessment, we find also that the assessment is consistent. Nowhere are large hides assessed more heavily than small hides. Nowhere does the acre replace the hide as the assessment unit. This fact in itself would be enough to justify at least the tentative assumption that the Berkshire system was general rather than local.

It should also be noted that the existence of forty-acre hides in Berkshire is by no means certain. James Tait has shown that the hides of Wiltshire and Dorsetshire contained only forty acres, but he cautions that the existence of small hides in other counties cannot be stated dogmatically.[3] There is, in fact, excellent evidence that the five-hide recruitment rule applied in a county of singularly large hides. In Devonshire where, as Eyton expresses it, 'the scope of the geld-hide was enormous',[4] the burghers of Exeter served in military campaigns as five hides of land, and the towns of Barnstaple, Lidford, and Totnes together served as Exeter did.[5] Thus five hides was the standard unit of military assessment in Devonshire as well as in Berkshire, and although we are not told explicitly that the Devonshire

---

[1] *A.S.C.*, A.D. 1008. See *Fl. Wig.* i. 160 where slightly different figures are given. Some versions of the *A.S.C.* refer to districts of 310 hides rather than 300. See below, pp. 108 ff.

[2] *Chron. Ab.* ii. 38, 113; *Fl. Wig.* ii. 40; H. of Hunt., p. 237; Liebermann, *Gesetze*, i. 636; S. K. Mitchell, *Taxation in Medieval England* (New Haven, 1951), pp. 164–5.

[3] Tait, 'Large Hides and Small Hides', *E.H.R.* xvii (1902), 282. The Berkshire hide may well have been small: 'The infrequent mention of acres in the Domesday of the southern counties and their small numbers when mentioned is much more easily explicable on the assumption of a 10-acre virgate [forty-acre hide], where areas could in most cases be stated in simple fractions of a virgate, than if we suppose that as many as thirty acres went to the virgate.' Ibid.

[4] R. W. Eyton, *A Key to Domesday, Dorset* (London, 1878), p 14. See also Round, *F.E.*, pp. 62–63, and Vinogradoff, *Engl. Soc.*, pp. 150–1.

[5] D.B. i. 100.

five-hide unit owed one man to the fyrd, we are certainly
left to infer it. The wording of the military obligation which
Domesday attributes to these four Devonshire towns is
strikingly similar to that of another Domesday passage
relating to Malmesbury in Wiltshire, which also serves on
military campaigns as five hides of land. But here Domesday
provides us with the additional information, scarcely necessary under the circumstances, that the burghers of Malmesbury sent one warrior-representative.[1] Wiltshire, as we have
seen, had unusually small hides, whereas the hides of
Devonshire were exceptionally large, but both had the same
military assessment system based upon the same five-hide
unit. And Stenton's argument as to the invulnerability of
Berkshire is singularly inapplicable to Devonshire, which
had two long coastlines to protect. In the light of my previous
discussion of the great-fyrd obligation it should be clear that
exposed shires defended themselves against hostile attack,
not by increasing the recruitment rate of the select fyrd, but
by resorting to the mass levy of freemen to back up the local
warrior-representatives of the five-hide units.

The general and widespread application of the five-hide
recruitment system in Anglo-Saxon England is paralleled
by a strikingly similar military structure on the continent of
Europe. We have already observed that the military obligations of certain continental towns correspond closely to the
select-fyrd and great-fyrd dichotomy of Old English custom.[2]
Evidently both the Frankish and the Anglo-Saxon systems
evolved along similar lines out of a common Germanic
tradition. Professor Lot has shown that in the time of
Charlemagne and his immediate successors there existed a
strong and ancient tradition that all free men owed military
service. But in order to raise an army of manageable size
and at least moderate skill for a service term of three months
as was then customary, the Carolingian monarchs recruited
their infantry normally on the basis of a military land unit
of four manses.[3] A tenant holding three manses served in

---

[1] D.B. i. 64b. See above, p. 23, and below, p. 76.

[2] Above, p. 28.

[3] Lot, *L'Art militaire* (2 vols., Paris, 1946), i. 91 ff.; Capitularies of A.D. 808,
829, and 864; *Capitularia Regum Francorum*, ed. Boretius and Krause (*M.G.H.*,
2 vols., Hanover, 1883–97), i. 137; ii. 7, 321. Similar arrangements existed in the

the army and was given financial support by an adjacent holder of a single manse. If two neighbouring tenants each held two manses, one served in the army and the other contributed money toward his support. Tenants holding single manses formed into groups of four, one serving in the army and the other three aiding him. In short, four manses owed one foot-soldier to the Frankish host and supported him exactly as the Berkshire hides contributed to the wages and provisions of their warrior-representatives. Nor does the parallel between the Frankish four-manse unit and the Anglo-Saxon five-hide unit end here, for Frankish manses, like English hides, could vary in acreage.[1] But as in England, the Frankish military unit retained its integrity regardless of the number of acres which it contained.

The uniformity of the Anglo-Saxon recruitment system is well illustrated by an episode in 1094. King William Rufus had a large body of Englishmen summoned for overseas duty, but instead of sending them across the Channel he collected 10s. from each of them—the money which they had received for their service—and sent them home.[2] The three chroniclers who report this event agree that no less than 20,000 men were assembled. Doubtless this figure is a gross exaggeration, but one can at least infer that the number was considerable and included warrior-representatives from many parts of England. The fact that each one of these warriors had received 10s. from the men of his locality proves the existence of a uniform system of support. It may be argued that the possession of 10s. by every fyrd soldier in 1094 is poor evidence for the universality of a 20s. support system such as is described in the Berkshire entry, but it does seem clear that the philosophy of local support described with such precision in Berkshire Domesday was generally observed throughout England and that at least

Lombard Kingdom of Italy: Aistulf, 2 (*M.G.H.*, *Lgg.* iv. 196), quoted in Vinogradoff, *Engl. Soc.*, p. 30 n. The same basic recruitment system is also to be found in Denmark and Sweden: Steenstrup, *Kong Valdemar's Jordbog*, pp. 185 ff.; Vinogradoff, *Engl. Soc.*, pp. 37–38; Hildebrand, *Sveriges medeltid Kulturhistorisk Skildring* (3 vols., Stockholm, 1879–1903), ii. 613 ff.

[1] F. Lot, 'Le Jugum, le manse et les exploitations agricoles', in *Mélanges d'histoire offerts à Henri Pirenne* (Brussels, Vromant, &c., 1926); see also *L'Art mil.* i. 91, 94.

[2] *Fl. Wig.* ii. 35; H. of Hunt., p. 217; *A.S.C.*, A.D. 1094. See above, p. 23.

in 1094 the amount of support was uniform. Nor are the two references necessarily contradictory. We are not told that the soldiers of 1094 were serving for wages of 10s. each, but merely that they had been given 10s. before setting forth on the campaign. It may well have been customary to pay them 10s. on their departure and another 10s. on their return. Payments in two equal instalments are encountered frequently in the documents of the period.[1] Moreover, the Berkshire passage makes clear that the 20s. were paid to the warrior-representative for two purposes: subsistence and wages.[2] The money was to support the soldier on his two-month campaign and also to pay him for his time and effort. It is by no means unlikely that the payment to cover his costs during the campaign would be rendered on his departure, whereas his wages, as distinct from his subsistence money, would be given him when he returned from the expedition. Florence of Worcester, describing the episode of 1094, states specifically that the 10s. had been allotted to each soldier *for his subsistence—ad victum.*[3] The 20s. of the Berkshire passage were for *victum vel stipendium.* There is no real contradiction here. The only doubt that remains is whether or not after returning from that abbreviated and bloodless campaign the warriors were treated generously by their neighbours and given their additional 10s. *stipendium.*

II

We have already seen that the five-hide recruitment unit can be traced beyond Berkshire into Wiltshire and Devon-

---

[1] e.g. *Facsimiles of Early Charters from Northamptonshire Collections*, ed. F. M. Stenton (Northamptonshire Record Society, iv, 1930), p. 132; *Sir Christopher Hatton's Book of Seals*, nos. 114, 337, 343, 373, 380, 402, and *passim*; *Regestrum Antiquissimum of the Cathedral Church of Lincoln*, ed. C. W. Foster and K. Major (Lincoln Record Society, 1931–), ii, no. 625; iv, nos. 1195, 1301, and *passim*; *Charters Relating to Gilbertine Houses*, pp. 7, 12, 17, 79, and *passim*.

[2] D.B. i. 56b: *victum vel stipendium.* I translate *vel* as 'and' in the sense of 'and also' rather than 'or'. 'Subsistence *and* wages' makes much better sense here than 'subsistence *or* wages'. Cf. Carl Stephenson's translation of the phrase as 'food and pay' in Stephenson and Marcham, *Sources of English Constitutional History* (New York and London, 1937), p. 45.

[3] *Fl. Wig.* ii. 35.

shire, where certain important towns are found to have military obligations which are expressed in terms of the five-hide rule. Malmesbury in Wiltshire and Exeter in Devonshire each serve as five hides of land, producing one man for the select fyrd.[1] Barnstaple, Lidford, and Totnes (all in Devonshire) together serve as five hides, and therefore have a joint obligation to send one warrior when the select fyrd is summoned.[2] The military obligations of several other English towns can also be determined, but unfortunately when the number of warriors is given, the number of hides is not, and vice versa. Thus, Warwick sent ten men when the king went on an expedition by land, Oxford sent twenty men, and Leicester sent twelve.[3] But it is impossible to determine the hidage assessments of any of these towns (unless we apply the five-hide rule and multiply each military assessment by five, but that would be begging the question).[4] We should note, however, that the towns whose military obligation we know, generally owe whole numbers of warriors. This is precisely what we should expect, for the independent nature of burghal organization would seriously impede any sort of co-operation with the surrounding countryside for the purpose of combining fractional obligations into whole warriors. Indeed, the three Devonshire towns of Barnstaple, Lidford, and Totnes, each of which owes a fraction of one warrior, do not combine with their surrounding regions but rather co-operate with one another to produce a joint quota of one man. We are not told that they are assessed at the rate of one and two-thirds hides or one-third warrior each, but rather that they serve *as a unit* at the rate of five hides. We should expect, therefore, that other English towns would follow suit—that their military obligation would also be assessed in terms of the five-hide unit. And this is exactly what we do find. The vast majority of towns whose hidage assessment can be determined are assessed either at five hides or at some exact multiple thereof. Below are some examples of this trend:[5]

[1] D.B. i. 64*b*, 100.　　　[2] Ibid. i. 100.　　　[3] Ibid. i. 238, 154, 230.

[4] The five-hide rule cannot have applied to Leicester, which is in a county assessed by carucates rather than by hides.

[5] Some of these town obligations are discussed by Round, 'Danegeld and the Finance of Domesday', pp. 119 ff.

Town	Hides	Domesday reference
Bath	20	i. 87
Bedford	50	i. 209
Bridport	5	i. 75
Cambridge	100	i. 189
Cheshunt	20	i. 137
Chester	50	i. 262b
Colchester	100	ii. 104
Dorchester	10	i. 75
Exeter	5	i. 100
Hertford	10	i. 132
Huntingdon	50	i. 203
Ipswich	50	ii. 290
Maldon	50	ii. 5b
Malmesbury	5	i. 64b
Northampton	25	. . 1
St. Albans	10	i. 135b
Shaftesbury	20	i. 75
Shrewsbury	100	i. 252
Sudbury	25	ii. 286b
Tewkesbury	95	i. 163b
Wareham	10	i. 75
Worcester	15	i. 172
Yarmouth	5	ii. 118

Surely figures such as these are significant illustrations of the widespread enforcement of a five-hide recruitment system. These towns would each owe, according to the five-hide rule, a whole number of soldiers to the select fyrd, a number ranging from one (Bridport, Exeter, Malmesbury, and Yarmouth) to twenty (Cambridge and Shrewsbury; Oxford, as we have seen, also owed twenty men). If any recruitment rule had been employed other than that of one man from five hides, the military obligation of these widely scattered towns would have been bewilderingly difficult to determine and enforce. But the remarkably systematic five-hide basis which underlies their assessments provides a striking confirmation of our previous evidence.[2]

[1] For the assessment of Northampton, see the Northamptonshire Geld Roll, printed in Ellis, i. 186 n.

[2] Of the few exceptions to this five-hide rule of town assessment, some are assessed at very low figures (e.g. Buckingham, one hide, D.B. i. 143) and may have combined with others to produce a warrior, as did the three Devonshire towns. Other assessments exceed or fall short of an even multiple of five hides by only a

Thus, the prevailing opinion among present-day historians that the five-hide system was limited to Berkshire and
possibly to one or two adjacent counties can no longer be
maintained. To begin with, it cannot be proven that Berkshire had the small hide. But even if the Berkshire hides
were small, this would be irrelevant to the problem, since
a five-hide obligation can be traced to four scattered towns
in Devonshire, a county with unusually large hides. The
argument that more vulnerable shires would require a
heavier assessment rate collapses before the fact of the great-
fyrd obligation and the additional fact that Devonshire, one
of the most vulnerable of all English counties, had the five-
hide system. We have seen that in all other kinds of assessment, e.g. danegeld, aids, and ship service, the hide retained
throughout non-Danish England its integrity as a standard
assessment unit, regardless of variations among individual
hides in acreage, value, or military potential. We have noted
the existence of a remarkably similar system of military
recruitment in Carolingian Frankland. There the manse,
analogous to the English hide, was the standard assessment
unit throughout the Empire, and the four-manse unit,
regardless of variations in acreage among individual manses
or variations of custom in different parts of Frankland,
owed one infantryman to the Carolingian host. We have
seen that a uniform system of support, compatible with the
recruitment and support system described in Berkshire
Domesday, governed the English fyrd in 1094. Finally, we
have shown that throughout England the hidage assessment
of towns was based upon the unit of five hides.

The system disclosed in Berkshire Domesday would
require close co-operation among the various tenants of the
five-hide unit. It suggests strongly that in Berkshire at least,
the assessment of land ought to reveal, on close examination,
the existence of five-hide groups—military-recruitment
units. Without such groups the recruitment-support system
would be virtually unworkable. And just as one would expect,
these five-hide groupings did abound in pre-Conquest

small fraction (e.g. Taunton, 54⅝ hides, D.B. i. 87*b*). A small minority appear
to be exceptions to the rule (e.g. Reading, 43 hides, D.B. i. 58). My list of towns
following the five-hide rule is, of course, far from exhaustive.

Berkshire. Round has shown that the hidage assessment of the county falls naturally into small regional units assessed at five hides or at simple multiples of that figure.[1] We have found direct evidence of the five-hide recruitment system in Wiltshire and Devonshire, and here, also, Round has discovered a strong and unmistakable tendency towards five-hide groupings.[2] But this tendency is by no means limited to Berkshire, Wiltshire, and Devonshire. Indeed, these five-hide groups abound in virtually every hidated shire. They constitute an underlying characteristic of the hide system throughout England from Staffordshire in the northern midlands to Essex in the east and Devonshire in the south-west.[3] They are particularly conspicuous in Cambridgeshire, a county with large hides of 120 acres.[4] Round describes this nation-wide tendency toward five-hide groupings as 'a vast system of artificial hidation, of which the very existence has been hitherto unsuspected'.[5]

Before drawing conclusions as to the significance of these five-hide groups, we must remember that the hide served as a unit of fiscal as well as military assessment. At the customary danegeld rate of 2s. on the hide, two five-hide units would pay one pound, and consequently the hide groups doubtless contributed to the efficiency of the Anglo-Saxon financial system. But granting that they may have been useful as administrative and fiscal subdivisions, their role as units of recruitment and military support was far

---

[1] F.E., pp. 65–66.

[2] Ibid., pp. 66, 62–63.

[3] J. C. Wedgwood, 'Early Staffordshire History' (Wm. Salt, 1916), pp. 175–8; V.C.H., Essex, i. 334; J. H. Round, 'The Domesday Hidation of Essex', E.H.R. xxix (1914), 477–9.

[4] Round, F.E., pp. 45–55. The five-hide unit is especially easy to trace in Cambridgeshire because of the existence of a unique survey, the Inquisitio Comitatus Cantabrigiensis, which is roughly contemporary with Domesday Book but differs from it in arranging the manors according to townships and hundreds rather than according to individual landholders. Hence, the organization of the Inquisitio is geographical rather than tenurial and consequently the five-hide groupings are much easier to identify than in Domesday.

[5] F.E., p. 49. For a general discussion of these five-hide groupings, see ibid., pp. 44–69. Round finds them in the following counties: Cambridgeshire, Bedfordshire, Huntingdonshire, Northamptonshire, Hertfordshire, Worcestershire, Devonshire, Oxfordshire, Berkshire, Buckinghamshire, Surrey, Wiltshire, and Middlesex.

more significant. They were absolutely essential to the successful operation of the Old English fyrd system and were, in fact, the units within which arrangements such as those disclosed in Berkshire Domesday could be implemented. And as Round has shown, these five-hide groups were by no means limited to Berkshire or even to the southern Midlands. They existed in profusion throughout most of England, and their abundance testifies unmistakably to the universality of the five-hide recruitment system.

III

But perhaps 'universality' is too strong a word, for there are certain regions of England where the five-hide unit cannot have applied. This is obviously the case in the Danish regions, where the lands were assessed in carucates rather than hides. For the carucated regions of England there is no evidence comparable to the Berkshire passage. The military structure of the pre-Conquest Danelaw is a matter of considerable obscurity. It is, however, by no means unlikely that fyrd service in the Danelaw was assessed on the basis of the carucate, just as in the remainder of England it was assessed by hides. This is suggested by the fact that in nearly every other respect the Danelaw carucate has the same function as the English hide. The services and obligations which 'went by hides and by hundreds' in central and southern England are said to 'run by carucates of land' in the Danelaw.[1] Domesday discloses that Stamford, on the border between Lincolnshire and Northamptonshire, gelded for 150 carucates for army service, ship service, and danegeld: 'Stanford burgum regis dedit geldum T.R.E. pro xii hundrez et dimidio [or 150 carucates, with twelve carucates to the hundred] in exercitu et nauigio et in danegeld.'[2] This passage can be interpreted in at least two ways. At first sight it would seem to imply that Stamford paid geld for army and navy service as well as danegeld, paying whatever amount

---

[1] *Danelaw Charters,* cxxvi, and no. 417: a later twelfth-century charter grants five bovates 'liberas et quietas a seruiciis que currunt per carrucatas terre . . .'.
[2] D.B. i. 336*b*.

150 carucates would normally owe. But it is quite unlikely, as we have seen, that any distinction existed between 'army geld' and danegeld. This fact suggests the alternative interpretation that the passage refers not to a military and naval tax but rather to actual military and naval service. The phrase *dedit geldum* would then be interpreted in the broad sense in which it is frequently used elsewhere in the Domesday Survey, not as 'gave geld' or 'paid geld' but 'was assessed'. Thus, Stamford was assessed for personal service in the select fyrd on the basis of 150 carucates, at some fixed and generally understood ratio of carucates to warriors analogous to the familiar relationship of one man from five hides. This interpretation, if valid, confirms our earlier hypothesis that select-fyrd duty was assessed in the Danelaw at the standard rate of one man from a particular number of carucates, a number which was generally known at the time but is unknown to us. Further evidence for this theory can be found in certain Domesday passages relating to Lincolnshire, which imply that military service was assessed according to carucates of land. One Lincolnshire tenant, for example, held a tenement of six bovates at Wilsford (one Danelaw carucate being equal to eight bovates) which was free of every obligation except military service.[1] There are several similar passages which report the assessment of a Lincolnshire estate in carucates and bovates and make clear that the estate owed the customary military service.[2] But these passages never stipulate the *amount* of fyrd service that the lands owe. One must conclude that the amount of service could always be calculated from the assessment— that the Wilsford tenement, for example, served for six bovates or three-quarters of a carucate at some predeter-

---

[1] D.B., i. 366: 'In Wivelesford habuit Siward ix carucatas terrae ad geldum. Terra xii carucis. De hac terra habuit Azor frater ejus vi bovatas et i molendinum quietum [*sic*] ab omni servitio praeter exercitum.'

[2] Ibid. i. 357*b*: Swaton, Lincolnshire: 'In eadem villa habuerunt Alsi et Adestan i carucatam terrae ad geldum. . . . Aluric frater eorum habebat socam super illos in Hazebi solummodo in servitio regis.' Ibid. i. 368: Somerby, Lincolnshire: 'In Summerdebi Adelid vi bovatas terrae ad geldum . . . . Haec soca talis fuit quod nichil reddebat, sed adiuvabat in exercitu regis in terra et in mari.' 2 Cnut 65 makes it clear that select-fyrd service was assessed on the same general basis in the Danelaw as in the remainder of England; the burden of the *trimoda necessitas* applied to both regions. On the Scottish military carucate see *Highland Papers*, ed. MacPhail, ii, 230.

mined rate. Notice also that Domesday does not state directly that the Wilsford estate owed military service, as though there were something extraordinary in that fact; it states rather that the six bovates were free of every custom *except* military service, implying that fyrd duty was a normal burden on the lands of Lincolnshire and that it was assessed by bovates and carucates.

Obviously the evidence in favour of a standard carucate recruitment rate, if not conclusive, is at least highly suggestive. And although it may lead us well into the realm of hypothesis, we are strongly tempted to take the further step of inquiring what the ratio may have been between carucates and warriors. As we have seen, the five-hide recruitment system is reflected clearly in the five-hide groups which Round traced throughout most of non-Danish England. At the end of his analysis of these five-hide groups, Round adds: 'I propose to adduce for my theory convincing corroborative evidence by showing that the part which is played in the hidated district of England by the five-hide unit is played in the Danish districts by a unit of six carucates.'[1] There follows an analysis of corroborative evidence for the six-carucate theory, based on an examination of seven carucated counties,[2] which demonstrates that the Danelaw region was characterized by a strong tendency toward six-carucate groups, and suggests, although it does not prove, that the six-carucate group was the military-recruitment unit of the Danelaw. It is extremely unfortunate that Domesday fails to give the carucate assessment of the town of Leicester, since this is the one major Danelaw burgh for which the amount of military service is given. Leicester owed twelve warriors to the fyrd,[3] which, on the basis of our hypothetical six-carucate rule, would give the town an assessment of seventy-two carucates or six hundreds of twelve carucates each. This is a perfectly reasonable figure, but there is no way of confirming it. Yet perhaps there is some significance in the very absence of any statement

---

[1] *F.E.*, p. 69.
[2] Ibid., pp. 69–90: Lincolnshire, Yorkshire, Derbyshire, Nottinghamshire, Rutland, Leicestershire, and Lancashire (between Ribble and Mersey).
[3] D.B. i. 230; see above, p. 45.

regarding the carucate assessment for Leicester. In Stamford, as we have just seen, military service seems to have been assessed on the basis of 150 carucates, which, according to the six-carucate theory, would come to exactly twenty-five men. But there is no positive statement that Stamford owed twenty-five men, perhaps because such a statement would be redundant. Conversely, the Leicester obligation of twelve warriors is stated expressly, but the carucate assessment is omitted, again, perhaps, to avoid redundance. Everything points to the existence of some relationship between carucates and military service, and the ratio of one warrior from every six carucates certainly seems the most likely hypothesis.

IV

There are certain other regions of England where the five-hide rule seems to have been inapplicable. Kent, for example, was assessed in *sulungs* and *juga* rather than hides and virgates, and although here, too, some ratio probably existed between land assessment and military service, it was obviously a relationship peculiar to the district.[1]

East Anglia presents problems that are in many ways unique.[2] Here, hides were not used as assessment units, but rather carucates as in the Danelaw. Yet the six-carucate unit is not observed. Among the peculiarities of this region are the remarkable number of freemen and sokemen, many of whom are free to choose their lord, and the fact that village and manor bear no clear relationship to one another. The fyrd of East Anglia was very active in Anglo-Saxon times, but the recruitment system on which it was based is impossible to reconstruct. Doubtless it was connected in some way with the geld system as elsewhere in England. The

[1] Four *juga* (yokes) make one *sulung*, which itself is usually taken as the equivalent of two hides. See J. E. A. Jolliffe, *Pre-Feudal England: The Jutes* (London, 1933). It is also somewhat doubtful that the five-hide unit governed recruitment in neighbouring Sussex. See *V.C.H., Sussex*, i. 351 ff., 359 ff.

[2] See Charles Johnson in *V.C.H., Norfolk*, ii. 1–38; Beatrice Lees in *V.C.H., Suffolk*, i. 357–416; Round, *F.E.*, pp. 98 ff.; Vinogradoff, *Engl. Soc.*, pp. 145, 301; Maitland, *D.B.B.*, pp. 429 ff.; D. C. Douglas, *The Social Structure of Medieval East Anglia* (Oxford Studies, ix, 1927), pp. 52 ff.

East Anglian geld arrangements were based on the hundred. For every pound of geld that the hundred paid, certain villages within the hundred owed a specified amount toward the total. The assessment seems also to have been based on a unit peculiar to the region, the leet. The typical hundred had twelve leets, and generally each of these owed 20*d*., i.e. one Danish ora, to the geld.[1] It appears also that the typical leet contained ten carucates, and therefore the typical hundred, 120 carucates. Each carucate would therefore owe 2*d*. to the geld. And, to carry the analysis one step farther, the typical bovate (assuming eight bovates to the carucate) would owe one farthing. Thus the heterogeneous land divisions of East Anglia are fitted by this theory into a neat system of geld assessment running from the bovate owing a farthing through the carucate owing 2*d*. and the leet owing an ora to the hundred owing a pound. There is good evidence to support the theory, although it is subject to many exceptions.[2] To the extent that all these divisions are interrelated, we can conclude that fyrd service, like the geld assessment, was fixed at some standard ratio of men to carucates, leets, or hundreds, a ratio which we are unable to determine from existing evidence.

There has been some uncertainty as to the relationship between demesne land and the hide system. Miss Hollings has assumed that inland or demesne land was not assessed for military service even though it might be rated in hides.[3] But the Berkshire Domesday passage, which gives us our most complete picture of the five-hide system in operation, makes no exceptions to the rule. Throughout the county, five hides owed one warrior. If an estate was assessed in hides, it owed military service to the full extent of its assessment. In many areas of England the royal demesne land was not hided and therefore evidently paid no geld and rendered no military service.[4] In Berkshire, however, although the king's demesne had never gelded it was assessed in hides, presumably for the purpose of levying the fyrd

[1] *V.C.H.*, *Suffolk*, i. 412–16.
[2] See Douglas, op. cit., pp. 55 ff.
[3] Hollings, p. 476.
[4] Demarest, 'Firma Unius Noctis', p. 83; D.B. i. 64*b*, 75.

obligation,[1] and the same was true of Gloucestershire, and parts of Surrey.[2] As for local, non-royal demesne or inland, Stenton has observed: 'The use which might be made of the term *inland* in any given text might legitimately vary; exemption from the geld was only one among a number of characteristics which might be made the basis of distinction.'[3] The same, of course, may be said of military service. Occasionally we find that inland is not assessed in hides, or in some other way we are allowed to conclude that it was exempt from gelds and military service. In Kent we are told specifically that the demesne did not geld or perform other services but that the warriors and tenants of the 'outland' defended for all.[4] But this passage leaves some doubt as to whether the demesne was absolutely exempt or whether the 'outland' tenants served and gelded for the demesne as well as for their own holdings. The bishop of Worcester's triple hundred of Oswaldslaw was divided into demesne land and loan land. We know that the tenants on the loan land owed royal service, and in view of the fact that the bishops frequently converted their demesne land into loan land it is difficult to believe that the tenants bore royal obligations which would not have rested on their land had they not been tenants. It seems extremely unlikely that the very act of converting demesne land to loan land, as was so often done by the bishops of Worcester, automatically instituted the select-fyrd obligation on a previously exempt estate. Accordingly, there seems to be no sound basis for assuming that hidated inland was necessarily exempt from the select-

---

[1] D.B. i. 56*b*, 57; Demarest, op. cit., p. 83.

[2] Ibid.; D.B. i. 30, 30*b*, 162*b*; C. S. Taylor, in *V.C.H., Glos.* i. 47.

[3] *Northern Danelaw*, p. 11. Stenton thinks it improbable that the Lincolnshire demesnes were exempt from the geld. For a masterly discussion of demesne geld liability in the post-Conquest period, see Robert S. Hoyt, *The Royal Demesne in English Constitutional History: 1066–1272* (Ithaca, N.Y., 1950), pp. 18 ff. Professor Hoyt concludes that the royal demesne manors paid geld unless specifically exempted. Feudal demesne lands were similarly liable, but the manorial demesnes of tenants-in-chief were exempt. There is, however, no indication that such an exemption existed before the Conquest, when the feudal term 'tenant-in-chief' was meaningless, or that it included fyrd service as well as geld assessments.

[4] Jolliffe, *Pre-Feudal England*, p. 42: 'Dominium et pars monachorum nunquam geldaverunt vel consuetudines fecerunt. Sed milites et ceteri homines per omnia defendebant.' Cf. D.B. i. 12*b* (Mongeham), and *An Eleventh-Century Inquisition of St. Augustine's, Canterbury*, ed. A. Ballard (British Academy Records, iv, 1920), p. 22.

fyrd obligation or outside the network of five-hide units which characterized the military structure of Anglo-Saxon England.

The military obligation of the hidated regions was subject to change, on occasion, as a result of alterations in the hidage assessment. The monarchs of the eleventh century occasionally reduced the hidage of certain favoured estates, and indeed, around the time of the Norman Conquest and shortly thereafter, the assessment of an entire county was sometimes systematically lowered. There are a number of instances in the Anglo-Saxon sources of this beneficial hidation. The manor of Chilcomb, belonging to the bishop of Worcester, was reduced prior to the Conquest from 100 hides to one hide. A manor of twenty hides at Wenlock, Shropshire, was reduced in the reign of King Cnut to sixteen hides, and Chippenham, Cambridgeshire, was reduced by Edward the Confessor from ten hides to five.[1] And these are merely examples of a number of instances in which the monarchy granted to favoured subjects a reduction in the assessment of their estates, thereby lessening their obligation to the select fyrd.[2] Such isolated reductions as these would have no drastic effect upon the prevailing structure of recruitment and support, although certain rearrangements must have been necessary in the localities where the beneficial hidation occurred. On the other hand, a systematic county-wide reduction in hidage assessments such as occurred, for example, in Berkshire and Northamptonshire[3] would

[1] Birch, *C.S.*, nos. 1159, 1160; D.B. i. 41. See also D.B. i. 252b, 197.

[2] D.B. i. 121b, 165b, 169, 175b. See *A.S. Writs*, pp. 374 ff., and Maitland, *D.B.B.*, p. 450. It has been argued that reductions in hidage assessment gradually subverted the five-hide basis of the select-fyrd obligation. But ordinarily beneficial hidation must have been accompanied by a corresponding reduction in fyrd duty, thus preserving the five-hide unit in terms of the new assessment. Thus, an estate reduced from ten hides to five would find its fyrd obligation cut from two men to one; e.g. *Facsimiles of Royal Charters in the British Museum*, ed. Warner and Ellis, i, no. 28 (*temp.* Stephen): '. . . quietum clamauit inperpetuum de geldatione vi hidarum et dimidie in omnibus rebus que siue ad coronam regis siue ad ministrorum suorum spectant consuetudinem.'

[3] Round, *F.E.*, p. 65; F. Baring, 'The Pre-Domesday Hidation of Northamptonshire', *E.H.R.* xvii (1902), 470–9, and 'The Hidation of Northamptonshire in 1086', *E.H.R.* xvii (1902), 76–83; *The Domesday Geography of Midland England*, ed. Darby and Terrett (Cambridge, England, 1954), pp. 386–8; Round, 'The Hidation of Northamptonshire', *E.H.R.* xv (1900), 78–86.

necessitate rather sweeping revisions in the recruitment system of the select fyrd. The nature of these revisions varies from one shire to another, and they are in almost every instance virtually impossible to trace. As an example of the difficulties which these county-wide reductions present, let us look a little more closely at the changes in the hidation of Northamptonshire. Here, the hidage reduction, as it emerges in Domesday, seems to have occurred in several steps, beginning in about 1065 and probably stemming from the ravages which occurred in the district during that year.[1] In the south-western half of the county there was an overall hidage reduction of 60 per cent. Estates which were assessed at ten hides prior to 1065 were rated at four hides by the time of the Domesday Survey, and the five-hide and ten-hide units which characterized the district in Anglo-Saxon times gave way to two-hide or four-hide groups in the Anglo-Norman period. How these reductions affected the recruitment system it is impossible to determine with precision. I would suspect, however, that the old recruitment groups retained their integrity and that the fyrd obligation was reduced accordingly from one man in five hides to one man in four hides. Thus, an estate rated at ten hides prior to the reductions would have owed two warriors to the fyrd according to the prevailing five-hide rule. After a 60 per cent. reduction the same estate, being assessed now at four hides, would owe four-fifths of a warrior according to the old custom. But this would throw the fyrd-recruitment system into chaos. The hide groups which had long sent a given number of soldiers to the fyrd would be rendered obsolete. Certainly four-fifths of a warrior is an impossibly awkward quantity with which to work. More probably, the 60 per cent. reduction in hidage assessment was accompanied by a reduction of only 50 per cent. in the fyrd quota. Thus, the four-hide groups which characterize the Domesday assessment of south-western Northamptonshire[2] would become

---

[1] Round, op. cit., p. 85; Round, *F.E.*, p. 149. Baring remarks that in Northamptonshire, 'The assessments were modified in the northern hundreds before 1065; within a dozen or at most twenty years after 1065 they were again rearranged, probably twice, perhaps three times, or even oftener': 'Pre-Domesday Hidation of Northamptonshire', p. 479.

[2] *Domesday Geography of Midland England*, p. 387; *V.C.H., Northants.* i. 257–68.

the basic units of the fyrd assessment, just as the five-hide groups elsewhere in England reveal a five-hide military system. The tenement which once owed two warriors for ten hides would now owe one warrior for four hides.

In the north-eastern half of the county, the situation is more complex, for here the percentage of hidage reduction seems to have varied from hundred to hundred, ranging from 50 to 60 per cent.[1] Probably the instances of a 50 per cent. reduction in hidage resulted in a halving of the select-fyrd quota and a retention of the five-hide group as the basic unit of recruitment, but even this is uncertain.[2] One can only conclude that these county-wide assessment reductions must have resulted in serious revisions and perhaps a certain amount of confusion in the recruitment system of the select fyrd, and that the nature of these revisions cannot be determined with precision, but can merely be hypothesized.

The confusion arising from such changes provides one illustration of the difficulties and ambiguities which must have beset the select-fyrd system in the years after Hastings. We can be quite certain that the Norman Conquest did not mean the end of the select fyrd, for we find it being summoned on a number of occasions in the Anglo-Norman period. The assembling of the select fyrd in 1094, which we have already discussed, is merely one illustration of this.[3] But the military resources of post-Conquest England were by no means unlimited, and the imposition of feudal military obligations on lands which were already burdened with select-fyrd duty cannot but have resulted in a deterioration in the quality of the select fyrd. This tendency was doubtless exacerbated by the destruction of the thegn class and the gradual decline of the upper peasantry. How long the select fyrd was able to endure we cannot say with precision; by the middle years of the twelfth century chroniclers are no longer alluding to its existence and no traces of the old five-hide system can be found in the records of the time. In the Assize of Arms of 1181 the select fyrd was apparently

---

[1] Baring, 'Pre-Domesday Hidation of Northamptonshire', pp. 470–9.
[2] There is some evidence suggesting the existence of six-hide units in north-eastern Northamptonshire: *V.C.H.*, *Northants*. i. 266 ff.
[3] Above, pp. 23, 43–44.

reconstituted, but the basis of recruitment was transformed from hide-units to individual incomes. The free laymen of clause 2 of the Assize, with annual incomes of 16 marks and 10 marks, are seemingly the institutional descendants of the Anglo-Saxon warrior-representatives, but one wonders whether these descendants would have been recognized by their ancestors.

IV

THE PERSONNEL OF THE
SELECT FYRD

I

AGAIN and again in the sources for the history of late-Saxon England, one encounters references to a three-fold obligation which rested upon the land. Almost without exception, tenants are said to owe military service, fortress work, and bridge repair. Even when a landholder is granted exemptions from almost every imaginable royal service, these three duties are reserved. They are mentioned in the laws of several pre-Conquest kings as obligations resting on everyone. Thus, according to 2 Cnut 65, 'If anybody neglects the repair of fortresses or bridges or military service, he shall pay 120s. as compensation to the king in districts under the English law, and the amount fixed by existing regulations in the Danelaw . . . '.[1] These obligations have traditionally been called the *trinoda necessitas*, or, more correctly, *trimoda necessitas*, and although the legitimacy of this term has been questioned, I find it a convenient label for the threefold obligation and will henceforth use it accordingly.[2]

The *trimoda necessitas* appear with regularity in Anglo-Saxon land charters. The earliest reference to the obligations comes from Mercia in the late eighth century.[3] In Latin

[1] Cf. 2 Ethelred 26. 1; 6 Ethelred 32. 3; 2 Cnut 10.

[2] On the use and meaning of this term, see W. H. Stevenson, 'Trinoda Necessitas', *E.H.R.* xxix (1914), 689–703.

[3] See Birch, *C.S.*, no. 203 (A.D. 770). Here fyrd duty itself is absent but fortress duty is expressed in military terms: '. . . praeter instructionibus pontium vel necessaris [*sic*] defensionibus arcium contra hostes.' The more normal formula appears first in ibid., no. 274 (A.D. 793–6): '. . . preter expeditionalibus causis et pontium structionum et arcium munimentum quod omni populo necesse est. . . .' This passage suggests that the custom was by no means novel at the end of the eighth century. See Stevenson, op. cit., p. 696, and Eric John, 'The Imposition of the Common Burdens on the Lands of the English Church', *Bulletin of the Institute of Historical Research*,

charters they are usually specified by such phrases as *expeditio et pontis arcisque restauratio*.[1] In Anglo-Saxon documents they appear under a variety of names. Military service might be expressed as *fyrd-faru, fyrd-foereld, fyrd-socne*, or simply *fyrd*.[2] To pick at random an example of the *trimoda necessitas* clause in an Old English charter, Ethelbert of Kent made an exchange of land with his thegn Wulflaf in 858, with the stipulation that Wulflaf's land should be free of all royal services and secular burdens except military service, the building of bridges, and fortress work—*absque expeditione sola et pontium structura et arcium munitionibus*.[3] Some variation of this reservation appears in most of the charters of the age. In 957 King Edwig granted an estate to Oda, archbishop of Canterbury, free from everything except for the three burdens which are common to all people, i.e. *expeditionis et arcis pontisque constructione*.[4] Exemptions from the *trimoda necessitas* are very rare in the Anglo-Saxon age, although they become rather common in the era following the Norman Conquest.[5]

We must now determine the relationship between the military obligation of the *trimoda necessitas* and the various sorts of fyrd service which have already been examined. At first glance, the statement that the *trimoda necessitas* were burdens common to all people might suggest an identification with service in the great fyrd. But on the other hand, there is strong evidence that the military obligation of the *trimoda necessitas* was based on hides and thus was identical

---

xxxi (1958), 117–29. It should be emphasized that the three obligations probably did not arise simultaneously, and that there are early instances of one or two of the obligations appearing in charters without the third.

[1] *Land Charters*, ed. Earle (Oxford, 1888), p. xxi.

[2] Ibid., pp. xxi, 242; Stevenson, op. cit., p. 689 n.

[3] *Land Charters*, p. 126; Kemble, *C.D.*, no. 281; Birch, *C.S.*, no. 496.

[4] Ibid., no. 999; *Crawford*, p. 10.

[5] Birch, *C.S.*, no. 1343; *Crawford*, p. 6; Kemble, *C.D.*, no. 240. Some documents grant general exemptions without mentioning the *trimoda necessitas*: e.g. *Wulfric Spot's Will*, ed. C. G. O. Bridgeman, Wm. Salt, 1916, pp. 13–14; Kemble, *C.D.*, no. 805. On the question of whether such general exemptions included immunity from the threefold obligation, see Stevenson, op. cit., pp. 701 ff., and R. Stewart-Brown, ' "Bridge-Work" at Chester', *E.H.R.* liv (1939), 87. Professor Stewart-Brown challenges Stevenson's statement that general exemption clauses did not exempt lands from the *trimoda necessitas*. However, Stewart-Brown's evidence dates from the thirteenth and fourteenth centuries, long after the age when the threefold burden was regarded as sacrosanct.

to the select-fyrd duty of producing warrior-representatives when the army was summoned. In a document of A.D. 801, confirming an earlier grant of an estate of thirty hides in Middlesex by Offa, king of Mercia, to Abbot Stithbert, we are told that the estate owed the three public burdens, 'i.e. the construction of bridges and forts and also, in the necessity of military service, only five men are to be sent'.[1] This is the only charter known to stipulate the *amount* of military service owed in accordance with the *trimoda necessitas*. The estate owes five men from thirty hides or one man from every six hides. This has led more than one historian to speculate as to the existence of a widespread six-hide unit, competing, as it were, with the five-hide unit.[2] Miss Hollings, on the other hand, finds this charter perfectly compatible with the five-hide rule. She assumes that twenty-five of the thirty hides owed military service and that the remaining five hides, being inland, were exempt.[3] But there is nothing in the charter to indicate that the estate had an inland of five hides, nor, as we have seen, is it safe to assume that inland was exempt from military service. This charter is important to us neither as an illustration of the five-hide rule nor as an indication of an otherwise unknown six-hide rule. Its importance lies in the fact that it proves the relationship between the military service of the *trimoda necessitas* and the warrior-representative arrangements of the select fyrd. Five men serve from thirty hides and are therefore the warrior-representatives of the estate. The service is exceptional, to be sure, because it does not conform to the five-hide rule, but its connexion with select-fyrd duty is unmistakable. Nor should we be overly disturbed by the discovery of an exception to the five-hide recruitment system. On the contrary, we can be quite certain that if the Middlesex estate had followed the customary five-hide pattern, the number of warriors which it owed would never have been

---

[1] 'Trium tamen causarum puplicarum ratio reddatur hoc est instructio pontuum [*sic*] et arcis verum etiam in expeditionis necessitatem vires [*sic*] v. tantum modo mittantur': Birch, *C.S.*, i, no. 201.

[2] e.g. Chadwick, *Origin of the English Nation*, p. 151.

[3] 'Survival of the Five Hide Unit', p. 476. On the five-hide unit in Middlesex, see Round, *F.E.*, pp. 66–67. Round writes (p. 66): 'In Middlesex the five-hide unit is peculiarly prominent.'

stipulated. We are told that the estate owed five warriors precisely because the assessment rate was exceptional. In no other grant is the amount of service specified. The normal charter states that the tenement contains a certain number of hides and that it owes military service. It was unnecessary to say more, since the service could always be calculated by dividing the total number of hides by five. We can perhaps appreciate more clearly the significance of King Offa's grant by comparing it with certain other unusual charters. In the mid-eleventh century Bishop Ealdred of Worcester granted a lease of $1\frac{1}{2}$ hides of land to Wulfgeat, who was to discharge the royal military obligations of this small estate at the rate of one hide.[1] In other words, Wulfgeat ought to have owed nearly one-third of a warrior to the select fyrd, but he owed instead only one-fifth. Or, to express the same thing in terms of the Berkshire support system, Wulfgeat was obliged to support the warrior-representative of his five-hide unit with 4s., the amount normally due from one hide, instead of 6s., the amount due from $1\frac{1}{2}$ hides. Again, Abbot Ælfweard of Evesham leased to Æthelmar an estate which was assessed at three hides for home service (*inware*) and $1\frac{1}{2}$ hides for national service (*utware*).[2] *Utware*, as we have seen, included royal military service, and would indicate here an obligation to pay 6s. toward the support of the warrior-representative of the five-hide unit. Accordingly, we can say that King Offa's grant in Middlesex involved an estate of thirty hides which was to discharge the royal military obligation at the rate of twenty-five hides.

There is good evidence that bridge repair and fortress work, the two remaining burdens of the *trimoda necessitas*, were also assessed in terms of hides. According to the Domesday survey, the reeve of Chester had the right to summon one man from every hide in the county for the repair of the city wall and the bridge, and the burden of constructing and repairing Rochester bridge rested upon the neighbouring lands.[3] Thus, all three of the obligations

---

[1] Kemble, *C.D.*, no. 804.   [2] *A.S. Chart.*, p. 156.

[3] D.B., i. 262b; *A.S. Chart.*, p. 106. The work for the seventh and eighth piers of the bridge, for example, is due 'from the Hoo people's *land*'. See Hasted, *History of Kent*, ii. 15–22. For fortress work at Malmesbury, see A. Ballard, *The Domesday Boroughs* (Oxford, 1904), p. 34.

were territorial rather than personal and were normally assessed in terms of hides. The military duty of the *trimoda necessitas* provides us with another avenue of approach to the structure of the select fyrd.

II

We have seen that service in the great fyrd was an obligation incumbent upon all freemen, but it may well be inquired what classes the select fyrd normally included. Stenton believes that the five-hide recruitment system described in the Berkshire passage of Domesday Book refers exclusively to peasants.[1] He maintains that there existed, apart from what I have termed the select-fyrd duty, an obligation incumbent upon all thegns to serve in the royal army as a consequence of their rank. The select-fyrd obligation was territorial rather than personal, whereas the military obligation of the thegn was personal rather than territorial.[2] We can certainly agree with Stenton that peasants served in the select fyrd, although it seems to me most doubtful that the select fyrd was limited to peasants. The Maldon poet describes the English force which Ealdorman Byrhtnoth led against the Danes in A.D. 991 as 'the flower of the East Saxons',[3] and if this is an accurate description rather than a mere rhetorical flourish we would assume that the personnel of Byrhtnoth's army included mercenaries and members of the select fyrd but excluded the great fyrd. If this assumption is valid, then we can be certain that the select fyrd included peasants, for a ceorl named Dunhere, armed with a lance, played an important role in the battle.[4] Indeed the very existence of a five-hide recruitment system implies the military service of peasants, for there were innumerable five-hide units throughout England which cannot possibly have been represented by thegns. For one thing, the unit might form only a part of a much larger estate held by a single thegn who had to find warrior-representatives for every five hides within his tenement. Again, the five-hide unit might not be part of any thegn's estate.

---

[1] *E.F.*, pp. 116–17.   [2] Ibid., pp. 118–19.
[3] line 68.   [4] ll. 255–64.

But on the other hand, the five-hide system disclosed by the Berkshire entry cannot have applied exclusively to peasants. For one thing, the Berkshire support system provided the warrior-representative with wages of 4*d.* per day, which seems unusually high for a peasant soldier. Fully armed mounted knights in the Anglo-Norman period were receiving wages of only 6*d.* per day,[1] and even in the late twelfth century the boatswains in the crusading fleet of King Richard the Lion-Hearted received 4*d.* per day and the sailors in the same fleet 2*d.* per day.[2] Moreover, the assumption that thegn duty was distinct from service in the select fyrd implies the existence of two mutually exclusive select armies. For that reason, as I have elsewhere observed,[3] the notion of a separate personal military obligation incumbent on all thegns is unreasonable on *a priori* grounds. The select peasant army would be if anything more exclusive than the military thegnhood. Numerous Domesday thegns held estates that were much smaller than five hides,[4] and might well have envied the prosperous peasant warrior with his 20*s.* for maintenance and wages. So I must take issue with Stenton and with the majority of modern scholars.[5] The military obligation of the English thegns was not personal but territorial; it was founded on the duty of every five-hide unit to produce a competent warrior, and was therefore identical with the obligation of the select fyrd. Thegns served in the select fyrd as well as peasants and on

---

[1] Hollister, 'Significance of Scutage Rates', pp. 580–1.

[2] Round, *F.E.*, p. 273; Vinogradoff, *Engl. Soc.*, p. 18.

[3] 'The Five-Hide Unit and the Old English Military Obligation', *Speculum*, xxxvi (1961), 71.

[4] e.g. D.B. i. 269*b*, 270, 356, 370*b*. See Little, 'Gesiths and Thegns', *E.H.R.* iv (1889), 729 n.; Maitland, *D.B.B.*, pp. 64 ff., 165, and the references there given.

[5] e.g. J. H. Beeler states that the military obligation of the thegn 'seems to have been purely personal, and was not due from the land': Oman, *The Art of War in the Middle Ages*, ed. Beeler (Ithaca, N.Y., 1953), p. 24. R. R. Darlington writes, 'Thegn and peasant alike were under the obligation to serve in war when called upon by the king to do so, but the obligation of the thegn . . . was a personal one, the outcome of his rank . . .': 'Last Phase of Anglo-Saxon History', p. 2. G. O. Sayles states, 'It was because of the ancient traditions and duties connected with their social rank, and not because of the lands they held, that the thegns rendered service in war. The obligation was purely personal and not territorial': *Medieval Foundations of England* (Philadelphia, 1950), p. 210. But modern scholars are not unanimous on this point. See Jolliffe, *Constitutional History*, p. 96, and Hollings, pp. 467 ff.

exactly the same basis as peasants. Nor is this fact sub-
versive to our conception of late-Saxon England as a strongly
aristocratic society, for it should be remembered that the
peasant warriors of the select fyrd constituted only a small
fraction of the whole English peasantry. They doubtless
represented the *élite* of their class and were, to say the least,
atypical. It would be grotesque to regard the select fyrd as
an illustration of Old Saxon democracy or a microcosm of
the classless society. But it would be equally wrong to insist
that thegns and peasants cannot possibly have fought side
by side, for we find them doing precisely that in every
important battle from Maldon to Hastings.

But since the majority of historians now favour the notion
that the thegn's military obligation was personal, we must
explore the problem in detail. Modern historical opinion on
the subject seems to be based on a passage in Stenton's
distinguished book, *The First Century of English Feudalism*,
and since the issue is so crucial to a correct understanding
of the pre-Conquest military system, I will quote the passage
in full:[1]

The thegn's obligation was of no less ancient origin [than that of
the peasants], but its basis was different. There is no doubt that in the
eleventh century a king's thegn, when summoned to an expedition,
must obey, under penalties which might amount to an entire forfeiture
of his land. The same service was demanded from thegns who held of
other lords than the king. In either case, so far as we can see, the
obligation was purely personal. There is nowhere any suggestion that
a thegn's military service was due in respect of an estate which the king
or any other lord has given him. It is a duty which follows from his
rank, the expression of the traditions of an order which, as a class,
represented the military companions of a lord, the *gesithas*, of ancient
times. These traditions were still strong in the century before the
Norman Conquest. They are nowhere more clearly brought out than
in the poem which relates the death of Byrhtnoth at Maldon in 991.
The men who are most prominent in the poem are naturally the
companions, the personal following of the earl, but they included
landed Essex thegns and their close kinsmen. The ideas which moved
these men must have been common to the whole class from which
they sprung (*sic*). It is more than probable that many thegns of the
eleventh century were country gentlemen, with no special aptitude

[1] *E.F.*, pp. 118–19.

for war. In most cases, the estates of a thegn of 1066 must have come to him by inheritance, and not by the gift of a king or any other lord. But his obligation to military service represented the ancient duty of attending a lord in battle.

In a later work, *Anglo-Saxon England*, Stenton summarizes his views as follows:[1]

The military service of the thegn was a duty which fell on him as a consequence of his rank, and was inherent in the constitution of Old English Society. There is evidence in Domesday Book suggesting that every thegn, or at least every thegn possessing rights of jurisdiction, would receive a personal summons to the host, and that if he disobeyed it the king was entitled to confiscate his land.

The evidence which Stenton cites to support his position consists of three passages from Domesday Book. The first passage relates to Worcestershire:[2]

When the king goes on a military expedition, if one who is summoned remains behind and if he is so free a man as to have his *soc* and *sac* [i.e. his rights of jurisdiction] and can go with his land to whomever he wishes, he is in the king's mercy for all his land. But if the freeman of another lord remains away from the army, and his lord leads another man to the host in his place, he pays 40*s*. to his lord who received the summons. But if nobody at all goes in his place, he shall pay his lord 40*s*.; but his lord must pay the entire amount to the king.

The second passage pertains to Berkshire and runs as follows:[3]

If anyone summoned on an expedition did not go, he forfeited all his land to the king. But if anyone for the sake of remaining behind

---

[1] *A.S.E.*, p. 575. But Stenton is not perfectly consistent. In an earlier work he states that thegnland 'denotes the holding of a thegn, land defended by military service' (*Northern Danelaw*, p. 13), and adds, 'Essentially, thegnland is a portion of an estate granted out to secure the performance of military service by the grantee' (ibid., p. 16, n. 2).

[2] These three passages are quoted in *E.F.*, p. 118 n. For the first, see D.B. i. 172: 'Quando rex in hostem pergit si quis edictu eius vocatus remanserit, si ita liber homo est ut habeat socam suam et sacam et cum terra possit ire quo voluerit, de omni terra sua est in misericordia regis. Cuiuscunque vero alterius domini liber homo, si de hoste remanserit, et dominus eius pro eo alium hominem duxerit, xl solidis domino suo qui vocatus fuit emendabit. Quod si ex toto nullus pro eo abierit, ipse quidem domino suo xl solidos dabit; dominus autem eius totidem solidos regi emendabit.'

[3] D.B. i. 56*b*: 'Si quis in expeditionem summonitus non ibat, totam terram suam erga regem forisfaciebat. Quod si quis remanendi habens alium pro se mittere promitteret, et tamen qui mittendus erat remaneret, pro l solidis quietus erat dominus eius.'

promised to send another in his place, and yet he who was to have been sent remained behind, his lord was freed of obligation by the payment of 50s.

Finally, an Oxfordshire passage reports that 'whoever was to go on an expedition and did not do so owed 100s. to the king'.[1] Stenton then concludes:

These passages leave innumerable points of detail unexplained, but they agree in suggesting that there lay on the landed thegn of the eleventh century a military duty which was essentially a personal obligation to obey a royal summons, and entirely distinct from his responsibility for seeing that the free men upon his estate served in accordance with local custom [i.e. in the select fyrd].

I have considerable difficulty in following Stenton's reasoning here, for I cannot discover in these Domesday passages the slightest suggestion that every landed thegn owed military service or that the thegn's military obligation was personal rather than territorial. Nor is there evidence that every thegn possessing jurisdictional rights was subject to the military summons. The Worcestershire passage, which is the only one that refers to jurisdictional rights, merely states that if the man who had been summoned to the fyrd and defaulted possessed rights of jurisdiction, he was to forfeit his land. But there were numerous landed thegns who lacked rights of jurisdiction. As Jolliffe has observed, 'it is clear that there was no common right of jurisdiction in the thegnage. Some king's thegns had their soke and some had not.'[2] More important still, the Worcestershire passage does not state that everyone with rights of jurisdiction received a summons. It merely reports that if the summoned defaulter happened to possess such rights he would be punished accordingly. Let us imagine for a moment that some assiduous scholar discovered a previously unknown Anglo-Saxon law stating that if anyone summoned to the fyrd was sick with the plague he would be excused from service. Would it be legitimate to conclude from this that every Englishman who was sick with the plague received a personal summons to the army? The truth of the matter

---

[1] Ibid. i. 154b: 'Qui monitus ire in expeditionem non vadit, c solidos regi dabat.'
[2] *Constitutional History*, pp. 145-6.

is that the Worcestershire passage tells us nothing whatever about the military obligation of thegns. The summoned man might be a thegn or he might be a peasant. He might have *sac* and *soc* or he might not. He might possess an estate or he might be landless (he loses his land only if he has rights of jurisdiction). He might, in fact, be anyone at all.

The second passage is much shorter but is also a little more helpful, for it suggests that the man who was summoned was ordinarily a landholder. But peasants held land as well as thegns, and the passage is conspicuously silent on the matter of the summoned warrior's social status. The Oxfordshire passage, which is the third and last that Stenton quotes to support his view, says merely that if the man who was to serve in the fyrd defaulted, he owed 100*s*.; again we are unable to discover whether the defaulter was a peasant or a nobleman.

Perhaps Stenton means to imply that the military service of these men was personal rather than territorial because they received a personal summons. But the receiving of a summons is by no means incompatible with territorial service. If, for example, a thegn possessed an estate of five hides, he might very well be expected to perform the military service due from the five-hide unit and would doubtless receive a summons from the sheriff whenever the king wished to assemble his select fyrd. The summons would be personal, but the basis of the service would be territorial. Thus, the town of Warwick owed ten burghers to the select fyrd; if one of these ten was summoned but failed to go, he owed the king a *fyrdwite* of 100*s*.[1] Nobody could possibly suggest that the receipt of a military summons by a Warwick burgher proves that all townsmen owed personal service in the fyrd as a consequence of their social rank, for we are told in the same passage that aside from the ten burghers who served as warrior-representatives the remaining Warwick townsmen were exempt. Again, the reeve of Cheshire had the right to summon one man from every hide in the county to repair the city walls and the bridge, on penalty of 40*s*. for default of service.[2] The summons was evidently personal but the service was clearly territorial.

[1] D.B. i. 238.   [2] Ibid. i. 262*b*.

We have already seen that the warrior-representative of the five-hide unit was not chosen by rotation, but was specially designated. The same man would normally serve on all campaigns, and it is to him that the military summons would go. Thus, Siwate and his three brothers inherited their father's estate in Lincolnshire, dividing it equally among them. In the event of a military expedition, Siwate normally served as the warrior-representative of the estate, his brothers giving him financial support on the pattern of the Berkshire system. Should Siwate be unable to go, one of his brothers served, and Siwate and the others aided him. But the passage concludes with the specific statement that Siwate was the king's man.[1] Was Siwate a thegn? So it would seem, but if he was, then the passage proves that all landed thegns did not serve in the army. For by the eleventh century thegnhood was hereditary and Siwate's brothers would be thegns as well as he.[2] In any event, Siwate was the specified warrior-representative of his estate, and therefore would receive the summons and, if necessary, pay the *fyrdwite*. Yet it is perfectly evident that Siwate's obligation was based on his land rather than his rank in society—it was territorial rather than personal.[3] Again, two brothers, Chetel and Turuer, divided their father's Lincolnshire estate in such a way that Chetel normally performed military service and Turuer supported him financially.[4] The service was territorial but the summons was personal. If the personal summons which Chetel received meant that he performed his service as a consequence of his rank, then why was his brother exempt? These examples could be multiplied almost indefinitely, but it should by now be perfectly evident that the receiving of

[1] Ibid. i. 375*b*: 'Siuuate et Alnod et Fenchel et Aschil equaliter et pariliter diuiserunt inter se terram patris sui, T.R.E., et ita tenuerunt ut si opus fuit expeditione regis et Siuuate potuit ire, alii fratres iuuerunt eum. Post istum, iuit alter, et Siuuate cum reliquis iuuit eum, et sic de omnibus. Siuuate tamen fuit homo regis.'

[2] On the hereditary status of thegns, see Little, p. 729, and H. M. Chadwick, *Studies on Anglo-Saxon Institutions* (Cambridge, England, 1905), pp. 79–80.

[3] There are many similar parage tenures recorded in Domesday Book: i. 7, 11*b*, 38, 40, 45, 46, 50*b*, 60 63*b*, 67*b*, 72, 83–84, 96*b*, 105, 116, 117, 145*b*, 146*b*, 152, 168*b*, 214, 291, 341, 354, 357*b*, 375; ii. 104, 229; iii (Exon Domesday), 202, 247, 329, 334, 354, 480. Cf. 2 Cnut 70, 78. See also Vinogradoff, *Engl. Soc.*, pp. 245–50, and Maitland, *D.B.B.*, p. 145.

[4] D.B. i. 354.

a military summons or the payment of *fyrdwite* is quite irrelevant to the question of whether the service has a personal or territorial basis. Stenton is probably correct in his statement that 'in the eleventh century a king's thegn, when summoned to an expedition, must obey, under penalties which might amount to an entire forfeiture of his land', but one cannot conclude from this fact that every thegn, or every landed thegn, or every thegn with jurisdictional rights owed personal military service. If any doubt remains on the matter, it should be dispelled by a passage from Ine's laws which alludes to common ceorls paying *fyrdwite* for failure to heed a military summons.[1]

Stenton goes on to state: 'There is nowhere any suggestion that a thegn's military service was due in respect of an estate which the king or any other lord has given him.' In connexion with this assertion, let us examine a passage from a well-known late-Saxon document, the *Rectitudines Singularum Personarum*: 'The law of the thegn is . . . that he shall contribute three things in respect of his land: armed service and the repairing of fortressses and work on bridges.'[2] This passage is the only one I know of that lists military service as a normal obligation of thegns. It is perfectly clear on the point that the thegn's military service is territorial—that he owes armed service *in respect of his land*. It also connects the thegn's service with the *trimoda necessitas*, which we have already associated with the select-fyrd obligation and which we have found to have a territorial basis.

The passage from the *Rectitudines* is not conclusive, however, for Stenton and others would maintain that this obligation was essentially supervisorial—that the thegn was to make certain that the peasants on his estates performed the service due from the land. According to this interpretation, the passage in the *Rectitudines* does not actually refer to the thegn's military service at all, but rather to his obligation to supervise the recruitment of his

---

[1] Dooms of Ine, clause 51.

[2] 'Þ he ðreo ðinc of his lande do fyrd-færeld ⁊ burh-bote ⁊ bryc-geweorc.' 'et ut ita faciat pro terra sua, scilicet, expeditionem, burhbotam, et brigbotam.' The document is printed in Liebermann, *Gesetze*, i. 444–53. For a discussion of it, see Seebohm, *English Village Community*, pp. 129–47; Maitland, *D.B.B.*, pp. 327–9; Vinogradoff, *Growth of the Manor*, pp. 231–5.

ceorls.[1] But it seems clear that the passage refers to both. The thegn possessing a five-hide tenement served personally for his estate in the select fyrd, while the thegn with an estate of, say, fifteen hides, answered the summons personally and was also responsible for the appearance of two additional warrior-representatives. To deny that the passage has anything to do with the military service of thegns seems to me a hazardous assumption.

The thegn with five hides or more, or the thegn with a smaller estate who served as warrior-representative for a five-hide unit, was expected to contribute personally—to *perform* the duties encompassed by the *trimoda necessitas*. Accordingly, Bishop Denewulf of Winchester leased fifteen hides to a thegn named Beornwulf, who was to contribute yearly to the repair of the church, to pay the church scots, and to *perform* (*hewe*) military service and bridge and fortress work 'as all others do'.[2] Around the middle of the eleventh century Bishop Ealdred of Worcester leased an estate of 1½ hides at Ditchford to his thegn, Wulfgeat, who, at the king's summons, was to redeem [*hredde*] it at the rate of one hide.[3] The same bishop granted to another of his thegns, Æthelstan the Fat, 'a certain piece of land, namely two hides along with what he had before and with the uninhabited land—and he shall discharge the obligations upon them at the rate of two hides. . . . This estate shall be free of every burden except wall and bridge work and military service and church dues.'[4] At Peterborough a tenant named Ansford, who was the immediate tenurial successor of the well-known English warrior-hero, Hereward, performed military service for half a hide, and another Peterborough

---

[1] Stenton, *A.S.E.*, p. 575; Reid, p. 171.

[2] Birch, *C.S.*, no. 599: 'ʒ fyrde ʒ brycge ʒ fester ge weorc hewe swa mon ofer eall folc do.' On the meaning of *hewe* in this passage see *Select English Historical Documents of the Ninth and Tenth Centuries*, ed. Harmer (Cambridge, England, 1914), p. 113, and Liebermann, *Gesetze*, ii. 331. Liebermann equates the term with *heawe* and suggests that it may apply here only to bridge and fortress work. But even if this is so, the passage proves that thegns actually performed at least two items of the *trimoda necessitas*. Dr. Harmer believes that the term applies to all three obligations (op. cit., pp. 29, 60, 113).

[3] *A.S. Chart.*, p. 208. On the meaning of the verb *hreddan* see p. 459, and Hollings, pp. 467–8.

[4] *A.S. Chart.*, pp. 208–10: 'ʒ he hig eac werige for twa hida.' See p. 460.

tenant, Robert de Guneges, served for three hides.[1] Bishop Oswald of Worcester stated explicitly that his leasehold tenants, most of whom were thegns, owed service to the king in proportion to the size of their holdings.[2]

It may perhaps be thought unlikely that a nobleman of the thegn class would be required to perform such menial services as bridge and fortress work. But in Domesday Book we find thegns who are obliged to do ploughing and to work at the harvest, and a twelfth-century charter of Bury St. Edmunds reports that knights customarily joined the free sokemen and burghers in repairing the ditch that surrounded the town.[3] A tenth-century Anglo-Saxon document, the Burghal Hidage, suggests that the obligation of fortress work was very closely associated with that of fortress defence, and that the same men performed both.[4] This view is strengthened by a passage from the *Anglo-Saxon Chronicle* reporting that King Edward the Elder went to Nottingham with his fyrd and had a fortress built on the south side of the river, exactly opposite an already-existing fort. He then had a bridge made over the Trent to connect the two strongholds.[5] Here we find fyrd soldiers apparently doing both bridge and fortress work as a function of their military service, and we are shown that all three of the *trimoda necessitas* could be military in nature.

The second of the three Domesday entries which Stenton cites in support of the personal nature of the thegn's military obligation appears on closer examination to suggest precisely the opposite, and is itself a convincing indication of the

---

[1] *Chron. Pet.*, p. 75. These holdings, however, are in Lincolnshire where gelds and military service were assessed by carucates. Why the obligations of these tenures were expressed in hides is unclear. On Ansford, see D.B. i. 346, 376b.

[2] Birch, *C.S.*, no. 1136: '. . . ad regale explendum semper illius archiductoris dominatui et voluntati qui episcopatui presidet propter beneficium quod illis prestitum est cum omni humilitate et subjectione subditi fiant secundum ipsius voluntatem *et terrarum quas quisque possidet quantitatem*.' Cf. Maitland, *D.B.B.*, pp. 305 ff.

[3] D.B. i. 269b; cf. Jolliffe, *Constitutional History*, p. 94; *British Borough Charters*, p. 93.

[4] *A.S. Chart.*, pp. 246–8, 494–6. See particularly p. 246: 'To anes æceres bræde on wealstillinge ꞇ to þære wære gebirigeað .XVI. hida. . . .' The editor translates this passage as follows: 'For the maintenance (?) and defence of an acre's breadth of wall 16 hides are required.' There is, however, considerable doubt as to the meaning of *wealstillinge*, translated above as 'maintenance'. See ibid., p. 496.

[5] *A.S.C.*, A, A.D. 924 [923].

territorial basis of thegn service. The passage comes from the Berkshire section of Domesday Book and is, in fact, immediately adjacent to the passage relating to the five-hide system which we have used to reconstruct the organization of the select fyrd. Let us look at the passage as a whole:[1]

> If the king sent an army anywhere, only one soldier went from five hides, and four shillings were given him from each hide as subsistence and wages for two months. This money, indeed, was not sent to the king but was given to the soldiers. If anyone summoned on an expedition did not go, he forfeited all his land to the king. But if anyone for the sake of remaining behind promised to send another in his place, and yet he who was to have been sent remained behind, his lord was freed of obligation by the payment of 50s.

According to Stenton's theory, the first half of this passage refers to the service of peasants in the select fyrd, whereas the last half refers to the personal obligation of thegns.[2] But again the peasant–thegn dichotomy can be sustained only by a forced and artificial interpretation of what otherwise would be a relatively clear statement. The section on default of service is illuminated by the examples of parage tenure which we have just discussed. Each five-hide unit had a more or less permanent warrior-representative who, like Siwate in Lincolnshire, was regarded as the king's man. It was upon him that the military obligation fell when the select fyrd was summoned. It was he who had to pay the *fyrdwite* or forfeit his land. As in the case of Siwate, the Berkshire warrior-representative might call upon a co-tenant in the five-hide unit to serve in his stead if he were unable to serve himself. But if the substitute failed to appear, the lord of the district paid a fine to the king and, presumably, collected a like sum from the defaulter. The entire Berkshire passage should be regarded as a self-consistent unit which refers neither to thegns exclusively nor to peasants exclusively but rather to the warrior-representatives of five-hide districts, whether thegn or peasant. This is surely the simplest and most reasonable interpretation of the passage and, when so interpreted, the passage makes perfectly good sense.

---

[1] D.B. i. 56b. For the Latin, see above, p. 38 n. 1, and p. 66 n. 3.
[2] E.F., p. 116 n. 3.

The next point which Stenton makes is that the alleged personal obligation of the thegn is 'the expression of the traditions of an order which, as a class, represented the military companions of a lord, the *gesithas*, of ancient times'. Here it is necessary to point out a certain ambiguity in Stenton's position. At one point he seems to be saying that every thegn with rights of jurisdiction served in the army,[1] and we have noted that a great many thegns lacked such rights. But elsewhere he seems to imply that every single thegn in England owed personal military service, although I do not believe that he attempts seriously to prove this notion. His observation regarding the ancient military traditions of the thegnhood as a class would be relevant only to the theory that every thegn owed military service. If there were numerous exceptions, then the military heritage would prove nothing. In other words, if the thegns actually inherited an all-inclusive personal military obligation from the *gesithas*, then every thegn without exception would be obliged to take up arms when summoned. This would hold true whether the thegn held half a county or half a virgate. But the parage tenures in Domesday prove quite conclusively, as we have seen, that every thegn did not serve. Anglo-Saxon records reveal a bewildering variety of thegns. There were Danish thegns as well as English thegns.[2] There were even Norman thegns.[3] The normal wergeld of a thegn was 1,200*s*., but we also encounter references to thegns with wergelds of only 200*s*.[4] The king's chamberlain was called a *bur-thegn*; the seneschal was a *disc-thegn* (dish-thegn); the steward was a *rail-thegn*.[5] Larson observes that in late-Saxon times 'the term came to be applied in Anglo-Saxon to almost every possible rank of men from serf to noble',[6] and Stenton himself declares, 'we are in virtually complete ignorance as to the social position occupied by the smaller thegns of King Edward's day . . . '.[7]

---

[1] *A.S.E.*, p. 575.   [2] *A.S. Chart.*, pp. 180, 208, 210.

[3] *A.S.C.*, E, A.D. 1123. The *Chronicle* uses the term 'thegn' in an exceedingly broad sense: e.g. E, 1086 [1087], 1123.

[4] Kemble, *C.D.*, no. 731 (A.D. 1013–20).   [5] Larson, pp. 128 ff.

[6] Ibid., p. 90. A tenant whom one Domesday passage calls 'Ketel teignus Stigandi' (D.B. ii. 254) is described in another passage as 'Ketel liber homo Stigandi' (D.B. ii. 266).   [7] *Northern Danelaw*, p. 22.

Hence, the theory that every thegn in the eleventh century was obliged to answer the military summons requires considerable documentation. It is not sufficient to speculate as to the significance of ancient Germanic military traditions unless it can be shown that these traditions actually applied to the late-Saxon thegnhood. But the only evidence to which Stenton alludes is the poetic account of the battle of Maldon:

These traditions were still strong in the century before the Norman Conquest. They are nowhere more clearly brought out than in the poem which relates the death of Byrhtnoth at Maldon in 991. The men who are prominent in the poem are naturally the companions, the personal following of the earl, but they included landed Essex thegns and their close kinsmen. The ideas which moved these men must have been common to the whole class from which they sprung.[1]

We have already seen that the warriors *par excellence* of Byrhtnoth's force were retainers—mercenaries—and this Stenton concedes. But he argues that the remainder of the army also included men who were motivated by the Old Germanic hero ideals. When Byrhtnoth fell dead, one of his warriors who was not a retainer rallied the army with the following words: 'He who thinks to avenge his lord, his chief in the press, may not waver or reckon for his life!' The poet then tells how the English advanced bravely against the Danes, thinking not of protecting their own lives but of avenging their lord's death.[2] All this is markedly reminiscent of the barbarian *comitatus* which Tacitus describes. But the warrior ethos cannot be said to apply exclusively to the thegns. Indeed, the man who uttered these heroic words was not a thegn at all; he was, as the Maldon poet expresses it, 'a simple ceorl'.[3] And he was used by the Maldon poet as a symbol of the attitudes of his whole class.[4] There were many heroes among the English at Maldon, but they were distributed among every class from the military retainers to the peasants. Surely one finds no grounds in this poem for

[1] *E.F.*, p. 119.
[2] *Battle of Maldon*, ll. 255–64.
[3] Ibid., l. 256.
[4] See Laborde, *Byrhtnoth and Maldon*, pp. 115, 132.

distinguishing between the military obligations of thegn and ceorl.[1]

Thus there is little support for the assumption that thegns owed a personal military service that was separate from the select-fyrd obligation. On the contrary, thegns and peasants coalesced into one force, which was recruited ordinarily on the basis of the five-hide unit. The obligation to serve in this force is identical with the military duty of the *trimoda necessitas* and is listed by the *Rectitudines Singularum Personarum* as a duty incumbent upon thegns in respect of their land. And it is possible to prove the point even more conclusively by demonstrating the existence of a direct relationship between the five-hide unit and the military thegnhood. This relationship is suggested in the Domesday passage relating to the military service of Malmesbury: 'When the king went on an expedition by land or sea, he had in this town either 20*s.* to feed his "buzecarles" or one man, as for an honour of five hides.'[2] Malmesbury conforms rigorously to the five-hide rule, but it should be noted that the town serves not only as five hides of land—it serves as an *honour* of five hides—as a five-hide *estate* such as is so frequently found to be possessed by Domesday thegns, and is, indeed, the typical thegn-holding of late-Saxon times.[3] A. G. Little believed that five hides was the normal and traditional holding of a Saxon king's thegn as far back as the seventh century.[4] We can perhaps never be sure whether originally the five-hide unit acquired its military significance because it was the normal thegn-holding, or whether the normal

---

[1] Another point to be considered is that the Maldon poet was writing in the old heroic tradition, and we cannot therefore be sure to what extent his own sentiments were actually shared by Byrhtnoth and his followers. See *Battle of Maldon*, ed. Gordon, p. 23: 'The aristocratic quality of *Maldon* is evident both in the glorification of the military ideals of the *comitatus* and in the close kinship in art and sentiment with other Old English court poetry.' See also ibid., pp. 23–28, and B. S. Phillpotts, 'The Battle of Maldon: Some Danish Affinities', *Modern Language Review*, xxiv (1929), 172–90.

[2] D.B. i. 64*b*: 'Quando Rex ibat in expeditione vel terra vel mari, habebat de hoc burgo aut xx solidos ad pascendos suos buzecarlos, aut unum hominem ducebat secum, pro honore v hidarum.' See below, pp. 23, 42.

[3] Birch, *C.S.*, no. 246; Liebermann, *Gesetze*, ii. 419; Hodgkin, ii. 597; Maitland, *D.B.B.*, p. 158; Vinogradoff, *Growth of the Manor*, pp. 127–8. Cf. Stenton, *A.S.E.*, p. 480.

[4] 'Gesiths and Thegns', *E.H.R.* iv (1889), 728–9.

thegn owed military service because he held an estate of five hides. But the military obligation of the thegn and of the five-hide unit evidently have a common origin and, indeed, remain intimately related until the coming of the Normans.

The relationship is proven by an early-eleventh-century document known as the Promotion Law, which lists among the criteria that entitle a ceorl to the rights of thegnhood the possession of five hides of land.[1] A Law of Wergelds dating from the same period reports that if a ceorl prospers to such an extent that he performs the king's *utware* on five hides of land, he is to be entitled to a thegn's wergeld.[2] The *utware* which the document refers to is, of course, primarily military. This fact is made clear by the next passage in the Law of Wergelds, stating that if a ceorl does not possess the five hides he cannot attain the thegn's wergeld even if he owns a helmet, a coat of mail, and a gold-plated sword.[3] It is not sufficient, in other words, merely to be a well-armed warrior-representative of a five-hide unit. The true thegn holds personally the five hides for which he serves. If a peasant becomes sole possessor of a five-hide unit, and if he meets certain other qualifications, he acquires the rights of a thegn,[4] and assumes the military role of the thegnhood. Moreover, if his son and grandson are also entitled to become thegns, then the status becomes hereditary. After a certain time, thegnhood becomes indelible, and thus we find numerous Domesday thegns with diminutive estates, much smaller than five hides. The Promotion Law is not also a demotion law. But it establishes the five-hide unit—the honour of five hides—as the crucial mark of the military thegnhood.

Both the Promotion Law and the Law of Wergelds

---

[1] Liebermann, *Gesetze*, i. 456 ff.: Gethynctho, sec. 2; cf. sec. 3. This passage has been much discussed. See Maitland, 'Northumbrian Tenures'; Chadwick, *Anglo-Saxon Institutions*, pp. 80 ff.; Larson, p. 101; Little, pp. 723–9; Maitland, *D.B.B.*, p. 164; W. H. Stevenson, 'Burh-geat-setl', *E.H.R.* xii (1897), 489–92.

[2] Liebermann, *Gesetze*, i. 456 ff.: *Northleoda laga*, sec. 9. A thegn might, of course, hold an estate of less than five hides without forfeiting his inherited social and legal status. [3] Ibid., sec. 10.

[4] There has been considerable dispute as to whether the ceorl who enjoys the rights of a thegn thereby actually *becomes* a thegn, but this controversy is not strictly relevant to our problem. Chadwick (op. cit., p. 83) suggests that the Promotion Law refers to a king's thegn whereas the Law of Wergelds applies to an ordinary thegn.

originated in northern England, but the customs to which
they allude seem to have existed in the south long before the
eleventh century. The Dooms of Ine, king of Wessex,
stipulate that a Welshman possessing five hides of land is to
have a wergeld of 600*s*.[1] This law would not at first sight
seem relevant to the thegn class, which was normally entitled
to a wergeld of 1,200*s*. But as H. M. Chadwick has pointed
out, the Welsh peasant of that age had a wergeld which was
about half the size of the English ceorl's wergeld. He concludes that in all likelihood the same ratio held good in the
case of the landed proprietor, and consequently that even in
the seventh century, when the Dooms of Ine were promul-
gated, the possession of five hides was a prerequisite to an
Englishman's acquisition of a 1,200*s*. wergeld.[2] Thus the
connexion between the thegn and the five-hide unit emerges
from a variety of Anglo-Saxon sources originating from
diverse regions and dating from the seventh to the eleventh
centuries.

It may be well at this point to anticipate a possible argument in favour of the thegn's personal military obligation.
It might be pointed out that the heriot of the thegn—the
payment which his lord received in the event of his death—
was usually military in nature, consisting of weapons,
horses, or armour. If some thegns did not owe military
service, why did they have a military heriot—why did they
possess military equipment? It should be observed that
many thegns did hold five hides or more, and many
others with lesser estates doubtless served as warrior-representatives of five-hide units. As for those thegns who did
not normally perform military service, it is important to note
that the ordinary thegn was given an option as regards his
heriot. According to 2 Cnut 71, his heriot was to consist of
a horse and its trappings and his weapons, or his *healsfang*,
the latter being a sum of money.[3] And it is by no means
unusual to find thegns' heriots being rendered in money
rather than arms.[4]

---

[1] Dooms of Ine 24. 2 (A.D. 688–95).
[2] Chadwick, op. cit., pp. 91–93. Cf. Little, pp. 728–9.
[3] See *Laws of the Kings of England*, pp. 297–8.
[4] *A.S. Wills*, pp. 74, 186, 202–3; D.B. i. 280*b*, 298*b*; *A.S. Writs*, pp. 549–50.
According to 2 Cnut 71, Mercian and East Anglian thegns had money heriots.

If any doubt remains as to the identity between the thegn's military obligation and the five-hide select-fyrd system described in the Berkshire Domesday, it should be dispelled by a careful analysis of a Wiltshire parage tenure which provides us with conclusive proof that the thegn's service is to be understood in the context of the Berkshire support system. Three Englishmen held a four-hide estate at Durnford, Wiltshire, which belonged to the church of Wilton. The conditions of the tenure were that two of the Englishmen rendered 5s. each and the third served as a thegn.[1] In itself, the passage leaves many points unclear, but it is possible to learn considerably more about this tenure by comparing it with other parage arrangements. First of all, we can be quite certain that the three Englishmen divided the four hides equally among themselves. Equal division is a characteristic of parage tenures, and, indeed, is required by law.[2] Hence, each of the three Englishmen held an estate of $1\frac{1}{3}$ hides. The 5s. which two of them rendered might have been paid to the king or possibly to the church of Wilton. But again, a comparison with similar parage tenures reveals that the money was paid neither to the church nor to the king, but rather to the third tenant—the man who 'served as a thegn'.[3] It was his military support money. Now according to the Berkshire passage each hide of the five-hide unit contributed 4s. to the support of the military representative. A Berkshire tenant who held $1\frac{1}{3}$ hides would therefore contribute 5s. 4d., or, in the round numbers which were usually preferred, 5s. And our Durnford passage shows that in Wiltshire also $1\frac{1}{3}$ hides supported the warrior-representative to the extent of 5s. Doubtless the four hides which the three Englishmen held were combined with an adjacent hide to form a five-hide recruitment unit, for we know that the five-hide unit governed recruitment in Wiltshire.[4] The

---

[1] D.B. i. 67b: 'Tres Angli tenuerunt T.R.E. et non poterant ab aecclesia separari. Duo ex eis reddebant v s. et tercius seruiebat sicut tainus.'

[2] e.g. ibid. i. 375, 375b: 'aequaliter et pariliter.' 2 Cnut 70. 1, 78. See also Ellis, i. 141 n.

[3] Cf. D.B. i. 354: 'Chetel et Turuer fratres fuerunt et post mortem patris sui terram diviserunt. Ita tamen ut Chetel faciens servitium regis haberet adiutorium Turuer fratris sui'. See also D.B. i. 375b.

[4] D.B. i. 64b: Malmesbury. See below, pp. 23, 42, 76.

warrior-representative of this unit was the third Englishman mentioned in Domesday. When summoned to the fyrd, he was given 5s. by each of his companions and an additional 4s. by the holder of the adjacent hide. Here is a beautiful illustration of the Berkshire support system operating in an adjoining county. But the Durnford passage provides us with an even more valuable piece of information: it discloses that the warrior-representative *served as a thegn!* It proves our contention that warrior-representatives perform the military service which has been associated with the thegnhood, and, conversely, that the military obligation of thegns arises from the duty of five-hide units to produce warrior-representatives for the select fyrd.

III

The five-hide system was therefore the basis of both ceorl service and thegn service. Well-armed and well-supported members of both classes served in the select fyrd. In general, the military recruitment unit provided the fyrd with its best available warrior, and consequently the masses of the lower peasantry did not fight unless the great-fyrd obligation was invoked. The thegn was the typical select-fyrd warrior but there must have been numerous recruitment units which had no thegn to represent them. Pre-Conquest Berkshire, for example, contained 2,502 hides[1] and would therefore owe a total of about 500 men to the select fyrd at the rate of one man from five hides. The population of Berkshire in 1086, as compiled from Domesday Book, breaks down as follows: tenants-in-chief, 80; under-tenants, 185; *alodarii*, 5; *bordarii*, 1,827; *cotarii*, 750; miscellaneous, 53; *milites*, 4; priests, 5; *servi*, 792; *villani*, 2,623.[2] Out of a total population of 6,324, the bordars, cottagers, slaves, villains, and priests amount to 5,997, leaving 327 among the remaining classes including *alodarii* and miscellaneous. Admittedly these Domesday figures may not be precise, but we can expect them to be rather accurate with respect to the higher classes at least. It is also true that the population changed

---

[1] See F. H. Baring, *Domesday Tables* (London, 1909), pp. 50–51, and the references cited therein.   [2] Ellis, ii. 423.

considerably in the two decades since 1066. Many thegns died at Hastings, and others went into exile or descended into the ranks of the peasantry. But on the other hand, the Domesday population figures include among the upper classes a substantial number of foreign newcomers. It seems most improbable that there were enough thegns in pre-Conquest Berkshire to meet its select-fyrd quota of 500 warriors.

In many instances the military representatives must have been chosen from one of the intermediate classes between the thegnhood and the ordinary peasantry. Certain sources allude to a class of people with wergelds of 600s.—*sixhynde* men—intermediate between the *twihynde* ceorls and the *twelfhynde* thegns. They are mentioned in Alfred 39, and again in several passages from the *Leges Henrici Primi*.[1] Chadwick shows that the men of this class were called *radcnihts*, and identifies them with the *radchenistres* and *radmanni* who are recorded in the Domesday sections relating to the western Midlands.[2] He believes that the *sixhynde* wergeld had virtually disappeared by the eleventh century and that *sixhynde* men became *twelfhynde* or *twohynde*.[3] But the old *sixhynde* classes continued, even though their wergeld may have changed. Vinogradoff observes that the *radmanni* of pre-Conquest times are frequently found to be the tenurial antecedents of Anglo-Norman military sergeants, and concludes that although there is no direct proof of military service being imposed upon them as a class, nevertheless they probably had a military function of some sort.[4] They served normally as mounted attendants of their lords, and therefore might well have been summoned, under certain circumstances, to the select fyrd. But like the thegns, the *radmanni* did not serve as a consequence of their rank but rather as warrior-representatives of territorial units of

---

[1] Sections 76. 3, 82. 9, 87. 4; Liebermann, *Gesetze*, i. 593, 599, 601. See also Dooms of Ine 70.

[2] Chadwick, op. cit., pp. 88–89; *Pseudoleges Canuti*, 6.

[3] Chadwick, op. cit., pp. 96–97. Stenton thinks that the *sixhynde* weregeld continued into post-Conquest times, although not in the Wessex shires south of the Thames. He agrees that the *sixhynde* man is probably to be identified with the *radcniht* of the west: *Northern Danelaw*, p. 18 n.

[4] *Engl. Soc.*, pp. 70–71. See also Vinogradoff, *Villainage in England* (Oxford, 1892), pp. 320, 323, 407; Maitland, *D.B.B.*, pp. 57, 305.

recruitment. If no thegn were available, a *radmannus* might very well be the best warrior that the five-hide unit could produce.

The obligation of riding for one's lord, either as an escort, a messenger, or a carrier, is ascribed to several classes, all of which were, for our purposes, nearly identical. Thus the *cnihts*, the *radcnihts*, the *radmanni*, the *geneats*,[1] and, in the north and west, the sokemen, may all be regarded as belonging to an intermediate group between the nobility and the common ceorls. In another sense, they can be considered members of the upper peasantry, for they often performed agricultural services of various kinds. But since they were good horsemen, many of them doubtless served as warrior-representatives. The military nature of the *cniht* is particularly striking, since the term was later used to describe the post-Conquest feudal cavalry. And, indeed, we find *cnihts* among the military lessees of the see of Worcester. A *cniht* named Æthelwold was granted an estate called Wolverton for three lives, free of all burdens except military service, bridge and wall work, and carrying service for the church. Another Worcester *cniht*, Osulf, was granted two manors for three lives, free of all burdens except *ferdfare*, *walgeweorc*, and *brygcgeweorc*.[2] As we have seen, the Worcester lessees were normally expected to perform personally the military service due from their lands.[3] Thus, the military obligations of *cnihts'* estates were ordinarily performed by the *cnihts* themselves.[4] The military nature of the *cniht* is further illustrated by the fact that the term is translated in Latin sources as *miles*.[5]

[1] See Stenton, *E.F.*, pp. 132 ff.; Vinogradoff, *Engl. Soc.*, p. 72; *Select English Historical Documents*, pp. 24, 108; *A.S. Chart.*, p. 206; *Rectitudines Singularum Personarum*, c. 2.

[2] *A.S. Chart.*, p. 114 (A.D. 977); p. 96 (A.D. 969).

[3] See above, pp. 71–72. But there were exceptions: e.g. *A.S. Chart.*, p. 86, where a woman named Ælfhild holds three hides which owe the *trimoda necessitas*. Osulf's two manors (ibid., p. 96) were to pass to his wife if she outlived his children, who were the immediate heirs.

[4] It should be remembered that the extent of the obligations of these Worcester estates is not specified. Here, too, the five-hide rule applied, and the leasehold tenements themselves were combined or divided into five-hide units for military-recruitment purposes. See above, Chap. III, and Round, *F.E.*, pp. 60 ff.

[5] e.g. *A.S. Chart.*, pp. 220, 472. D. C. Douglas writes of the term *cniht* as follows: 'And often in the later preconquest charters it is used in such a way that we are far

The military obligations of the pre-Conquest sokeman are somewhat less clear, although in at least one instance the same individual is referred to as a sokeman in one document and a *knihte* in another.[1] Indeed, there are a number of references to the military service of sokemen or of men living on their lord's sokeland. The Lincolnshire Domesday reports that one sokeland helped in the king's army on land and at sea.[2] The military obligation of certain sokemen on the estates of the abbey of Peterborough is mentioned in an intriguing twelfth-century document, the *Descriptio Militum de Abbatia de Burgo*. Here, all the sokemen of six specified vills are required to serve along with the feudal knights— *cum militibus*.[3] It seems evident that the obligations of these sokemen originated in the Anglo-Saxon age, but it is difficult, at first sight, to identify them either with the great-fyrd or the select-fyrd obligation. There were numerous vills on the estates of Peterborough, in addition to the six mentioned in the *Descriptio Militum*, and most of them contained sokemen,[4] so we must conclude that only an isolated minority of the Peterborough sokemen were burdened with military service. Hence, the obligation of this specified group cannot have been connected with service in the great fyrd. On the other hand, the military sokemen cannot very well have been the direct military representatives of hide-units, since they are all clustered in six vills rather than being spread over the land. The problem which we face here is a very difficult one,

from sure that we have not to deal with some sort of military tenure, however vaguely expressed': *Feud. Docs.*, p. ci, n. 2, citing *Diplomatarium Anglicum Aevi Saxonici*, ed. B. Thorpe (London, 1865), pp. 571, 574, 583. See also *A.S.C.*, A.D. 1083, where a group of armed Normans are described as *cnihtas*. Cf. ibid., A.D. 1088, 1094. Stenton regards the *cniht* as a retainer attached to the personal service of a nobleman (*E.F.*, pp. 132–5), and in the will of an Anglo-Saxon ealdorman we find a reference to his *hired cnihtas*: *A.S. Wills*, p. 24.

[1] *A.S. Wills*, p. 82. Cf. D.B. i. 195*b*, and *Inquisitio Comitatus Cantabrigiensis*, 90*b*. The matter is discussed in *A.S. Wills*, pp. 194–5.

[2] D.B. i. 368: 'Haec soca talis fuit quod nichil reddebat, sed adiuabat in exercitu regis in terra et in mari.' See Stenton, *Northern Danelaw*, pp. 28–29, where three other passages from the Lincolnshire Domesday are quoted. These passages relate to military service, but their relevance to the problem of sokemen seems a little doubtful.

[3] *Chron. Pet.*, pp. 172–3: Great Easton, Leicestershire; Walton, Wirrinton, Pilsgate, and Irthlingborough, all in Northamptonshire; and Elton, Huntingdonshire.

[4] This fact appears from an examination of the Domesday entries relating to the estates of Peterborough, and the *Liber Niger*, an early-twelfth-century Peterborough survey printed in *Chron. Pet.*, pp. 157–68.

and, since our information is based on a twelfth-century source, it is perhaps not entirely relevant to this study. I will therefore refrain from examining the problem in detail at this time, and will merely suggest what seems to me the proper avenue of approach. As we will see in the next chapter, an important territorial lord of Anglo-Saxon times would ordinarily be expected to lead the select fyrd which was recruited from his own lands, and would be held responsible for assembling it. Such were the obligations, for example, of the abbot of Peterborough. The select fyrd would be recruited, as elsewhere, on the basis of a specific ratio of men to hides or carucates, but it is entirely possible that the lord might choose to raise his army in some way other then demanding one man from every five hides. Thus, a lord with, say, 200 hides would owe forty men to the select fyrd. The king would not be concerned with how the men were recruited so long as they appeared properly armed and in proper numerical strength. The lord might demand two men from each of twenty hides and leave his remaining 180 hides exempt. He might maintain forty landless warriors in his own household. Or he might, as the abbots of Peterborough seem to have done, place the bulk of the military burden on six particular vills.

The personnel of the select fyrd was heterogeneous because the obligation was based upon units of land rather than social rank. Throughout much of England, each five-hide unit was obliged to produce a warrior-representative. The *miles* who was produced was normally a thegn, but if no thegns were available he might be a man of lower status. He might be a member of one of the intermediate groups— a *cniht*, a *radmannus*, a sokeman. And he might, if necessary, be a well-armed and well-supported member of the ordinary peasantry. The important thing was that he represented an appreciable territorial unit which was obliged to give him generous financial support. As such, he belonged to an exclusive military group which can, in a sense, be considered a class in itself. And he may well have taken considerable pride in his connexion with the select territorial army of Saxon England.

V

SPECIAL ASPECTS OF THE SELECT-FYRD OBLIGATION

I

BERKSHIRE Domesday, which has been so helpful to us in other respects, provides the one explicit statement as to the length of the service term in the select fyrd: each hide gave the warrior-representative 4s. for maintenance and wages for two months.[1] This two-month term may be compared with the three-month period of the earlier Carolingian army,[2] and the forty-day period which was prevalent throughout most of feudal Europe.[3] I have noted elsewhere in this connexion that for about a century after the Norman Conquest the feudal host of England apparently owed an identical term of war-time service, and have suggested that the significance of the post-Conquest fyrd was such as to necessitate a common duty period for the Anglo-Saxon army and the force of feudal knights.[4] It was not until the reign of King Stephen that the knights' duty term was reduced from two months to the more customary forty days.

The sixty-day service term was not, however, of great antiquity. It cannot have existed, for example, in the ninth century when King Alfred divided the fyrd into two groups which served alternately so as to provide a continuously existing military force.[5] Indeed, during Alfred's reign the fyrd seems to have been in action almost all the time. In 871 it fought nine major battles against the Danes besides innumerable minor engagements,[6] and this pace was maintained through much of the reigns of Alfred and Edward

---

[1] D.B. i. 56b.   [2] Lot, *L'Art mil.* i. 91 n. 3.

[3] See my article, 'The Annual Term of Military Service in Medieval England', *Medievalia et Humanistica*, xiii (1960), 40–47.

[4] Ibid. See also Hollister, 'Significance of Scutage Rates', *E.H.R.* lxxv (1960), 582 ff.

[5] *A.S.C.*, A, A.D. 894 [893].   [6] Ibid., A, A.D. 871.

the Elder. Alfred's system of rotating the two groups was still in effect as late as 920,[1] and long afterwards English monarchs seem to have expected almost unlimited service from the select fyrd in times of grave emergency. Thus, Edmund Ironside summoned the fyrd five separate times in the year 1016.[2]

But normally the service term was limited, at least in the eleventh century, by the problem of provisioning the soldiers. As we have seen, the bulk of the logistical burden was assumed by the tenants of recruitment units. It was they who were responsible for the subsistence of their warrior-representatives. However advantageous this arrangement may have been to the monarchy, it set a limit on the service term, for as Berkshire Domesday informs us, the soldier was given a subsistence allowance sufficient to cover only two months. And we have seen that this same support system prevailed throughout most of England if not all of it. Accordingly, several passages from the pre-Conquest chronicles report instances when the fyrd was obliged to disband and return home because its provisions ran out. Florence of Worcester states that in July 1006 a huge Danish army landed at Sandwich and began to pillage Kent and Sussex. King Ethelred assembled the fyrd in Mercia and Wessex to oppose the Danes, but they refused battle, harassing the fyrd throughout the whole autumn. At length, on the approach of winter, Ethelred was compelled to disband the fyrd.[3] It is impossible to determine from this episode the exact term that the fyrd served during the summer and autumn of 1006. Presumably, it was summoned some time in July, and it was disbanded as autumn ended and winter began. This would seem offhand to be a period considerably in excess of two months. But elsewhere Florence of Worcester is more specific in explaining what he means by the end of autumn and the beginning of winter. He reports that in 1066 King Harold stationed his army at suitable points along the coast in preparation for the Norman invasion, and kept watch *throughout the summer and autumn*. But provisions gave out around the time of the feast of the

[1] *A.S.C.*, A, A.D. 921 [920].   [2] Ibid., A.D. 1016
[3] *Fl. Wig.* i. 159.

nativity of St. Mary, and the force was disbanded.[1] So presumably the fyrd was sent home, as in 1006, when autumn ended and winter began. But the feast of the nativity of St. Mary occurs on 8 September. The chroniclers of the time must have regarded winter as beginning at a singularly early date. It would seem, then, that the duty periods of 1066 and 1006 ended at about the same time of year, namely, early or mid-September, and that the period which the fyrd served in 1006, running apparently from July to September, fits in quite well with the two-month term of service which Berkshire Domesday discloses.

The term of Anglo-Saxon fyrd service differs from that of post-Conquest knight service in one important respect. The knights of Norman England were expected not only to serve two months in war-time but also to serve forty days each year in time of peace.[2] This peace-time duty was apparently a training period during which the knights practised their military craft in preparation for actual campaigns. The warriors of the select fyrd do not seem to have had any such annual training period. Their two-month obligation was exacted only in time of war. To what extent this custom hindered their military effectiveness cannot be determined. Perhaps they trained privately or in small local groups, but if so, there is no indication of it in the sources. It should be noted, however, that the select fyrd was composed entirely of men who fought on foot—of warriors who might ride to the scene of the battle but who dismounted before the fight began.[3] Many scholars have called attention to the fact that the tactics of the medieval heavy cavalry required far more intensive training than those of the infantry, and even though the knights of Norman England themselves frequently fought on foot,[4] nevertheless they were expected to be competent cavalrymen as well. An annual training period would therefore be considerably more important to the Anglo-Norman knight than to the Old English warrior-representative.

---

[1] Ibid. i. 225. See also *A.S.C.*, C, A.D. 1066.
[2] Hollister, 'Annual Term of Military Service', *Medievalia et Humanistica*, pp. 41–42.   [3] See below, pp. 137 ff.
[4] See my article, 'Norman Conquest and Genesis of English Feudalism', pp. 655–6, and below, pp. 131–2

Accordingly, numerous sources relating to the Anglo-Saxon age testify that the select fyrd was to be summoned only in time of war or emergency. In the Berkshire entry itself, we are told that the five-hide unit sent its representative only when the king sent an army on a campaign.[1] The burghers of Warwick sent ten warrior-representatives to the select fyrd *when the king went on a campaign by land,* and four boatswains or four pounds *if he went against his enemies by sea.*[2] At Malmesbury and Leicester, too, warrior-representatives were summoned only in the instance of an actual military campaign.[3] A land grant by Oswald of Worcester which exempts the holder from all secular obligations except the usual *trimoda necessitas,* stipulates that the fyrd obligation will be assessed only in time of war,[4] and the confirmation of the grant by King Offa of Mercia to Abbot Stithbert of thirty hides in Middlesex, which also reserves the *trimoda necessitas,* states that warrior-representatives are to be sent only *in expeditionis necessitatem.*[5] According to Ethelred's Laws, the *trimoda necessitas* 'shall always be diligently performed, *whenever the need arises'*,[6] and such language as this is surely incompatible with the notion of an annual training period. But if the sixty-day service period was not normally enforced every year, there is, on the other hand, nothing in the sources to suggest that it might not be enforced more than once a year in cases of emergency. The summoning of the fyrd five times in 1016 was obviously exceptional, but it was not strictly incompatible with the custom that the fyrd could be summoned at times of war or emergency. Usually, however, campaigns were several years apart and select-fyrd duty was normally much less than an annual obligation.[7]

---

[1] D.B. i. 56*b.*   [2] Ibid. i. 238.   [3] Ibid. i. 64*b,* 230.

[4] *A.S. Chart.,* p. 126, *c.* A.D. 985: '. . . pontis et arcis restaurationem et *contra hostes* expeditionem'.

[5] Birch, *C.S.,* no. 201; Kemble, *C.D.,* no. 116.

[6] 2 Ethelred 26. 1. Cf. 6 Ethelred 32. 3, and 2 Cnut 10.

[7] This was obviously so in such relatively peaceful reigns as those of Edgar, Cnut, and Edward the Confessor. Even in the reign of Edward the Elder, a landholder from Kent who was subject to fyrd duty is reported to have gone at least seven years without performing military service: Kemble, *C.D.,* no. 499; Birch, *C.S.,* no. 1064.

II

The problem of the select-fyrd obligation is complicated somewhat by the fact that certain sources make a distinction between a summons to an expedition led personally by the king and a summons to an expedition in which the king is not present. The laws of Ethelred state that a person who deserts an army under the king's personal command does so at the risk of losing his life or his wergeld. If he deserts any other army, he is to forfeit 120s.[1] The wording of several Domesday passages relating to the select-fyrd obligation suggests that the obligation was operative only when the king led the army. Leicester performed its military obligation 'when *the king* marched with his army through the land' or 'if *the king* went overseas against the enemy'.[2] At Warwick, ten burghers joined the fyrd 'whenever *the king went personally* in any expedition by land'.[3] The town also owed military service 'if *the king* went against his enemies by sea'.[4] Other passages, however, make it equally clear that military obligations were enforceable in the absence of the king. The burghers of Shrewsbury were obliged, when summoned, to join the great fyrd 'when *the sheriff* went into Wales',[5] and at Lewes, if the king wished to send his men '*without going himself* to guard the sea, 20s. were collected from all the men, no matter whose tenants they might be, and those who handled the arms in the ships had this money'.[6] It should be noted, however, that neither of these two passages has to do with the normal select-fyrd obligation.

The notion that the select fyrd can be summoned only when the king is present on the expedition may cast some light on a passage from the *Anglo-Saxon Chronicle* of A.D. 1016:

Then Prince Edmund [Ironside] began to assemble the fyrd; and when the fyrd soldiers had been brought together, nothing would satisfy them but that the king should be with them and that they should have the support of the citizens of London. So they abandoned the expedition and each of them went home.[7]

---

[1] 5 Ethelred 28. Cf. 6 Ethelred 35.
[3] Ibid. i. 238. [4] Ibid.
[6] Ibid. i. 26. See above, p. 21, and below, p. 121.
[7] *A.S.C.*, E, A.D. 1016. Cf. D, 1016, and *Fl. Wig.* i. 171: 'Quod ut audivit clito

[2] D.B. i. 230.
[5] Ibid. i. 252.

This restriction on the summoning of the select fyrd might prove most awkward, as indeed it did in 1016, but it could also be a blessing for the king. In so far as the rule applied, the select fyrd could not be brought together by dissident nobles for purposes of revolt. This may be one of the reasons why, after the Norman Conquest, the fyrd invariably appears on the side of the monarchy, never on the side of rebelling barons.[1]

But the rule was obviously not always adhered to. On other occasions in 1016, Edmund Ironside did raise an army, and Earl Godwin was successful in summoning the select fyrd of his earldom during the revolt of 1051–2.[2] Indeed, the evidence cited above is quite insufficient to prove that the summoning of the select fyrd was always limited to instances when the king led the army. The Berkshire passage states that warrior-representatives were to be sent by every five-hide unit in the county whenever the king *sent* an army anywhere.[3] We may perhaps conclude that the necessity of the royal presence was an ancient tradition derived from the days when the king was above all a warrior-chief of a tribe. We find traces of the same tradition (and the same exceptions to it) on the Continent: at Verneuil the burghers were obliged to perform military service only when the king was actually serving in the same army, whereas at Beaumont the burghers were bound to serve wherever the king wished.[4] Indeed, the necessity of the royal presence is stated in at least one feudal charter of post-Conquest England. In 1107 King Henry I granted a fief to the church of Evesham in return for the service of four and one-half knights 'in military expeditions when I am present'.[5]

Eadmundus, cognomine Ferreum Latus, exercitum festinato congregavit, sed cum congregatus esset, cum West-Saxonicis et Danis nolebant congredi Mercenses, nisi cumi llis essent rex Ægelredus et cives Lundonienses: quapropter expeditione dimissa, unusquisque redit in sua.'

[1] This is true at least after the initial English revolts had been suppressed and the Conquest stabilized (after about 1070 or 1071).

[2] *A.S.C.*, A.D. 1051; *Fl. Wig.* i. 205.

[3] D.B. i. 56*b*: 'Si rex *mittebat* alicubi exercitum. . . .'

[4] *British Borough Charters*, p. cxi. Cp, Boutaric, *Institutions militaires*, pp. 146–7.

[5] *C. Ch. R.* i. 257. The land is to be held free of 'omni seculari servicio et opere servili et de scutagio, salvo tamen et retento servicio quatuor militum et dimidii in expeditione, me presente'. For the date of this charter, see *R.R.A.N.* ii, no. 831.

In the period with which this study is concerned, the king would usually be present to lead a large army on an important campaign, and therefore the question of the necessity of the royal presence would be in many instances an academic one. Nevertheless, there were also times when the select fyrd of a particular district would be assembled, perhaps for a local defensive campaign. The narrative sources disclose many such local armies, usually led by an earl or a sheriff, and aside from the one instance in 1016 the sources are silent as to any objection by the fyrd soldiers to the fact that the king was not present.[1] The necessity of the royal presence is therefore a rather ambiguous aspect of the select-fyrd obligation. It seems doubtful that this qualification was generally accepted, and even more doubtful that it was rigidly followed. We are perhaps safe in concluding that it was a custom of great antiquity, extending far back into the Germanic past, existing on the Continent as well as in England, and in both places gradually falling into disuse. Some regions of England reported the custom to the Domesday commissioners; others did not. It continued into post-Conquest times, but only in one rather singular feudal charter. For the time was fast arriving when the king need no longer be his own general. Indeed the time had come, although perhaps prematurely, with the accession of Edward the Confessor.[2]

III

The most cursory examination of the narrative sources discloses that the select fyrd was organized, by and large, according to shires. Subdivisions of the fyrd are persistently referred to as 'the men of Kent', 'the people of Gloucestershire and Herefordshire', 'the people of Devonshire and

---

[1] In 1016, it will be recalled, the fyrd objected not only to the absence of King Ethelred but also to the absence of the citizens of London. Thus, the reasons for their objection are by no means clear. It may very well have been merely that they felt they were not getting sufficient support.

[2] Under the Confessor, one finds border campaigns being led by earls, particularly Earl Harold of Wessex. The same is true, of course, of the Marcher lords after the Conquest.

Somersetshire', &c.[1] As we have seen, the narrative sources do not enable us to distinguish clearly between the great fyrd and the select fyrd, but the practice of dividing the Anglo-Saxon army according to counties is so common as to indicate that a shire organization characterized both fyrds. Accordingly, all the warrior-representatives of a shire are usually summoned to the fyrd at the same time; they seem to have their own leaders and to fight as a unit. Thus, we encounter in a tenth-century charter an allusion to all the Kentish troops being summoned to battle,[2] and the narrative sources contain numerous references of a similar nature, e.g. 'A large body of the men of Hampshire and Wiltshire assembled and marched boldly against the enemy'.[3] At a dark moment during Ethelred's reign, the *Anglo-Saxon Chronicle* reports: 'Finally there was no leader who would collect an army but each fled as best he could, and ultimately no shire would even help the next.'[4] The distinction between shire fyrds continued even into battle. In May 1010, for example, an invading force of Danes was met by Ulfkytel, the ealdorman of East Anglia. In the desperate battle that followed, the East Anglian fyrd gave way, but the men of Cambridgeshire stood firm until they were at last defeated and forced to withdraw.[5] Here we see the fyrds of each district acting as a unit. The East Anglian fyrd retreats, but the Cambridgeshire fyrd fights on. Ealdorman Ulfkytel was the commander of the entire force, but under him the Cambridge and East Anglian fyrds must each have had its own

---

[1] The fyrds of the following shires are mentioned in the *Anglo-Saxon Chronicle* and Florence of Worcester: Kent (*A.S.C.*, A.D. 853; C, 902; A, 905; E, 999; *Fl. Wig.* i. 154, 205); Gloucester (*A.S.C.*, A, A.D. 918 [917]; *Fl. Wig.* i. 203); Hereford (*A.S.C.*, A, A.D. 918 [917]; *Fl. Wig.* i. 203); Sussex (*Fl. Wig.* i. 205); Oxford (*Fl. Wig.* i. 205); Somerset (*A.S.C.*, A.D. 848, 878; E, 1001; *Fl. Wig.* i. 155, 205, 208); Berks. (*A.S.C.*, F, A.D. 871; *Fl. Wig.* i. 205); Essex (*Fl. Wig.* i. 205); Huntingdon (*Fl. Wig.* i. 205); Cambridge (*A.S.C.*, E, A.D. 1010; *Fl. Wig.* i. 162, 205); Devon (*A.S.C.*, A, A.D. 823 [825]; A.D. 850; E, 1001; *Fl. Wig.* i. 155, 208); Hants (*A.S.C.*, A.D. 860; F, 861; 878; A, 1001; 1003; *Fl. Wig.* i. 156); Wilts. (*A.S.C.*, A, A.D. 800; 878; 1003; *Fl. Wig.* i. 156); Dorset (*A.S.C.*, A.D. 837 [840]; 848); Surrey (*A.S.C.*, A.D. 853, 860); York (*A.S.C.*, A.D. 866); Nottingham, Derby, and Lincoln (*A.S.C.*, A.D. 1065). East Anglia is treated as a unit (*A.S.C.*, E, A.D. 1004, 1010; *Fl. Wig.* i. 157, 162, 205), but early references to Mercia and Wessex (*A.S.C.*, A.D. 850, 867, 875, 876, &c.) give way to references naming their component shires (*A.S.C.*, A.D. 1065 and *passim*).

[2] Kemble, *C.D.*, no. 499.

[3] *Fl. Wig.* i. 156.

[4] *A.S.C.*, E, A.D. 1010.

[5] Ibid.; *Fl. Wig.* i. 159.

leaders—men whose importance was insufficient to warrant their being mentioned by name. Occasionally, however, the chroniclers disclose by name the commanders of shire fyrds who are participating in joint campaigns. In 860 Ealdorman Osric and the men of Hampshire together with Ealdorman Æthelwulf and the men of Berkshire defeated an army of Danes.[1] But it is exceptional later on for an ealdorman or earl to be found commanding the forces of a single county, and men of lesser rank are seldom mentioned by the chroniclers.

But if the chronicles are obscure as to the leaders of the individual shire levies, they frequently disclose the leader of an entire military expedition. A large military force consisting of the fyrds of several shires would frequently, of course, be led by the king. But such forces were also led on many occasions by ealdormen or earls.[2] It is they who are mentioned again and again by the chroniclers as the leaders of local or regional military forces. The relation between the ealdorman or earl and his military force was psychologically somewhat similar to that between a feudal lord and his vassals. The *Battle of Maldon*, for example, discloses that the warriors in Ealdorman Byrhtnoth's force, whether retainers, thegns, or ceorls, regarded him as their lord, and although the Maldon poet may have been guilty of a certain amount of heroic exaggeration on this point, nevertheless it seems clear that the old *comitatus* idea lingered on, at least in attenuated form, among the Anglo-Saxon fyrd leaders and the warriors who fought under them.

Once in a while, bishops served as military commanders. We find Bishop Ealdred of Worcester, for example, leading the fyrds of Gloucestershire and Herefordshire in an unsuccessful defensive campaign against a plundering expedition of Norsemen from Ireland.[3] Two of the king's reeves

---

[1] *A.S.C.*, E, A.D. 860. Cf. ibid. 845 [848].

[2] From about the time of Cnut, the term *ealdorman* is superseded by earl (*eorl*). On ealdormen or earls as military commanders, see Chadwick, *Anglo-Saxon Institutions*, pp. 168 ff.; *A.S.C.*, A, A.D. 800; 837 [840]; 848; 850; 860; 991; A, 1001; 1003; 1004; 1010; E, 1015; 1051; 1055; 1065; 1066; *Fl. Wig.* i. 151 (cf. E. A. Freeman, *Norman Conquest* [6 vols., Oxford, 1867–79], i. 281, 624–5), 156, 157, 162, 203, 205, 225.

[3] *Fl. Wig.* i. 203; *A.S.C.*, D, 1050 [1049]. See also ibid., A.D. 848, 1056.

participated in a campaign of 1001, presumably as commanders or sub-commanders, and were killed in battle;[1]
and as the Anglo-Saxon era drew to a close, sheriffs came
to play an increasingly significant role in the leadership of
the fyrd, a role that grew still more important in the years
following the Norman Conquest.[2] The sheriff, as 'shire
reeve', was the obvious figure to lead the military force of
the individual shire. But references to sheriffs in positions
of military command are relatively rare in late-Saxon sources
as compared with references to earls. While this may be
explained in part by the fact that earls were more illustrious
than sheriffs and therefore considered more worthy of
mention, nevertheless we are probably safe in concluding
that a major military force was usually led by the earl of the
district if not by the king himself. Indeed, the pious pacifism
of the Confessor resulted in the military burden shifting
significantly from the monarch to his earls, and it is such
men as Harold and Swein, Siward and Leofric, Edwin and
Morcar—the great earls of the realm—who bear the weight
of military responsibility in the last years of the Saxon age.[3]

During the reign of Edward the Confessor, the earls were
exceptionally strong. The kingdom of England was divided
into six or seven great earldoms, each consisting of a number
of counties. These political divisions were reflected in the
organization of the fyrd. The chronicles still divide the fyrd
into shire levies, but they also group these levies into larger
units which correspond with the boundaries of the earldoms.
Thus one may speak of the Wiltshire fyrd or the Hampshire
fyrd, but these two forces, together with the fyrds of other
shires, constituted the fyrd of Earl Godwin or Earl Harold.
Accordingly, the Anglo-Saxon chronicler writes on the
occasion of the Northumbrian revolt of 1065:

> They [the Yorkshire thegns] sent for Morcar, son of Earl Ælfgar,
> and chose him to be their earl. He marched south with all the men of
> the shire, together with men from Nottinghamshire, Derbyshire, and

---

[1] *A.S.C.*, A, A.D. 1001.

[2] Besides the Domesday references already noted (i. 179, 252), see W. A. Morris,
The Medieval English Sheriff (Manchester, 1927), pp. 27–28, 58–60, and the
references cited therein. See also *A.S.C.*, A.D. 897; A, 1001.

[3] *A.S.C.*, A.D. 1051, 1065, 1066.

Lincolnshire, until he came to Northampton, where he was joined by his brother Edwin and the men from his earldom, among whom were many Welshmen.[1]

In 1051, on the occasion of Godwin's rebellion:

> Earl Godwin . . . began to assemble troops throughout his earldom and Swein, his son, throughout his, and Harold, his second son, throughout his earldom. . . . King Edward was then residing at Gloucester. He sent then for Earl Leofric and to the north for Earl Siward, and asked them for troops. At first they arrived with modest reinforcements, but when they understood the situation in the south they sent north all over their earldoms and had a great fyrd summoned to the assistance of their lord, and Earl Ralph did likewise throughout his earldom.[2]

Florence of Worcester, describing the same episode, enumerates the shires within each earldom from which the fyrds were raised.[3] We may conclude, then, that in the last phase of Anglo-Saxon history, the echelons of military organization and command were the shire, the earldom, and the kingdom, and that these echelons were led, at least ideally, by the sheriff, the earl, and the king.[4]

IV

This neat, simple, and symmetrical organization is marred, however, by the existence of a complicating element —that of private lordship. I suggested in an earlier chapter

---

[1] Ibid., D, A.D. 1065.   [2] Ibid., D, A.D. 1052 [1051].
[3] *Fl. Wig.* i. 205.
[4] Probably there were subordinate units of organization below the shire level. One such unit was the ship-soke, discussed below, pp. 108 ff., which consisted of three hundreds or 300 hides and therefore of sixty warriors, one from each five-hide unit. A charter of Henry II's reign refers to the royal service which was performed by hides and by hundreds: 'Et Fulcherus adquietabit terram de forensis seruiciis que uadunt per hidas et per hundreda': *Danelaw Charters*, p. cxxvi. Since the charter relates to Derbyshire, a county with neither hides nor hundreds, Stenton believes that the passage was an ancient alliterative formula. It raises for us the question of whether the hundred, with its normal complement of twenty men, was also an important unit of fyrd organization. A post-Conquest sergeant is required to carry the banner of the infantry force of the Hundred of Wootton in Oxfordshire (*Bk. of Fees*, i. 253; cf. ibid. i. 11, 104; ii. 830), but this duty is not recorded until 1219, and even if it reflected pre-Conquest custom, it doubtless related to the great fyrd rather than to the select fyrd. In the absence of additional evidence, we are obliged to leave the question open.

that the abbot of Peterborough, a monastery with far-flung lands in Northamptonshire, Lincolnshire, Nottinghamshire, Huntingdonshire, and Leicestershire, was personally responsible for fyrd recruitment throughout his estates.[1] Several Domesday passages refer to the responsibility of a lord for the recruitment of the warrior-representatives due to the select fyrd from his lands. In Berkshire, 'if anyone for the sake of remaining behind [when the fyrd was summoned] promised to send another in his place, and yet he who was to have been sent remained behind, *his lord was freed of obligation* by the payment of 50s.'. In Worcestershire, 'if the freeman of another lord remains away from the army, and his lord leads another man to the host in his place, he pays 40s. *to his lord who received the summons*. But if nobody at all goes in his place, he shall pay his lord 40s.; but his lord must pay the entire amount to the king.'[2] These passages have already been discussed in another context. They contribute to our present discussion by making it clear that the royal summons was sent to an important lord directly. The lord would then have the responsibility of summoning the warrior-representatives of each military recruitment unit on his estate. The warrior-representative, if he held his land under an important lord, would be responsible to that lord for his service, and the lord would be responsible to the king for the appearance of the appropriate number of warrior-representatives.[3]

It would follow from this that the lord might well be the leader of his own military contingent consisting of the warrior-representatives from his estates. This supposition is borne out by at least one piece of evidence, in which a certain Eadric is designated as steersman of the ship of the bishop of Worcester and commander of the bishop's troops at the time of Edward the Confessor.[4] The bishop, who was

---

[1] See above, pp. 83–84.

[2] D.B. i. 56*b*, 172; see above, pp. 66 ff.

[3] See Chadwick, *Anglo-Saxon Institutions*, p. 102; *Origin of the English Nation*, p. 152; Maitland, *D.B.B.*, pp. 301 ff.

[4] *Heming's Cartulary*, i. 81: 'Edricus qui fuit, tempore regis Edwardi, stermannus navis episcopi et ductor exercitus eiusdem episcopi ad servitium regis'. Cf. D.B. i. 173*b*; Maitland, *D.B.B.*, p. 308; Stenton, *E.F.*, p. 127; Ballard, *Domesday Inquest*, p. 102; see below, pp. 105, 112,

not himself able to serve in a position of military command, had evidently selected Eadric as his representative, to perform the function ordinarily incumbent on a great lord. The notion that the fyrd soldiers of the bishop of Worcester were regarded as a discrete military unit receives further support from a document which records a suit between the see of Worcester and the abbey of Evesham. The bishop claimed successfully that the men of Hampton were obliged to discharge their military obligation in his own contingent along with the men of Oswaldslaw Hundred.[1] Similarly, the men of Taunton were obliged to go to the fyrd with the contingent of the bishop of Winchester.[2] Moreover, certain important landholders such as the bishop of Worcester and the abbot of Bury St. Edmunds were given the privilege of collecting *fyrdwite*—the fine for non-performance of the military obligation, which was normally reserved to the king.[3] According to Cnut's Laws, *fyrdwite* was one of the dues to which the king was entitled unless he wished to show special honour to anyone by granting it to him.[4]

On the basis of these facts it is safe to conclude that a lord might, if he wished, raise the select-fyrd quota from his lands by some means other than the five-hide system. This would not be a real exception to the five-hide rule, since all the estates of a lord taken together would owe an exact number of men to the select fyrd, the number being equal to the number of hides under the lord's jurisdiction divided by five (or by however many hides the recruitment units contained). Accordingly, I suggested earlier that a lord with an estate of 200 hides, owing forty warriors to the fyrd according to the five-hide rule, might recruit them in any way he pleased.[5] He might place an unusually heavy burden on some hide-groups and leave others exempt. He might keep forty retainers in his household. Or he might follow the normal custom of demanding one warrior from each five-hide unit. There is reason to believe, as we have seen, that the abbot of Peterborough took the first course, enforcing

---

[1] *Heming's Cartulary*, i. 77; *V.C.H.*, *Worcs.* i. 249.
[2] D.B. i. 87*b*: 'Istae consuetudines pertinent ad Tantone. . . . profectio in exercitum cum hominibus episcopi.'
[3] *A.S. Writs*, nos. 18, 24; *V.C.H.*, *Worcs.* i. 249; *A.S. Chart.*, p. 236.
[4] 2 Cnut 12, 15.   [5] Above, pp. 83–84.

the service of every sokeman from certain designated vills and leaving the remainder of his lands exempt from fyrd duty. The bishops of Worcester, on the other hand, maintained the normal five-hide arrangements on their estates, for in the numerous land leases which these bishops granted, the military obligation is always expressed in terms of the *trimoda necessitas* due from the land.[1] There is no concentration of military service in certain areas or any diminution of it in others.

Ever since the late nineteenth century there has been an exceptional amount of interest in the land leases or land loans granted by the bishops of Worcester. This has been especially true of the series of about seventy leases granted by Bishop Oswald in the triple hundred of Oswaldslaw between 962 and 992. Almost all these leases were for three lives, that is, for the life of the grantee, that of his heir, and that of his heir's heir. V. H. Galbraith believes that some of the leases of late-Saxon times were hereditary, although this is a matter that cannot be proven conclusively.[2] There is also some uncertainty as to the terms according to which the leases were held. What did the grantee owe the grantor in return for the lease? Maitland discusses this matter at some length. He finds that the conditions of the lease, as set forth in the individual charters, are discouragingly vague. The fealty and service of the grantee are usually mentioned, but in such a way as to imply that the lease was granted in return for *past* service. As Maitland expresses it, 'Any thing that could be called a stipulation for future service is very rare'.[3] Nevertheless, he contends that these leases were an anticipation of post-Conquest feudalism. 'Dependent tenure is here', he writes, 'and, we may say, feudal tenure, and even tenure by knight's service. . . .'[4]

It should be remembered that these words were written only a short time after the publication of Round's famous

---

[1] e.g. *A.S. Chart.*, pp. 134, 138, 180, 208, 210. The same may be said of the estates of the see of Winchester: ibid., p. 26; Birch, *C.S.*, nos. 543, 599.

[2] Galbraith, 'An Episcopal Land Grant of 1085', p. 366: 'Even before 1066 the churches had found it necessary to make large grants of lands to thegns and cnihts: these grants were certainly not, as a rule, life grants. Often they were for three lives, and often we are left to infer that they were hereditary.'

[3] *D.B.B.*, p. 304; see ibid., pp. 303 ff.   [4] Ibid., p. 309.

essay on the introduction of knight service into England.[1] They are intended as a rebuttal to Round's contention that knight service and the feudal military system were introduced into England by William the Conqueror and were in no way anticipated during late-Saxon times.[2] Maitland argues that the Worcester leases were indeed such an anticipation. He bases his contention on a memorandum written by Oswald to King Edgar which Maitland regards as 'for our purposes the most important of all the documents that have come down to us from the age before the Conquest'.[3] This letter sets forth in some detail the conditions on which Oswald granted his leases. The grantees are to fulfil the whole law of riding (*equitandi lex*); they are to pay church dues; they are to swear, so long as they hold their land, to be humbly subject to the commands of the bishop; they are to lend him their horses, ride for him themselves, build bridges, burn lime, erect a hedge for the bishop's hunt, lend him their hunting spears, and, in general, meet many other needs of the bishop whether for the fulfilment of the service due to him or of that due to the king. Maitland feels that these obligations are distinctly feudal in character: the grantee is the bishop's man—his *fidelis*; he owes definite services in return for his land.

But above all, he is a horseman, a riding man and must fulfil 'the law of riding'. For a moment we are tempted to say 'the law of chivalry'. This indeed would be an anachronism; but still he is bound to ride at the bishop's command. Will he ride only on peaceful errands? We doubt it. He is bound to do all the service that is due to the king, all the forinsec service we may say. A certain quantity of military service is due from the bishop's lands; his thegns must do it. As already

---

[1] *Domesday Book and Beyond* was published in 1897. Round's essay appeared in his *Feudal England*, published in 1895, and had appeared earlier in the decade in article form in the *English Historical Review*. In the preface to *Domesday Book and Beyond*, Maitland writes: 'I knew that Mr. Round was on the eve of giving to the world his *Feudal England*, and that thereby he would teach me and others many new lessons about the scheme and meaning of Domesday Book. That I was well advised in waiting will be evident to everyone who has studied his work. In its light I have suppressed, corrected, added much.'

[2] On this problem and the historical controversy which it engendered, see my article, 'Norman Conquest and Genesis of English Feudalism', *A.H.R.* lxvi (1961), 641–63.

[3] *D.B.B.*, p. 305. For the document, see Kemble, *C.D.*, no. 1287; Birch, *C.S.*, no. 1136. A convenient abstract of this document is printed in *D.B.B.*, pp. 305–7.

said, the obligation of serving in warfare is not yet so precisely connected with the tenure of certain parcels of land as it will be in the days
of Henry II, but already the notion prevails that the land owes soldiers
to the king, and probably the bishop has so arranged matters that his
territory will be fully 'acquitted' if his *equites*, his *milites* take the field.[1]

Maitland concludes, 'It may well be that the thegns and
knights of other churches held on terms very similar to those
that the bishop of Worcester imposed',[2] and that therefore,
presumably, English feudalism, at least in its essentials,
antedated the Conquest.

Maitland's views have been challenged vigorously by
subsequent historians. Round later observed in connexion
with Maitland's writings, 'It is probably little realised how
much conjecture and hypothesis have found their way into
the work of this brilliant scholar',[3] and Stenton devoted a
section of his *First Century of English Feudalism* (pp. 122 ff.)
to a refutation of Maitland's views on pre-Conquest feudalism. Discussing Oswald's letter, Stenton comments:

But between these services and those which were imposed by
enfeoffments of the [later] eleventh and twelfth centuries there are
two essential differences. The services for which Oswald stipulated were
miscellaneous, and he left their exact nature vague. There is no trace
in his memorandum of the feudal ideas that the services to be rendered
for a tenement should admit of a close definition, and that if more than a
single form of service is required from the same holding, the services
with which it is associated should be of a cognate character. The
services set out by Oswald form a very incoherent series of obligations. . . . It is more significant that Oswald made no attempt to define
any of these duties. At every critical point in the memorandum, its
language shades off into vague assertions of general obligation. It is
not the memorandum itself, but a comparison of it and other evidence,
which shows that the famous 'law of riding' meant not military service,
but the duty of escorting a lord from place to place. This vagueness
was due to the circumstances under which the memorandum was
written. It was not intended as a precise formulation of rights and
duties like a later feudal custumal. It was a retrospective document,
drawn up to cover a number of grants already made in still more
general terms. . . . There can have been no real movement towards
any conceptions which can properly be called feudal in a society where
such a relationship needed to be clarified in such a way.[4]

[1] *D.B.B.*, pp. 307–8.   [2] Ibid., p. 312.
[3] *Family Origins* (London, 1930), p. 259.   [4] *E.F.*, pp. 124–5.

It seems to me that Stenton's criticism is just, up to a point. At least from the standpoint of military organization Bishop Oswald's memorandum tells us very little. It tells us merely that the bishop's grantees owned horses and knew how to ride them. One can hardly dispute with Maitland that mounted men would be helpful on a military campaign, but the 'law of riding' does not relate explicitly to military service. What, then, is the military service expected of these grantees? It is not to be found in Oswald's letter, but rather in the individual grants themselves, for almost all of these grants specifically reserve the *trimoda necessitas*. Bridge-building is mentioned in the memorandum, but we know from the charters that these grantees owed fortress work and fyrd service as well. And, as we have seen, the fyrd duty of the *trimoda necessitas* consisted of service in the select fyrd. The five-hide unit is common throughout the see of Worcester, and here, as elsewhere, it constituted the basic recruitment unit. The military obligation of the Worcester lessees was simply the select-fyrd obligation which was normally due from the land: each five-hide unit produced a warrior-representative when the select fyrd was summoned. When they granted their leases, the bishops of Worcester were anxious that the alienated lands should continue to produce their required warriors. It was the bishop, as we have seen, who was responsible for raising the select-fyrd quota due from all his estates. St. Oswald's memorandum serves as convincing negative evidence that the see of Worcester placed no unusual military burden on its men. It simply expected them to do what was customary. It expected every five hides under its jurisdiction to produce a warrior.

One further point needs clarification. It has been suggested by some writers that the post-Conquest feudal military obligation was somehow more exact—more specific —than that of the late-Saxon fyrd. This is, perhaps, the implication of Stenton's statement that 'At every critical point in the memorandum, its language shades off into vague assertions of general obligation'. But it should be clear from what I have previously said that this was decidedly not the case. The obligation of military service in the select fyrd was at least as specific as the feudal military obligation. The fact that the individual Worcester leases do not specify in so many words the amount of military service owed by the grantee should not mislead us. The amount was known. It was determined by custom and could be easily calculated from the number of hides in the tenement. By virtue of the five-hide recruitment system, the fyrd obligation was just as specific as the later feudal obligation, and was at the same time considerably more systematic. The fact that every feudal charter stipulates the number of *milites* owed to the lord does not indicate that the feudal obligation was more exact, but rather that it was less uniform than that of the select fyrd. The latter was national in scope and was based on a standard relationship between land and service. The former was based on individual fees which varied among themselves in both hidage and military obligation and which were created by discrete private contracts. These feudal contracts were of the nature of bargains, for in the absence of any accepted ratio of hides to service the feudal lord would be likely to demand whatever he could get. Consequently, the amount of service is always specified in a feudal contract but almost never in an Anglo-Saxon land charter. The military structure of late-Saxon England differs from that of Norman England, but not in the way that many historians have thought.

As to the aptness of the term *feudal* to describe the pre-Conquest military system, I would prefer not to commit myself. Feudalism can be and has been defined in a bewildering variety of ways. Let us say merely that an important Anglo-Saxon lord owed the service of an exact number of warriors as a result of his tenement. But the same land would owe the same service whether held by one lord, several lords, or no lord at all. The military obligation of the Anglo-Saxon nobleman was therefore merely one aspect of a larger structure—a national structure—which in other aspects was far less reminiscent of the feudal military arrangements of the Continent. As a whole, the Old English system was decidedly unlike that of Norman feudalism. Was it feudal at all? That question I will leave to others who may be more certain than I as to how feudalism ought to be defined.

VI

THE LATE-SAXON NAVY

I

The genesis of the English navy is heralded by a well-known passage from the *Anglo-Saxon Chronicle*:

Then King Alfred ordered that warships be built to meet the Danish ships. They were nearly twice as long as the others; some had sixty oars; some more, and they were both swifter and steadier and had more freeboard than the others. They were built neither after the Frisian design nor after the Danish, but as it seemed to him that they could be most serviceable.[1]

With this act King Alfred provided an essential ingredient to the defence of his island kingdom. The evolution of the English navy runs continuously from his reign onward. It is interesting to note that before the Norman Conquest the dukes of Normandy did not command a navy. The chroniclers agree that the fleet which carried the Conqueror's army across the English Channel was raised on a volunteer basis.[2] But when William established control over England, he inherited an active maritime force and a complex of rights which permitted him to order new ships to be built and to summon men to duty in the fleet.

The exact nature of the mid-eleventh-century fleet and of the naval obligations which rested upon Englishmen is obscure. The source material is both scattered and thin, and it would be presumptuous, under the circumstances, to suggest that the problem can be fully clarified. I will say little on the subject of naval mercenaries, since they were discussed in Chapter I. It will perhaps be sufficient merely to repeat that these mercenaries were of great importance

---

[1] *A.S.C.*, A, A.D. 897 [896].
[2] On this subject, see F. W. Brooks, *The English Naval Forces, 1199–1272* (London, n.d.), p. 160.

in the late-Saxon fleet. Apart from the mercenaries, naval service was obtained according to two broad principles. First, there was a general territorial obligation to perform sea duty and, at least on certain occasions, to provide ships. This duty was analogous to the select-fyrd obligation. Second, certain coastal towns bore special and precise obligations to provide warships and to man them. These obligations were characteristic of the towns which were later to be associated with the organization of the Cinque Ports,[1] but they also applied to towns outside the Cinque Ports region. Let us turn first to the general territorial obligation.

II

The intimate connexion between the obligation of naval service and that of the select fyrd does not seem to me to have been sufficiently stressed. The Anglo-Saxon dooms make clear that the military obligation of the *trimoda necessitas* included both land duty and sea duty. In the laws of Ethelred, the *trimoda necessitas* included, in addition to bridge and fortress work, *fyrdunga* and *scipfyrdunga*, and one of Cnut's laws states that the duties to be performed for the common need include the repair of fortresses and bridges and also *scipfyrdunga* and *fyrdunga*.[2] Since we have earlier identified the military obligation of the *trimoda necessitas* with select-fyrd duty, we are now driven to the conclusion that the ship fyrd was a parallel institution to the select land fyrd. The Berkshire passage, which describes the organization of the select fyrd, opens with the statement, 'If the king sent an army *anywhere*, only one soldier went from five hides, &c.', and we are left to conclude that 'anywhere' might very well include the sea. This conclusion is supported by numerous other passages. One of the laws of Cnut discloses the territorial nature of sea duty and its close connexion with the select fyrd: 'And whoever, with the cognizance of the shire, has performed the services demanded from

---

[1] The Cinque Ports organization included Hastings, Romney, Dover, Hythe, Sandwich, and smaller towns subordinate to one of these five. On the antiquity of the Cinque Ports as an organization, see Round, *F.E.*, pp. 552–71.

[2] Ethelred 32–33; 2 Cnut 10.

a landowner both in the *scypfyrde* and in the *landfyrde*' shall
hold his land freely during his life.[1] The town of Malmesbury, performing the military service of five hides of land,
sent one warrior on royal expeditions 'by land or sea'. The
same is true of the Devonshire towns. Exeter served as five
hides on expeditions by land or sea and Barnstaple, Lidford,
and Totnes together performed the same service as did
Exeter. Domesday reports that the sokeland of Somerby
near Grantham in Lincolnshire helped in the king's army
on land and at sea. On an estate of the church of Worcester,
four *liberi homines* rendered to the bishop, T.R.E., *sac* and
soc, et expeditiones et nauiga, and the same duties were owed
by the tenants who held the land at the time of the Domesday Survey.[2] We should recall, in this connexion, that
Eadric, the chief military officer of the see of Worcester,
who was discussed in the preceding chapter, was not only
the commander of the bishop's troops but also the steersman
of the bishop's ship. The nature of the office of steersman is
not entirely clear. He may have been a pilot, but was more
probably the ship's master.[3] Here, then, the select fyrd and
the ship fyrd appear to have a common leader. Again, a
thegn of Earl Leofric of Mercia, having devastated an estate
of the monastery of Worcester, was given the estate by the
prior of the monastery on the condition that the thegn
should perform the military service of the abbey *by land and
sea*, and that he should recognize the prior's lordship.[4] In all
of these passages the sea duty is clearly territorial and is
coupled with the obligation to serve in the select fyrd. This
fact should not surprise us. We have already seen that the
select fyrd differed from the great fyrd in that it was not
necessarily local in its operations. It was subject to service
in remote parts of the country and also, it would seem, in
foreign lands.[5] It would follow from this that warrior-

[1] Cnut 79.   [2] D.B. i. 64*b*, 100, 368, 173.
[3] See Brooks, p. 41. On Eadric, see above, pp. 96–97 and below, p. 112.
[4] *Heming's Cartulary*, i. 264: 'expeditionem terra marique monasterio serviret';
see also Vinogradoff, *Engl. Soc.*, p. 243. Another passage which couples land and
sea service is the Domesday description of the obligations of Colchester (ii. 107):
'Preterea de unaquaque domo per annum vi denarios quae reddere potest ad victum
soldariorum regis vel ad expeditionem terrae vel maris. . . .'
[5] In 1025 King Cnut brought a large force of Englishmen to Denmark to support
his campaign against the Swedes: *A.S.C.*, E, A.D. 1025.

representatives might well be expected to serve on expeditions overseas and on the sea as well.

The close parallel between land and sea duty is reflected also in the chronicles. In 973 eight tributary kings swore fealty to King Edgar, 'binding themselves to military service *et terra et mari*'.[1] Again in 1064, after a successful campaign against Wales, King Edward received an oath from the Welsh that they would be faithful to him and to Earl Harold and would obey their orders by sea and land (*mari terraque*).[2] Moreover, there are several references to the joint summoning of a ship fyrd and a land fyrd and to the use of the two forces in combined operations.[3]

The *Anglo-Saxon Chronicle* discloses that during the reigns of Cnut and his son Harold, ship men were being paid at the annual rate of 8 marks per oar.[4] This amounts to a sum slightly in excess of $3\frac{1}{2}d.$ per day, which is significantly close to the daily pay of a warrior in the select fyrd, which, as of 1066, was $4d.$ per day.[5] The similarity of these wages is particularly striking when allowance is made for the slight increase in the cost of living which probably occurred between 1040 and 1066. It is interesting also that the wages of ordinary seamen during the reign of King John were only $3d.$ per day, at a time when military wages had risen to a point considerably above their mid-eleventh-century level.[6] Not until the reign of Edward I in the later thirteenth century did sailors' wages return to $3\frac{1}{2}d.$[7] This fact suggests strongly that the shipman of 1040 and the sailor of the thirteenth century had distinctly different functions and that the oarsman of the Anglo-Saxon ship fyrd was regarded as a much more valuable and important person than his thirteenth-century counterpart. I would suggest that the difference lay in the fact that the duties of the thirteenth-century sailor were confined to his ship whereas the eleventh-

---

[1] *Fl. Wig.* i. 142–3; cf. *A.S.C.*, E, A.D. 973.

[2] *Fl. Wig.* i. 222.

[3] e.g. *A.S.C.*, C, A.D. 1065 [1066]; D, 1066.

[4] Ibid., E, A.D. 1039 [1040]; cf. Vinogradoff, *Engl. Soc.*, pp. 17 ff. See also *A.S.C.*, C, A.D. 1040 where a tax of 8 marks per oar is mentioned.

[5] D.B. i. 56*b*; Hollister, 'Significance of Scutage Rates', *E.H.R.* lxxv (1960) 584.

[6] Brooks, p. 41; Hollister, op. cit., pp. 578, 580–1, 586.

[7] Brooks, p. 41.

century oarsman was expected to be both sailor and warrior. He was, as it were, the twin of the warrior-representative who fought in the select fyrd on land. The oarsmen whose wages are disclosed by the *Anglo-Saxon Chronicle* were evidently mercenaries rather than territorial warriors, but as I have shown elsewhere[1] the wages of mercenaries and the support payments of territorial warrior-representatives were at least theoretically identical. So the fact that the wages reported in Berkshire Domesday relate to warrior-representatives while the payment of oarsmen described in the *Chronicle* applies to mercenaries in no way diminishes the importance of their similarity. The oarsmen of the *Chronicle* doubled as warriors, and as such performed the same dual function which we earlier attributed to the lithsmen and which we can now attribute also to the members of the territorial ship fyrd.

But although the ship fyrd and the select fyrd were obviously parallel institutions, they were by no means identical. Occasionally we encounter statements to the effect that the land obligation and the maritime obligation of the same territory were quite distinct. The burghers of Leicester, for example, owed twelve warriors in the event of a land expedition, but if the army went by sea the burghers instead sent four horses as far as London to carry arms or supplies. Ten burghers went from Warwick on land campaigns, but if the king went by sea the burghers provided either four boatswains or four pounds.[2] These customs are obviously local exceptions. The more normal practice is illustrated by the numerous references to a territorial military obligation which is the same whether the service is in a land fyrd or a ship fyrd. With the exception of these two towns and certain others which I will discuss presently, the recruitment system for the ship fyrd paralleled that of the select land fyrd. Indeed, since the two fyrds were recruited according to precisely the same principles, it would be more correct to say that they shared the same recruitment system. And we are also left with the conclusion that when the two forces were not summoned jointly they were manned by the same

---

[1] Hollister, op. cit., pp. 577–88, and above, pp. 22–24.
[2] D.B. i. 230, 238.

people. The Anglo-Saxon warrior-representatives, like the lithsmen and *butsecarls*, were expected to fight both on land and at sea. And the ship fyrd, like the select fyrd on land, was based upon the recruitment unit of five hides.

III

Florence of Worcester provides us with a good description of an exceptionally well-built and well-equipped Anglo-Saxon ship of the mid-eleventh century:

Godwin, in order to win the king's friendship, gave him a ship of excellent workmanship, having a gilded figurehead, equipped with the best armaments, and manned with eighty well-armed select warriors each of whom had a golden bracelet on each arm, a triple coat of mail, a partly gilded helmet on his head, a sword with a gilded hilt on his side, a Danish battle-axe inlaid with gold hanging from his left shoulder, a shield in his left hand the boss and studs of which were also gilt, and in his right hand a lance which in the English language is called *ategar*.[1]

This ship can by no means be regarded as typical. It is, in fact, only natural that a historian such as Florence of Worcester would dwell upon the exceptional rather than the normal. The more ordinary ship of Anglo-Saxon times must have been manned by warriors who were distinctly inferior to those described by Florence—inferior both in ability and in equipment. Moreover, the typical Old English ship seems to have been manned by about sixty warriors rather than eighty. As we have seen, the ships built during Alfred's reign had sixty oars or more.[2] Archbishop Ælfric of Canterbury granted to his lord his best ship together with sixty helmets and sixty coats of mail, and Bishop Alfwold of Crediton bequeathed to his lord a ship with sixty-four oars.[3] Here again we are left to infer that the warriors were also oarsmen.

A very important if somewhat obscure passage occurs in the chronicles under the year 1008. We are told that in this year King Ethelred ordered ships to be built throughout

---

[1] *Fl. Wig.* i. 195.
[2] *A.S.C.*, A, A.D. 897 [896]; cf. Vinogradoff, *Engl. Soc.*, pp. 31–32, and above, p. 103.   [3] *A.S. Wills*, p. 52; *Crawford*, p. 23.

England, one ship being furnished by every 300 or 310 hides. The figure of 310 is given by Florence of Worcester, Henry of Huntingdon, and by the C, E, and F manuscripts of the *Anglo-Saxon Chronicle*, and is accepted by many historians.[1] The D manuscript, whose version other historians accept, sets the figure at 300 hides to provide a *scip* and ten hides to provide a *scegð*,[2] the latter being a light, swift sailing ship similar to those used by the Vikings. Plummer argues that the D manuscript is less reliable than the others and that, moreover, the disproportion between the number of hides required to provide a *scip* and the number owing a *scegð* is unbelievably large, the ratio being 30:1. Although the *scegð* was a light ship it was not necessarily small. The ship of sixty-four oars which Bishop Alfwold bequeathed was termed a *scegð*,[3] and it is difficult to understand how such a ship as this might be worth only one-thirtieth of another kind of ship. On the other hand, the *scegð* of the 1008 passage may very well have been small; it is explained in Wülker's gloss as *litel scip*.[4] And it seems to me that the D version makes much better sense than those of the other manuscripts, which leave the impression that certain words have been omitted.[5]

However this may be, the 1008 passage discloses a district of 300 or 310 hides which is responsible for producing a ship. The same passage stipulates that every eight hides should provide a helmet and a coat of mail. Here, too, there is some confusion, for Florence of Worcester sets the figure at nine hides.[6] Doubtless the figure of eight hides reported by the *Anglo-Saxon Chronicle* is the more trustworthy of the two. The discrepancy is not important, since neither figure appears before or after 1008, and we must assume therefore

---

[1] *Fl. Wig.* i. 160; H. of Hunt., p. 176; *A.S.C.*, A.D. 1008 and Plummer's comments, ibid. ii. 185–6. See also *A.S. Writs*, p. 266, and above, p. 41.

[2] See Vinogradoff, *Engl. Soc.*, pp. 31–32; G. N. Garmonsway, *The Anglo-Saxon Chronicle* (London, 1953), p. 138; H. A. Rositzke, *The Peterborough Chronicle* (New York, 1951), p. 86 n. 156.

[3] *Crawford Charters*, p. 23. [4] Cited in *A.S.C.* ii. 185.

[5] D: 'of þrym hund scipum ꝼx be tynum anne scægð.' C: 'of þrim hund hidum ꝼ of tynum ænne scegð.' E: '[of] þrym hund hidum ꝼ of x hidon ænne scegð.' In full, the E manuscript reads: 'Her be bead se cyng þ man sceolde ofer eall Angel cynn scipu feastlice wircean þ is þonne [of] þrym hund hidum ꝼ of x hidon ænne scegð. . . .' [6] *Fl. Wig.* 160.

that the requirement was extraordinary. It seems clear from the context of these passages that the helmet and coat of mail were to be provided in connexion with the ship, but I see no reason to infer, as some historians have done, that the eight-hide districts of 1008 were each to send a warrior along with the armour.[1]

But even though the formation of eight-hide districts for the purpose of providing armour may have been a temporary expedient, naval obligations roughly similar to those disclosed by the 1008 passages were a permanent part of the late-Saxon military system. In 992 King Ethelred had collected at London all the ships in the kingdom that were of any value and had them manned by a force which the *Anglo-Saxon Chronicle* calls a *fyrd* under the command of two ealdormen and two bishops.[2] It may well be that this expedition was raised according to principles similar to those described in 1008. In 1003 or 1004 Archbishop Ælfric bequeathed three ships, one to his lord, one to the people of Kent, and one to Wiltshire.[3] The only evident reason for these grants, particularly the grant to the inland shire of Wilts., was to help the people in fulfilling their ship assessment, and therefore Ælfric's will provides us with strong evidence that a ship tax existed prior to 1008. One of Ethelred's dooms, issued in the very year 1008, orders that the fitting out of ships be carried out with all possible diligence so that each year they may all be ready for service soon after Easter, and a similar law was published later in the same reign.[4] In both instances, the references to ship duty immediately follow laws relating to the *trimoda necessitas*. The sequence is logical in view of the fact that both were terri-

---

[1] See, for example, Vinogradoff, *Engl. Soc.*, pp. 31–32; and Little, 'Gesiths and Thegns', p. 728, who interpret this passage as implying the obligation of a warrior. But although all of the accounts are unanimous in mentioning the obligation to provide armour, none contain any reference to the necessity of providing a warrior: *A.S.C.*, A.D. 1008; *Fl. Wig.* i. 160; H. of Hunt., p. 176. Florence of Worcester's account contains a strong implication that the hide-units which provided armour did not send warriors: 'Rex Anglorum Ægelredus de cccx cassatis unam trierem, de novem vero loricam et cassidem fieri, et per totam Angliam naves intente præcepit fabricari: quibus paratis, *electos in eis milites* cum alimentis posuit. . . .'

[2] *A.S.C.*, E, A.D. 992. Cf. *Fl. Wig.* i. 150.

[3] *A.S. Wills*, p. 52. Cf. ibid., p. 163. Ælfric had been prelate in these districts. See *A.S.C.* ii. 186.   [4] 5 Ethelred 27; 6 Ethelred 33.

torial obligations. The reference to Easter doubtless stems
from the fact that it was shortly after Easter that the Danish
raids normally began.[1]

Thus, the obligation to provide ships for the navy was a
general duty. If the provisions of 1008 are any indication,
it was a territorial obligation which was, like the select-fyrd
and the ship-fyrd obligations, assessed by hides. It seems
a little peculiar that interior districts were obliged to provide
ships, but such evidently was the case. In 1008 hide-
districts throughout all of England were expected to produce
ships, and Archbishop Ælfric's gift of a ship to Wiltshire
allows of no other explanation. Indeed, the units of approxi-
mately 300 hides which owed ships in 1008 were apparently
permanent ship-assessment districts.[2] A twelfth-century
copy of what is alleged to be a charter of King Edgar, and
which was probably based upon actual custom, stipulates
that the triple hundred of Oswaldslaw was to be held by
the bishop of Worcester on the condition that it constitute
a *naucupletionem*, or in the English tongue, a *scypfylleð* or
scypsocne.[3] It is not entirely clear whether the *scypsocne* or
ship-soke was under the obligation of producing a ship
or providing its crew or both. In the former instance the
hundred of Oswaldslaw with its 300 hides would be identical
to the districts mentioned in connexion with the assessment
of 1008. If Oswaldslaw was obliged to produce a ship's
company rather than a ship, then we would have here a
splendid example of the five-hide recruitment system. For
the normal ship was, as we have seen, a vessel of about sixty
oars, and a district of 300 hides such as Oswaldslaw Hundred
would yield, according to the five-hide rule, exactly sixty
armed oarsmen.[4] But probably the Worcester document is
an illustration of both the 300-hide district which owed a

[1] *Laws of the Kings of England*, p. 330.

[2] See *A.S.C.* ii. 185–6; H. M. Cam, *Liberties and Communities in Medieval England* (Cambridge, England, 1944), pp. 93–94; *A.S. Writs*, pp. 266–8, 483. The unit
of 300 hides appears also as a legal district in 2 Cnut 22. 1.

[3] Birch, *C.S.*, no. 1135. Vinogradoff interprets this as a ship's complement of
sixty armed oarsmen (*Engl. Soc.*, p. 84). Professor Cam regards *scypfylleð* as a ship's
complement (op. cit., p. 93), but she also connects it with the obligation to provide
ships (ibid., p. 94).

[4] This fact was pointed out by Liebermann (*Gesetze*, ii. 638). See also Vinogradoff, *Engl. Soc.*, pp. 31–32.

ship to the navy and the five-hide district which owed one armed oarsman. We should recall in this connexion the passage discussed earlier which named Eadric the commander of the bishop of Worcester's troops and the steersman (i.e. the master) of the bishop's ship.[1] The bishop's ship was evidently the ship which was owed by his ship-soke of Oswaldslaw. And Eadric commanded the bishop's men, whether they were serving on land campaigns or aboard his ship. Accordingly, a ship-soke seems to have been a district of 300 hides or thereabouts which produced and maintained a ship for the royal navy and which also provided the necessary armed oarsmen to man it.

We must next inquire whether these ship-sokes existed throughout England or whether the ship-soke of Oswaldslaw was unique. In 1008 the obligation of 300 or 310 hide districts to provide a ship was a nation-wide duty. The universality of the ship-soke is supported by a passage from the *Leges Henrici Primi* relating to pre-Conquest custom, which states that all shires were divided into hundreds and ship-sokes.[2] Professor Cam has observed that two Warwickshire Pipe Rolls from the reign of Henry II refer to three different hundreds as ship-sokes.[3] At least one of these, Knightlow Hundred, is composed of three Domesday hundreds and therefore presumably contained 300 hides.[4] Combinations of hundreds in groups of three have also been traced to Buckinghamshire and, with less certainty, to Cambridgeshire.[5] C. S. Taylor has shown that the Mercian shires, which he believes to have been formed around 1008 in connexion with the ship levy, were based on a unit of 1,200 hides and its multiples which broke down easily into 300-hide units. In Worcestershire, for example, in addition to the 300 hides of Oswaldslaw belonging to the church of

---

[1] *Heming's Cartulary*, i. 81; above, pp. 96–97, 105.

[2] *Leges Henrici*, 6, i: 'Regnum Anglie triphariam dividitur: in Westsexiam, et Mircenos, et Danorum provinciam. Habet . . . comitatus xxxii. Ipsi vero comitatus in centurias et *sipessocna* distinguntur.'

[3] *Sibbesoka* or *sipesocha*: P.R. *21 Henry II*, p. 94; *26 Henry II*, pp. 90, 91. Cited in Dugdale's *Warwickshire*, and in Cam, op. cit., p. 93.

[4] Mertone, Bomelau, and Stanlei. The other two hundreds which are termed 'ship-sokes' in the Pipe Rolls are Kineton and Hemlingford. Kineton is composed of four Domesday hundreds. See ibid.

[5] Ibid., p. 92; *A.S. Writs*, p. 267 n., and the references cited therein.

Worcester, Westminster held an estate of 200 hides, Pershore held 100 hides, Evesham held 65 hides, and the remaining 539 hides of the county were divided among numerous holders.[1] The 200 hides of Westminster and the 100 hides of Pershore combined into a 300-hide unit which is referred to in a twelfth-century survey as the 'Hundred of Pershore',[2] and the remaining 604 hides of the county can be regarded as the approximate equivalent of two ship-sokes.

Parallels to the ship-soke can be found in the Swedish *skiplag*, the Norwegian *skiprei ð*, and the Danish *skipaen*, all of which are described in Scandinavian laws of the thirteenth century as districts which were obligated to supply ships.[3] This fact has led some historians to speculate whether the English borrowed the institution from the Norsemen or vice versa, and in the absence of any direct evidence on this point I can only suggest that the Anglo-Saxon ship-soke arrangements fit so neatly into the select-fyrd system that the notion of a Scandinavian genesis seems unlikely.[4]

The tracing of the ship-soke to several English shires, combined with the evidence of the 1008 passage, the Dooms of Ethelred, and the *Leges Henrici Primi*, casts a strong presumption in favour of the generality of the ship-soke system although it does not prove it. Corroborative evidence is to be found in certain documents which refer to gifts or bequests of ships. We have already noted that in the late tenth or early eleventh century, Bishop Alfwold gave a ship of sixty-four oars to his lord, and that Archbishop Ælfric left ships to the king, to Kent, and to Wiltshire.[5] Between 975 and 1016, Ælfhelm of Wratting, a Cambridgeshire thegn, bequeathed a ship to the abbot and monks of Ramsey.[6]

---

[1] Taylor, 'The Origin of the Mercian Shires', in *Gloucestershire Studies*, ed. Finberg (Leicester, 1957), pp. 17–45.

[2] *V.C.H., Worcs.* i. 327–9.

[3] On these districts and their antiquity, see Cam, op. cit., pp. 93–94, and the references cited therein.

[4] Ibid.; Liebermann, *Gesetze*, ii. 638. Professor Cam, although she favours the theory of a Scandinavian genesis for the ship-soke, points out that our direct evidence for this institution is confined to regions outside the Danelaw: op. cit., p. 94.

[5] *Crawford*, p. 23; *A.S. Wills*, p. 52. Alfwold's ship was not a bequest but a part of his heriot. See above, p. 108; *A.S. Wills*, p. 52.

[6] Ibid., p. 32.

In all likelihood this grant, like the others, was for the purpose of helping the recipients with their obligations to
provide ships,[1] in which case all three of these gifts can be
understood in the context of a general ship-soke system.

One is still left with the problem of how interior districts
could comply with the obligation to produce ships. The
solution may perhaps be found in the tax known as *ship-scot*
(*scypgesceot*), which was apparently a sum of money paid
to the king for the purpose of building and equipping ships.[2]
It is logical to infer that an interior ship-soke might fulfil its
obligation by paying a certain amount of ship-scot, and this
view is supported by at least one piece of evidence. In a
document of the early eleventh century, Bishop Æthelric
complained that the see of Sherborne had lost control of
certain territories which had formerly aided him in fulfilling
his ship-scot obligation. After specifying the alienated land,
the bishop states: 'This amounts, in all, to thirty-three hides
which are lacking from the 300 hides that other bishops had
for their diocese.'[3] Evidently the district of 300 hides to
which the bishop alludes constituted a ship-soke, and at
least in this one instance the ship-soke was privileged to
commute its obligation to provide a vessel and maintain it.
Doubtless the five-hide units on the bishop's estates owed
warrior-seamen to the navy, for this, as we have seen, was
one of the duties embraced by the *trimoda necessitas*, but they
could escape their obligation of providing a ship by paying
a sum of money instead. Ship-scot may have replaced the
actual shipbuilding obligation over large areas of inland
England, but it is impossible to establish the generality of
this form of commutation in the absence of additional
evidence. One might, however, bring this Sherborne
evidence into line with the gift of a ship to Wiltshire and the
fact that the see of Worcester possessed a ship, by supposing
that ship-scot, like other kinds of commutation, constituted
the exact sum necessary to build and maintain a vessel, and
that when it was built, presumably in a coastal town, it was

---

[1] This is the opinion of Professor Whitelock: *A.S. Wills*, p. 137.

[2] This is the view of Stenton and Dr. Harmer. It has also been suggested that this
tax was a contribution in sheep. For a brief discussion of the problem, see *A.S. Writs*,
p. 483.

[3] Ibid., p. 269. Discussed in ibid., pp. 266–9 and on pp. 482–6 below.

regarded in some sense as a possession of the ship-soke which paid for it. According to this hypothesis, every ship-soke had a ship, and although the men of the ship-soke did not personally build it or maintain it they were responsible financially, through the ship-scot obligation, for its construction and its upkeep.

III

In general, then, the five-hide unit was basic to the recruitment system of the ship fyrd as well as to that of the select land fyrd. The recurring phrase 'by land or sea', or its equivalent, shows that in no case was the five-hide unit obliged to provide a man for *both* fyrds at the same time. The obligation was never more than one man per recruitment unit, but that man might be called upon to serve in either the land or the ship fyrd. Sixty such units—at least in many regions—constituted a ship-soke and would provide not only the normal crew of sixty armed oarsmen but also the ship on which they served. But we have also seen that in two towns, Leicester and Warwick, the ship-fyrd obligation differed from that of the select land fyrd. The same was true of Maldon.[1] This town, located on the Blackwater estuary in Essex, owed a horse for an expedition and a ship. Assessed at fifty hides, Maldon ought to have owed, according to the five-hide system, ten warriors to the select fyrd. Whether the obligation of a single horse represented the extent of Maldon's select-fyrd duty is not entirely clear, but so it would seem. On the other hand, the burghers of Maldon were burdened with an exceptionally heavy ship obligation. The assessment of Maldon was only one-sixth that of the normal 300-hide ship-soke, yet the town owed an entire ship.[2] The reduction of the select-fyrd obligation for a sea-port town in order that the burghers might contribute more heavily to the ship fyrd seems a logical expedient, but it is

[1] D.B. ii. 48.
[2] The size of the ship is not stated. The obligation continued into the post-Conquest decades, and is mentioned in a charter of Henry II (*Cal. Ch. R.* [1290], 351–2), which gives us the additional information that the ship owed royal service for forty days and had owed the same service under Henry I. We should be cautious, however, in applying this typically feudal service term to the eleventh century.

none the less an exceptionally significant deviation from the standardized sea and land obligations which prevailed elsewhere. The Maldon ship duty is unique. It is a discrete obligation which fits into no system, and can be regarded as a kind of private bargain between the monarchy and the burghers of Maldon. As such, it is distinctly closer to the feudal military arrangements of Anglo-Norman times than anything that we have examined thus far.

Nor was Maldon the only coastal town where such arrangements existed. They are also to be found in connexion with a group of towns in Kent and Sussex which appear in later sources as members of the Cinque Ports' organization. In addition to the five principal ports or Head Ports—Hastings, Romney, Hythe, Dover, and Sandwich—there were numerous limbs or Member Ports, each of which was subordinate to one of the Head Ports. Our most precise and detailed information regarding the Cinque Ports comes from sources of the twelfth and thirteenth centuries, but at least some of the obligations disclosed in these later sources can be shown to date from pre-Conquest times. In the later twelfth and thirteenth centuries the five Head Ports owed the king a total of fifty-seven ships and their crews for fifteen days a year. The subordinate ports aided the Head Ports by providing specified numbers of ships to help meet their quotas.[1] Under Henry II, the ports were regarded as a single unit, and their ships played a significant role in the naval warfare of the thirteenth century.

The special ship obligations of some of these ports are mentioned in Domesday Book, but there is no evidence of such obligations prior to the reign of Edward the Confessor. The feudal aspects of the Cinque Ports' ship duties have led some historians to conclude that these duties cannot have existed before Edward's time but were a natural outgrowth of the Norman influence which the Confessor brought to England.[2] On the eve of the Conquest, the Cinque Ports,

---

[1] On the customs of the Cinque Ports, see K. M. E. Murray, *The Constitutional History of the Cinque Ports* (Manchester, 1935). The customs are summarized in the introductory pages of an article by the same writer, 'Faversham and the Cinque Ports', *T.R.H.S.*, 4th ser. xviii (1935), 53 ff.

[2] Murray, *Cinque Ports*, pp. 23–26. Miss Murray suggests that the Cinque Ports' obligations replaced the mercenary navy which the Confessor is said to have dis-

or at least some of them, were bound together by similar naval obligations, but they do not seem to have been united in any real administrative sense until long after Hastings.[1] The general pattern of the Cinque Ports' ship obligations follows that of Maldon, where select-fyrd duty was abnormally light but naval duty was heavy and was specified precisely. The Cinque Ports, in fact, had no select-fyrd obligation at all, but instead were expected to provide a significant portion of the kingdom's naval strength. Domesday reports that the burgesses of Dover owed twenty ships to the monarch, each with a crew of twenty-one men, and a steersman and his assistant, for fifteen days annually.[2] It is made clear that these obligations were operative at the time that William the Conqueror came to England. The Survey adds that the burghers owed these obligations because the king had granted them *sac* and *soc*, and it also discloses that the burghers were exempt from toll throughout England. Thus, in return for these special privileges the burghers owed a specified, discrete amount of military service, i.e. twenty ships with crews to guard the sea for fifteen days.[3]

The naval obligations of Sandwich are reported by Domesday as being exactly the same as those of Dover, and as in the case of Dover the burghers of Sandwich received important privileges in return for their service.[4] Domesday provides us with no detailed accounts of Hastings, Romney, or Hythe, yet there is fairly good evidence that these three ports provided ships and crews for the king's navy according to arrangements similar to those of Dover and Sandwich.

missed at mid-century. But the activities of naval mercenaries continued up to the time of the Norman Conquest, as I have shown above (p. 17). On the parallel between the Cinque Ports' ship duty and feudal military service, see Brooks, pp. 79–80.

[1] See Murray, *Cinque Ports*, p. 26, and Round, *F.E.*, pp. 552–71.

[2] D.B. i. 1. Note that these are much smaller ships than the sixty-oar vessels owed by the ship-sokes.

[3] Cf. *An Eleventh-century Inquisition of St. Augustine's, Canterbury*, pp. 23–24: 'Et quando rex dedit burgensibus illorum sacam et socam tunc burgenses e contra dederunt regi xx naves semel in anno per xv dies ad custodiendum mare. Et in unaquaque navi xxi homo.' Domesday, after describing the obligations, states: 'Hoc faciebant pro eo quod eis perdonaverat saccam et socam' (i. 1).

[4] D.B. i. 3. The same information is given in *St. Augustine's, Canterbury* (p. 20), and in the *Domesday Monachorum*. For a collation of all three versions, see ibid., p. 89.

Domesday reports that twenty-one burghers at Romney rendered sea service and in return were granted broad privileges.[1] If we can assume that the twenty-one burghers in question served personally, then they would constitute the crew of one ship of the type owed by Dover and Sandwich. The burghers of Hythe enjoyed much the same privileges as those of Romney,[2] and although the incidental references to this port do not mention ship service, it seems likely, under the circumstances, that Hythe's naval obligation began in pre-Conquest times and that it was similar in nature to those of the other Cinque Ports. The virtual absence of information in Domesday Book relating to Hastings caused Round to suggest that this port, 'which ought to have figured at the head of the county survey (as did Dover in Kent), was one of the important towns wholly omitted in Domesday'.[3] Accordingly, the silence of the Survey on the subject of Hastings' ship obligation should not lead us to conclude that the burghers of Hastings had no such duty. Indeed, one passage from the *Anglo-Saxon Chronicle* suggests quite the reverse. In 1049 the 'men of Hastings' are reported to have served the king in a military capacity aboard their own ships, capturing two vessels belonging to the rebellious Earl Swein, and slaying the earl's crews.[4] That the 'men of Hastings' (*men of Haestinga*) were mercenaries is unlikely. They can more reasonably be regarded as the shipmen whom the burghers of Hastings owed to the king. In later years the ship service of Hastings was similar to that of the other Head Ports,[5] and the passage

---

[1] D.B. i. 4*b*: 'Ad hoc manerium pertinent xxi burgenses qui sunt in Romenel de quibus habet archiepiscopus iii forisfacturas latrocinium pacem fractam foristellum. Rex uero habet omne seruitium ab eis. Et ipsi habent omnes consuetudines et alias forisfacturas pro seruitio maris.' Cf. *Domesday Monachorum*, p. 92: 'Ibique pertinebant ac pertinent xx et i burgenses de quibus rex in mare habet seruitium. Ideoque quieti sunt per totam Angliam exceptis tribus forisfactis quae habet Rodbertus in Rumene.' Cf. D.B. i. 3.

[2] *Domesday Monachorum*, p. 93; *St. Augustine's, Canterbury*, p. 24.

[3] *F.E.*, p. 568.   [4] *A.S.C.*, D, A.D. 1050 [1049].

[5] *R.R.A.N.* ii, no. 1135; Murray, 'Dengemarsh and the Cinque Ports', *E.H.R.* liv (1939), 664: A precept of Henry I grants to the men of Dengemarsh their customs on sea and land 'as the men of Hastings have'. They are to perform service at sea like the men of Hastings. This service was given to the monks of Battle by William I and William II, and is here confirmed by Henry I. The charter, although of doubtful authenticity, suggests the antiquity of the Hastings ship service.

from the *Chronicle* enables us to trace the Hastings obligation back to the Confessor's reign. Probably, then, the ship service of Dover, which Domesday describes in some detail and which served as the model for the obligation of Sandwich, served also as the model for the ship service of the three other Head Ports—Hythe, Romney, and Hastings. The service of these last three probably differed from that of Dover only in the number of ships owed to the king.[1]

There is some reason to believe that the development of Member Ports which contributed to the quotas of the Head Ports was also under way during the Confessor's reign. The burghers of Fordwich, for example, owed an unspecified amount of ship service T.R.E.[2] In the thirteenth century Fordwich was a Member Port subordinate to Sandwich and responsible to the burghers of Sandwich for providing a part of their ship quota.[3] Miss Murray thinks that the same relationship existed at the time of the Conquest, although in the twelfth century Fordwich does not appear to have been connected with Sandwich or the Cinque Ports organization, nor did it owe a special ship obligation. She suggests that Fordwich was a Member of Sandwich in 1066 but that the relationship was later discontinued for a time, only to be renewed in the thirteenth century.[4] The *Domesday Monachorum* and *St. Augustine's, Canterbury*, both state expressly that Fordwich performed sea service at the time of Edward the Confessor but had discontinued it by the time the two surveys were made.[5] Although Miss Murray's hypothesis cannot be proven, it seems plausible that during the Confessor's reign Fordwich assisted the burghers of Sandwich in meeting their heavy quota of twenty ships, just as it was later to do in the reign of Edward I.

A somewhat questionable charter of Henry I represents William the Conqueror as granting the ship service of

---

[1] The ship service of Dover as described in Domesday remained virtually unchanged in the centuries to follow, and later sources confirm the implications of earlier ones by stating specifically that Hastings, Hythe, and Romney, like Sandwich, followed the pattern of the Dover obligation. See Murray, *Cinque Ports*, pp. 21 ff. See also *St. Augustine's, Canterbury*, pp. xxiii–xxiv.

[2] Ibid., pp. 17–18; Murray, *Cinque Ports*, pp. 22–23.

[3] Ibid., pp. 22–23, 46.

[4] Ibid., p. 23.

[5] *Domesday Monachorum*, p. 82.

Dengemarsh to the abbot of Battle.[1] This document gives the impression that Dengemarsh's ship service antedated the Conquest, although the fact is by no means proven. Dengemarsh appears later on, in the reign of Henry II, as a Sub-Member Port, subordinate to Lydd, which in turn was a Member Port of Romney.[2] How early such relationships as these began is uncertain, for our sources tend to be thin in the earlier period, and by the time definite evidence appears, the relationships are spoken of as having existed for some time. The connexion between Lydd and Romney, for example, is first mentioned in a charter of 1156.[3] At the same time, we learn that parts of Dungeness also aided Romney in meeting its ship quota. Miss Murray writes: 'Most significant is the fact that Dungeness was one of the places from which Earl Godwin collected ships during his revolt in 1052.'[4] But the *Anglo-Saxon Chronicle*, which Miss Murray cites as her authority, does not state expressly that Earl Godwin took ships from Dungeness but rather that he *went* to Dungeness, taking possession of all the ships in Romney, Hythe, and Folkestone. And even if Godwin had collected ships in Dungeness, we could not be certain that they were connected with any special ship duty of the town. There could be a number of reasons for the ships being there. We know that the kingdom had many warships in 1052, and there is nothing astonishing in the fact that some of them should be found in seaports. So again definite conclusions are impossible. A similar arrangement between Folkestone and Dover can be traced back as far as the reign of Henry I,[5] but no farther.

On the basis of this evidence, Miss Murray concludes that during the Confessor's reign:

It seems that the five Head Ports were selected by the king as the most important harbours situated at fairly regular intervals on the south-east coast. Each was made responsible for the provision of a definite quota of ships and was given a suitable reward for the trouble,

[1] R.R.A.N. ii, no. 1135; Murray, 'Dengemarsh and the Cinque Ports', E.H.R. liv (1939), 664 (or 665).   [2] Ibid., pp. 664–72.
[3] *Cal. Ch. R.* iii. 220.
[4] Murray, 'Dengemarsh and the Cinque Ports', ibid.; *A.S.C.*, A.D. 1052.
[5] Murray, *Cinque Ports*, p. 23. Folkestone was one of the ports from which Earl Godwin gathered ships in 1052: *A.S.C.*, A.D. 1052.

but it was tacitly understood that these ships might be partly drawn from the lesser creeks [i.e. Member Ports] in the area of each Head Port.[1]

Our evidence proves beyond doubt that the ship service of Dover and Sandwich was assessed prior to the Conquest on the same basis as in the thirteenth century. And there is good reason to believe that the pre-Conquest ship service of the other three Head Ports paralleled that of Dover and Sandwich. The evidence for the existence of Member Ports prior to the Conquest is suggestive but not conclusive. We know that Fordwich and possibly other towns owed ships T.R.E., but whether their ships were intended to aid particular Head Ports in meeting their quotas, as was the case in the twelfth and thirteenth centuries, cannot be determined. Miss Murray may well be correct in her belief that the Head Ports had Members before the Conquest, but the point is nevertheless somewhat hypothetical.

One more example of special naval service remains to be mentioned. The burghers of Lewes paid 20s. to support armed ship men whenever the king sent his men to guard the sea.[2] No mention is made of select-fyrd service, so whether it was assessed here or not we cannot tell. All we can say is that the burghers were burdened with a special obligation of 20s. toward the support of the English sea force, and in this respect were similar to the burghers of other towns who paid a special military tax.

If the ship services which we have been discussing were a product of Edward the Confessor's reign, it may well be asked in what way did this new aspect of naval organization affect the existing structure? As the Cinque Ports and other towns came to provide an important part of the war fleet, did the mercenary arrangements or the ship-soke system become less important? Miss Murray suggests that the rise of the Cinque Ports' ship service corresponded to the dismissal of the mercenary lithsmen by Edward the Confessor in 1050 and 1051. The naval mercenaries, she points out, had to be paid throughout the year, whereas the ships and crews of the Cinque Ports could be summoned whenever

---

[1] Murray, *Cinque Ports*, p. 23.
[2] D.B. i. 26. See *V.C.H., Sussex*, i. 382, and below, pp. 21, 89.

needed and were not at other times a financial burden on the royal treasury.[1] There are several objections to this theory, the most important being that only a portion of the amphibious mercenaries were dismissed in 1050 and 1051, the remainder of them continuing to play an important role right up to the time of Hastings.[2]

It might be argued, on the other hand, that the special ship obligations tended to supersede the older ship-soke system. Evidence for the existence of ship-sokes is rather thin in the decades immediately preceding the Conquest. And it should be remembered that the vessels which the ship-sokes contributed were manned largely by warrior-representatives from inland districts, a situation which might well be repugnant to any seafaring man. One can see the advantage of a navy manned by inhabitants of coastal towns rather than lubbers from the interior. But the fifteen-day service term of the Cinque Ports' ships was much too short for the average campaign, and it is unlikely that the monarchy would cease to summon the ship fyrd with its service term of two months simply because it had acquired additional naval strength from the coastal towns. Indeed, the *Anglo-Saxon Chronicle* makes clear that the ship fyrd was assembled in 1066 to defend the southern coast against the threatened invasion from Normandy, and again in 1071 by the Conqueror to help suppress the English rebels at Ely.[3] And the ship-fyrd obligation is mentioned repeatedly, as we have seen, in Domesday Book and other Anglo-Norman sources. The ship-sokes appear in the *Leges Henrici* and in the Pipe Rolls. Thus, the development of ship duty in connexion with particular coastal towns did not signal the disappearance of any of the older forms of naval service but rather represented a significant augmentation of Anglo-Saxon naval power. On the eve of the Norman Conquest the navy was supplied from several sources: from ships owned by the king or his earls and staffed by their own men; from ships operated by mercenaries of various kinds; from private merchant ships

---

[1] *Cinque Ports*, pp. 25–26.
[2] See above, p. 17.
[3] *A.S.C.*, A.D. 1066, 1071. Moreover, the Cinque Ports owed much smaller ships than those of the ship-sokes. See above, p. 117 n. 2.

impressed into duty during an emergency;[1] from ships and crews provided by particular coastal towns in return for specified liberties and privileges; and from ships owed by the 300-hide ship-sokes and manned by the warrior-representatives of the territorial ship fyrd.

IV

Frequent references to the activities of the English navy can be found in the narrative sources of the late-Saxon age. Most of these, however, are vague as to the composition of the fleet or its organizational structure. They leave us with the impression that it was exceptionally active and important, but tell us little more. In 911, for example, when the Northumbrian Danes broke their truce with Edward the Elder, the *Anglo-Saxon Chronicle* reports that the king mustered about 100 ships against them. That is all we are told, and numerous allusions to the fleet in subsequent years are no more helpful.

Occasionally a naval campaign is described in such a way as to suggest strongly that the ship fyrd of warrior-representatives participated. The *Anglo-Saxon Chronicle* reports that in 1049, at the news that hostile ships were harrying off the west coast, 'Earl Godwin sailed westward with two ships of the king's navy with Harold in command of one and Tostig, his brother, in command of the other, together with forty-two *landes manna scipa*'.[2] This last phrase probably refers to ships manned by warrior-representatives. Immediately after Godwin set forth, King Edward allowed the Mercian contingent of the fleet to return home, and here again we are evidently dealing with a part of the territorial ship fyrd.[3] There are also several references to campaigns in which the land fyrd and the ship fyrd participated jointly, and in these instances, also, the territorial system of recruitment is suggested.[4]

The commanders of the Anglo-Saxon fleet were similar to those of the land fyrd. Occasionally a body of ships might

---

[1] Brooks, p. 79; Murray, *Cinque Ports*, p. 3.
[2] *A.S.C.*, E, A.D. 1046 [1049].   [3] Ibid., C, A.D. 1049.
[4] e.g. ibid., A.D. 1054, 1063, 1066, 1071.

be commanded by a person such as Thorkell the Tall, who was essentially the chieftain of a band of sailor-mercenaries, but more often the fleets of pre-Conquest times are found to be led by the king himself, by one or more of his ealdormen or earls, or occasionally by bishops.[1] Nothing is said specifically about the term of service except, of course, in connexion with the special duties of Dover and Sandwich. But the close similarity between the select land fyrd and the ship fyrd suggests strongly that the latter served the same two-month term as did the former. This is confirmed by the *Anglo-Saxon Chronicle*'s description of King Harold's preparations for the Norman invasion in 1066. In order to meet the threatened attack, Harold collected an exceptionally large ship fyrd and land fyrd. The two forces guarded the Channel coast during the summer, but in early September, when provisions had been exhausted, both were dismissed.[2]

In one respect, however, the obligation of ship-fyrd duty differed from that of the select land fyrd. We have seen that the latter was not subject to annual training periods, but was only summoned to serve in actual campaigns. The ship fyrd, on the other hand, was summoned yearly at least for a time. Florence of Worcester reports that King Edgar the Peaceable formed a fleet of 3,600 stout ships and that each year after Easter he would summon them to his service, dividing them into three fleets of equal size and stationing them on the eastern, western, and northern coasts. The three fleets would then sail along the coasts according to a set plan, joining with one another on occasion, then separating again, in such a way that the entire island was circumnavigated each summer. Florence points out that these yearly expeditions not only served to defend the land against invasions from abroad, but also accustomed the English people to warlike exercises.[3] According to the Dooms of Ethelred, that unfortunate monarch sought to continue the yearly manœuvres,[4] but eventually the custom seems to have fallen into disuse for it is nowhere mentioned in the later sources. During the Confessor's reign the ship fyrd was apparently

---

[1] *A.S.C.*, E, A.D. 992, 1052, 1054, 1063.
[2] Ibid., A.D. 1066. See above, pp. 86–87.
[3] *Fl. Wig.* i. 143–4.   [4] 5 Ethelred 27; 6 Ethelred 33.

levied only in time of war or in order to meet some specific
military need.

Long before the age of the special ship duty, the towns of
the later Cinque Ports' organization were important bases
of naval operations. By far the most important of these bases
was Sandwich, which was used repeatedly as a central
assembly point for the ship fyrd. Sandwich had long been
used as a base by marauding fleets of Danes,[1] and it was here
that the great fleet was assembled which had been raised by
the summons of 1008, when every 300 hides throughout
England was ordered to give a ship to the king.[2] Here, also,
King Harthacnut stationed his ships during his brief reign,
and the Confessor used Sandwich on several occasions as
a point of assembly for large fleets.[3] The capture of Sandwich was perhaps the chief goal of Earl Godwin in 1052
when he was trying to force his way back into England from
exile, and of Tostig in 1066 when he was seeking revenge
against his royal brother.[4] Finally, Sandwich was the principal base of King Harold's fleet during the critical middle
months of 1066 when he was attempting to protect the
Channel coast against invasion.[5]

The importance of the fleet to the Old English military
structure cannot be gainsaid. In an island kingdom whose
greatest military danger was invasion from abroad, the
possession of a strong navy was crucial. In 1052, when Earl
Godwin won to his cause the bulk of the English fleet, he
had by that very act won his rebellion. Had the term of ship-
fyrd service not expired in the early autumn of 1066, the
Conqueror might never have managed a landing on the
English coast.[6] The fame of the Saxon fleet was international.
In 1047 envoys of King Swein of Denmark asked the
Confessor to send fifty ships to his assistance against King
Magnus of Norway, but Edward, following the advice of
his counsellors, declined to do so.[7] Two years later, when

---

[1] *A.S.C.*, A.D. 850, 991, 1006, 1009, 1013–15.   [2] Ibid., A.D. 1008, 1009.
[3] Ibid., E, A.D. 1039 [1040], and A.D. 1045, 1049, 1052.
[4] Ibid., A.D. 1052, 1066.   [5] Ibid.
[6] As is well known, William's invasion was delayed for many weeks by adverse
winds. It is quite possible that if the winds had been right and the Norman invasion
had occurred earlier than it did, its outcome might have been quite different.
[7] *A.S.C.*, D, A.D. 1048 [1047]; *Fl. Wig.* i. 200.

Emperor Henry III was invading the lands of Count Baldwin of Flanders, the emperor sent a message to King Edward requesting that he assemble a fleet to prevent Baldwin escaping by sea. This time the Confessor complied, summoning a large body of ships to Sandwich which remained on guard until Baldwin had capitulated to Henry.[1] There were times during the unhappy reign of Ethelred when, owing to poor or traitorous commanders, the fleet appeared ineffective and even helpless. But during the more typical periods of able leadership and national cohesion it was a formidable weapon indeed.

[1] *A.S.C.*, A.D. 1049; *Fl. Wig.* i. 201.

VII

TACTICS AND STRATEGY

SINCE this study is concerned with institutional history
rather than with the history of wars and battles, no attempt will be made to treat in any detail the tactics of
the Anglo-Saxon army. But it would be a serious error to
attempt too radical a separation of military organization from
military techniques, since the necessities of battle in large
measure govern the structure of the army. If, for example,
a medieval state depended heavily upon a territorial army of
well-armed mounted knights, the arrangements for recruitment would have to take into account the necessity of regular
training and the problem of enabling the knights to equip
themselves properly. Accordingly, a general discussion of
Anglo-Saxon tactics and strategy is necessary to a study such
as this, even though the particulars of individual battles need
not concern us except in so far as they illustrate broad
tendencies.

To begin with, the various components of the Old
English army which have been discussed previously often
fought jointly, each having its own particular role to play in
the total operation. Sometimes the land fyrd and the ship
fyrd combined against an enemy, the sea force supporting
a land invasion by putting bands of warrior-seamen ashore
at strategic points,[1] or co-operating with coastal defenders
in thwarting an attack from abroad.[2] On numerous occasions
members of the great fyrd and the select fyrd fought as a
body, and frequently they were joined by mercenaries. At
Maldon in 991, the English army seems to have been composed of two forces: the select fyrd, made up of both thegns
and well-armed peasants,[3] fought alongside Ealdorman

---

[1] e.g. *A.S.C.*, A.D. 1063, 1072; *Fl. Wig.* i. 212.

[2] As in the summer and early autumn of 1066.

[3] *Battle of Maldon*, ll. 205, 255 ff.; cf. Stenton, *E.F.*, p. 119; Laborde, p. 132. Elements of the great fyrd may also have been present, but this seems doubtful in view
of the Maldon Poet's description of the entire English force as 'the flower of the
East Saxons' (l. 69). See above, pp. 10–11, 75.

Byrhtnoth's retainers, who constituted the *élite* corps of the Saxon host.[1] After the conquest of Swein and Cnut, the role of the retainers was taken over by the housecarles, but the pattern was otherwise the same.[2] On at least one occasion prior to the Conquest, the fyrd joined with a group of Norman knights in an unsuccessful campaign against the Welsh.[3] This combination was to recur under the Anglo-Norman monarchs, who retained the fyrd and used it in conjunction with their feudal army on numerous occasions.

Historians have traditionally regarded the territorial fyrd of post-Conquest times as a motley and somewhat disreputable infantry force which played a rather inconsequential supporting role to the feudal cavalry, whereas in Anglo-Saxon times it has been regarded as a part—probably the lesser part—of an all-infantry army. The retainers and housecarles, with whom it so often combined, are usually described as performing the same functions as the select-fyrd soldiers, but performing them more skilfully. In other words, the Anglo-Norman combination of fyrd and feudal host was also, it is thought, a combination of infantry and cavalry, whereas the typical Anglo-Saxon army, consisting of warrior-representatives and highly trained mercenaries, was merely an army of foot-soldiers of greater or lesser skill. Nor are the Anglo-Saxons usually credited with having archers in any significant number. In the view of many historians, therefore, they are condemned to the tactics of stationary defence behind the shield wall, without cavalry and without missile weapons of any greater sophistication than the spear. On the offensive they are reduced to disorganized infantry charges. Such tactics as these might win occasional battles against rude foes such as the Scots and Welsh but could not possibly be successful against the more advanced military techniques of continental feudalism.

Such have been the views of numerous historians. Recently, however, many of these statements have been questioned, and with good reason. It is not only disappoint-

---

[1] These retainers are called *heorðwerod* (l. 24) or *hiredmen* (l. 261). Early in the poem (ll. 17–24) they are contrasted with the men of the select fyrd. Cf. *English and Norse Documents*, p. 10; Gordon, p. 43 n.; Laborde, p. 6.

[2] e.g. *Fl. Wig.* i. 195–6 (A.D. 1041). See above, pp. 12 ff.

[3] *Fl. Wig.* i. 207 (1052). This was probably also the case in 1055 (ibid. i. 213).

ing but almost incredible that a highly systematic recruitment system such as the Anglo-Saxons possessed should
produce such a miserably ineffective military force. And the
most cursory examination of Anglo-Saxon military history
demonstrates that the Old English army cannot have been
as helpless as it has so often been described. For more than
a century after the battle of Edington (879) the English
showed themselves fully capable of coping successfully with
the Danish threat, and although they failed to meet the
Scandinavian challenge during Ethelred's reign, they re-
deemed themselves at Stamford Bridge. The battle of
Hastings should be considered in the light of Richard
Glover's penetrating observations as to the extreme caution
which the Conqueror displayed in the weeks between his
original landing at Pevensey and the day of battle.[1] William
evidently had a great deal more respect for King Harold's
army than do many twentieth-century historians, and it
should be added that none of the latter have been in a
position to evaluate the strength of the English military
organization as accurately as the Conqueror himself.

The pessimistic views of these modern scholars are open
to criticism on two basic points: first, that the significance
of infantry in medieval warfare prior to the fourteenth
century has been grossly underestimated, and second, that
the Anglo-Saxon army may have included, in addition to its
ordinary foot-soldiers, a large number of archers and
perhaps even a cavalry force. Let us consider first the question
of infantry strength.

Until quite recently, scholars have tended to accept
Oman's dictum that

Infantry was in the twelfth and thirteenth centuries absolutely
insignificant. . . . There was . . . no really important part for them to
play. . . . If great bodies of foot occasionally appeared upon the field,
they came because it was the duty of every able-bodied man to join the
arrière-ban when summoned, not because the addition of 20,000 or
100,000 half-armed peasants and burghers was calculated to increase
the real strength of the levy.[2]

[1] Glover, 'English Warfare in 1066', *E.H.R.* lxvii (1952), 1 ff.
[2] Oman–Beeler, *Art of War*, pp. 63–64. Dr. Beeler comments that the figures of
20,000 or 100,000 are 'hopelessly exaggerated'.

But on the very face of it this statement is difficult to accept. Oman does not satisfactorily explain why these huge bodies of foot-soldiers were summoned at all. If they were really valueless from the military standpoint, it is hard to understand why any military commander would impose upon himself the overwhelming logistical and organizational problems which the assembling of such a force would raise.[1] One also wonders why medieval generals were unable to use infantry effectively in conjunction with cavalry as was done in other ages. This question, however, is answered by another of Oman's dicta, namely, that medieval warfare was characterized by an almost total absence of rational tactics. Oman writes:

> An engagement like Brémule or Bouvines or Benevento was nothing more than a huge scuffle and scramble of horses and men over a convenient heath or hillside. The most ordinary precautions, such as directing a reserve on a critical point, or detaching a corps to take the enemy in flank, or selecting a good position in which to receive battle, were considered instances of surpassing military skill.[2]

But again, one wonders how medieval infantry can possibly have been so much weaker than cavalry, if cavalry itself was in such a deplorable condition. And, in fact, this unattractive picture of medieval tactics has been questioned increasingly by recent historians both in England and on the Continent.[3] J. F. Verbruggen has shown that medieval armies were far better organized than Oman believed, that they were, as a rule, well disciplined and intelligently led, that their commanders employed sound tactical and strategic

---

[1] I discuss this matter in my article, 'Norman Conquest and Genesis of English Feudalism', *A.H.R.* lxvi (1961), 659 ff.

[2] Oman–Beeler, p. 60. Hans Delbrück expressed much the same view: *Geschichte der Kriegskunst im Rahmen der politischen Geschichte* (2nd ed., 3 vols., Berlin, 1923). For a brief discussion and criticism of this position, see J. F. Verbruggen, 'La tactique militaire des armées de chevaliers', *Revue du Nord*, xxix (1947), 161 ff.

[3] One of the first to question this view was Piero Pieri, 'Alcune quistioni sopra la fanteria in Italia nel periodo comunale', *Rivista Storica Italiana*, l (1933), 567–8 (I am indebted for this reference and for several others in this chapter to Professor Lynn White jr.). See also Verbruggen, 'La tactique militaire', and *De Krijgskunst in West-Europa in de Middeleeuwen* (Brussels, 1954); R. C. Smail, *Crusading Warfare* (Cambridge, England, 1956), and 'Art of War', in *Medieval England*, ed. A. L. Poole (2 vols., Oxford, 1958), i. 136 ff.

concepts, and that cavalrymen and foot-soldiers were often combined with skill and imagination. Not infrequently the infantry's role in a battle was as important as that of the cavalry, or even more so.[1]

This was particularly true in the warfare of post-Conquest England, when the Norman kings frequently strengthened their infantry by commanding all of their mounted knights or a large portion of them to dismount and to fight as foot-soldiers.[2] If cavalry completely overshadowed infantry in medieval times, it is impossible to understand why any commander should order his knights to dismount, yet it was done again and again, usually with marked success, in the decades after the Conquest. According to Oman, Hastings was 'the last great example of an endeavour to use the old infantry tactics of the Teutonic races against the now fully-developed cavalry of feudalism'. With the victory of the Normans, 'the supremacy of the feudal horseman was finally established'.[3] Yet in every important battle of the Anglo-Norman age, the bulk of the feudal cavalry dismounted to fight. At Tinchebrai, in 1106, an eyewitness account reports that 96 per cent. of King Henry's army was on foot, including the king himself and all his barons.[4] In 1119 a high percentage of King Henry's force at Brémule was made up of dismounted knights, and according to one contemporary, the battle was won by a charge of closely packed infantry.[5] At Bourg Théroulde (1124), most of the Anglo-Norman knights again fought on foot, and at North-allerton (1138), they dismounted to a man and fought behind a shield wall such as had been employed earlier by

---

[1] *Krijgskunst*, pp. 148–94 and *passim*.

[2] On this matter see Hollister, 'Norman Conquest and Genesis of English Feudalism', *A.H.R.* lxvi (1961), 655–6.

[3] Oman, *Art of War*, i. 149, 167.

[4] *E.H.R.* xxv (1910), 296. This account, by a priest of Fécamp, gives a total of 1,700 cavalry, including 1,000 held in reserve, out of an army of 40,000. It also states that 'in secunda [acie] uero rex cum innumeris baronibus suis, omnes similiter pedites [erant]'. Henry of Huntingdon explains that King Henry and Duke Robert 'et acies caeterae pedites erant, ut constantius pugnarent' (p. 235).

[5] H. of Hunt., p. 241. See also Suger, *Vie de Louis le Gros*, ed. A. Molinier, in *Collection de textes pour servir à l'étude et à l'enseignement de l'histoire* (Paris, 1887), p. 45; Ord. Vit. iv. 359. These three sources are not in agreement as to the details of the battle, but all of them allude to a large body of dismounted knights. According to Ordericus, King Henry and his barons fought on foot as at Tinchebrai.

Anglo-Saxon armies.[1] At Lincoln (1141) the king and his
knights again dismounted and fought as infantry.[2]

In these five battles, the only ones of any importance in
the whole Anglo-Norman age, the knights fought on foot
far more frequently than on horseback. Their tactics at the
battle of the Standard (Northallerton) are remarkably
similar to those of Harold's troops at Hastings.[3] The age of
the infantry was far from being over in 1066. The fact that
the Norman kings, who probably understood military tactics
as well as anybody in Europe, chose to emphasize infantry
so heavily, proves that foot-soldiers could be of the highest
military importance. And the fact that King Stephen's forces
won the crucial battle of Northallerton in 1138 with essentially the same battle-order that Harold employed at Hastings
shows that 'the old infantry tactics of the Teutonic races' were
by no means obsolete at the time of the Norman Conquest.

How, in general, are Old English tactics to be described?
The most famous and best-known example of Anglo-Saxon
warfare was, of course, Hastings itself, and modern scholarly
reconstructions of Hastings are legion.[4] Harold's forces
fought from a good defensive position on high ground
behind a closely formed shield wall. The best troops, including the housecarles, were in the front of the line, backed
by the lesser forces, including members of the great fyrd.
The shield wall had been used earlier by the Anglo-Saxons
at the battle of Maldon[5] and doubtless on numerous other
occasions, and it was also used frequently by the Danes.[6]

---

[1] Ord. Vit. iv. 457–8; Ælred of Rievaulx, *Relatio de Standardo* (R.S., Howlett),
iii. 189 ff., 196; *Fl. Wig.* ii. 111–12; H. of Hunt., p. 264; Richard of Hexham,
De Gestis Regis Stephani et de Bello Standardii (R.S., ed. Howlett), iii. 163–5. See Lot,
L'Art mil. i. 286–7; Round, *Commune of London*, p. 41; Norgate, *England under the
Angevin Kings* (2 vols., London, 1887), i. 291.

[2] A small royal cavalry force played an inglorious role in this battle. See H. of
Hunt., p. 274.

[3] Round writes: 'The fact is that the Battle of the Standard, for which we have
excellent authorities, is of no small value for the study of the Battle of Hastings'
(*F.E.*, p. 363).

[4] The most detailed account of Hastings, that of Freeman, is also probably the
most dramatic. But many of his most important conclusions have been superseded
by those of Round (*F.E.*, pp. 332 ff.) and others. A good recent account is C. H.
Lemmon, *The Field of Hastings* (2nd ed., St. Leonards-on-Sea, 1960).

[5] *Battle of Maldon*, ll. 101–2. See Gordon, pp. 49–50 n.

[6] For example, at Brunanburh: *A.S.C.*, A, A.D. 937.

Perhaps the most striking fact about the Saxon tactics at Hastings was the absence of a cavalry force and the scarcity of archers. But despite these weaknesses, Harold's force acquitted itself well throughout the long day, and not until evening, when the king himself was severely wounded by an enemy arrow, did the English force break into flight. Indeed, there were moments during the day of battle when the Normans seemed on the verge of defeat. Under the circumstances, much credit must be given to the shield-wall formation, which proved capable of turning back repeated charges by the Norman cavalry. Nor was this lesson lost on the Normans, for we find them using versions of the shield wall in their own campaigns later on.[1]

An interesting variation of the closely packed Anglo-Saxon infantry formation is illustrated by Edmund Ironside's tactics at the battle of Sherston in 1016. Here, as at Hastings, the front line of the English formation was composed of the best troops drawn tightly together; the inferior troops were to the rear. But at Sherston, the entire English formation advanced as a body toward the enemy, moving slowly so as not to break formation,[2] whereas at Hastings the English remained stationary in their excellent defensive position except for a few wild and undirected charges against the Norman knights as the latter were withdrawing from unsuccessful attacks against the shield wall. Edmund's tactics at Sherston were by no means novel. His Danish foes employed a similar moving infantry formation,[3] and we find it being used much earlier by the Franks of late-Roman times.[4] But it was also used with great success later on in conjunction with cavalry. A Syrian eyewitness to the Third Crusade, who was much impressed by the skilful tactics of the Christian armies, reported that the infantry often surrounded the cavalry with a shield wall reinforced by lancers and crossbowmen. Then the whole formation would march toward the enemy like a moving city. At an appropriate moment, the infantry would open a corridor through which

---

[1] e.g. Northallerton and Jaffa. Cf. W. G. Collingwood, *Northumbrian Crosses of the Pre-Norman Age* (London, 1927), p. 172, fig. 211, a relief of *c.* 1000 from Cumberland showing an English force forming a wall of round overlapping shields. [2] *Fl. Wig.* i. 174–5.
[3] Ibid. [4] Oman, *Art of War*, i. 36–37: battle of Casilinum.

the cavalry would charge. Should the charge be unsuccessful, the knights would return through the opening in the infantry ranks, which would thereupon close behind them to protect the knights from attack and allow them to regroup for another charge.[1] The Syrian observer was impressed by the sophistication of these tactics, and we should note that in a number of important respects they were similar to those used by the Anglo-Saxons. To the typical feudal cavalry charge is added the shield wall and the advancing infantry formation.[2]

During the twelfth and thirteenth centuries, infantry was frequently used in this capacity, forming a defensive line to protect its own cavalry and to turn back the charges of enemy knights. This was the case in numerous battles of the High Middle Ages: at Arsouf and Jaffa in the Holy Land, at Legnano, Bouvines, the battle of Steppes, Worringen, Norman Sicily, and elsewhere.[3] Indeed, a strong infantry force was normally regarded as an essential prerequisite to victory.[4]

But even though it be admitted that infantry played a significant role in medieval warfare, and that several of the most characteristic Anglo-Saxon tactics were developed and widely employed by commanders of the High Middle Ages, the fact remains that these later commanders were far better off than Harold at Hastings because they possessed numerous archers, including crossbowmen, and a heavy cavalry. This brings us to the problem of whether or not the Anglo-Saxons had archers and mounted warriors. Until quite recently historians were unanimous on the point that the Anglo-Saxons were unable to fight on horseback. Since the

[1] H. Ritter, 'La Perure des cavaliers [of ibn Hudail] und die Literatur über die ritterlichen Künste', Der Islam, xviii (1929), 146–7.

[2] The shield wall does not appear to have been used in continental warfare during the era prior to the Norman Conquest: Round, F.E., pp. 401, 415–16.

[3] Smail, Crusading Warfare, pp. 188–200; Itinerarium peregrinorum et gesta regis Ricardi, in Chronicles and Memorials of the Reign of Richard I, ed. Stubbs (R.S., 1864), pp. 249–75, 413–24; Lot, L'Art mil. i. 163; Delbrück, iii. 427–8; R. Grousset, Histoire des croisades et du royaume franc de Jérusalem (Paris, 1934–6), iii. 62–71,' 114–16; Verbruggen, Krijgskunst, pp. 346 ff., 390 ff., 399 ff., 435 ff.

[4] On the infantry in Latin Syria, see Smail, Crusading Warfare, pp. 115 ff., and Verbruggen, Krijgskunst, pp. 213–16. On medieval infantry in general, see ibid., pp. 196–335.

appearance of J. H. Clapham's article, 'The Horsing of the Danes', fifty years ago, it has been understood that Old English warriors frequently rode on horseback, but it was believed that they always dismounted before engaging in battle.[1] Clapham also pointed out that the practice of riding to battle began prior to the age of the Danish invasions. The fyrd did not learn horsemanship from the Danes. If anything, the reverse is true. Clapham concluded with some perceptive insights into the effectiveness and the organization of the Old English army. He rejected the notion that the fyrd was essentially a huge immobile *levée en masse*:

> I do not then regard the chronic helplessness of the fyrd as proved. But I do not think that the term always implies a force of one definite type. It probably covers at least two kinds of forces—expeditionary forces, riding divisions, and mixed forces of foot and horse.[2]

He cites numerous references in the narrative sources which are quite definite on the point that the Anglo-Saxon army, or at least part of it, had mounts.[3]

The belief that the Anglo-Saxons did not actually fight on horseback is based on the examples of Maldon and Hastings in which the English forces fought on foot,[4] on the absence of any positive reference in Old English sources to the participation of Anglo-Saxon cavalry in battles, and on an episode which occurred in 1055 and is reported by the *Anglo-Saxon Chronicle* and by Florence of Worcester.[5] The

---

[1] *E.H.R.* xxv (1910), 287–93. The fact that Anglo-Saxon warriors often went on expeditions mounted was widely accepted long before Clapham's article, but he verified the point with an impressive body of evidence. See also Oman, *Art of War*, i. 148 ff.; Round, *Commune of London*, pp. 39 ff.

[2] 'Horsing of the Danes', pp. 292–3.

[3] *A.S.C.*, A.D. 755, 800, 866, 877, 896, 1014. There are also references to the Danes defeating the fyrd and taking its horses: ibid. 994, 999, 1010. See also D.B. i. 179, which reports that upon the death of a Hereford burgher who served in the army with his horse, the king had his horse and arms. If he served without a horse, the king received 10s. or his land and houses.

[4] *Battle of Maldon*, ll. 1 ff., reports that Byrhtnoth ordered his warriors to leave their horses, drive them away, and go forth on foot. This may be taken as an additional illustration of the Anglo-Saxon practice of riding to the scene of the battle. Some significance may perhaps be attached to the fact that the English did not abandon their mounts as a matter of course, but did so according to specific orders, as though under different circumstances they might have fought on horseback.

[5] *A.S.C.*, C, A.D. 1055; *Fl. Wig.* i. 213: 'Anglos contra morem in equis pugnare jussit.'

Anglo-Saxon Chronicle discloses that in that year Earl Ralph
of Herefordshire summoned a large fyrd against Ælfgar
and the Welsh, but that before a spear was thrown the
English fled because they had been made to fight on horseback. According to Florence of Worcester, Earl Ralph
ordered the English, contrary to their custom, to fight as
cavalry. Accordingly, most historians would agree with
D. C. Douglas when he wrote: 'The English thegn might
use horses to take him to the battle but in the actual engage-
ment his practice was, as at Hastings, to fight on foot.'[1]

Despite this evidence, one historian has recently questioned the belief that the Anglo-Saxons lacked a cavalry
force. Richard Glover published an exceptionally original
article in 1952 in which he argued that elements of the late-
Saxon army were perfectly capable of fighting on horseback
and often did so.[2] He maintained, moreover, that their arms
and their tactics were virtually identical with those of the
Norman knights who fought at Hastings. He also argued
that the English army included a sizeable body of archers,
and that both cavalrymen and archers fought effectively in
Harold's force at Stamford Bridge. He bases the latter
statement on the evidence of Snorri Sturluson's *Heimskringla*, in which there appears an account of Stamford
Bridge that lays much emphasis on the role of English
cavalrymen who charged the Norse lines, throwing their
spears before them, and on the English archers whose shafts
decimated the Scandinavian ranks. This account was rejected by previous scholars as hopelessly inaccurate, but
Glover himself finds it to be in remarkable accordance with
other evidence. The Bayeux Tapestry shows the Norman
knights at Hastings throwing their spears overhand rather
than couching them beneath their arms as was customary in
feudal charges of a later period. By throwing their spears,
the knights sacrificed much of the impact of their charge,
but the fact that Snorri describes English horsemen doing
the same thing at Stamford Bridge gives considerable
credibility to his account. And there is additional evidence

[1] 'The Norman Conquest and English Feudalism', *Economic History Review*,
ix (1939), 132–3, n. 6.
[2] Glover, 'English Warfare in 1066', *E.H.R.* lxvii (1952), 1–18.

for the existence of an Anglo-Saxon cavalry force. Several passages from the *Anglo-Saxon Chronicle* describe English horsemen pursuing bands of Danes and slaying them as they were overtaken.[1] Florence of Worcester uses such terms as *equitatus* to describe Anglo-Saxon forces operating against the Welsh, the Scots, and other enemies.[2] Glover finds it significant that the weapons of Harold's army at Hastings as depicted in the Bayeux Tapestry are identical with those of the Normans.[3] Weapons, he observes, dictate tactics. As for the episode of 1055, we can conclude from it only that the Englishmen engaged in this particular campaign—the fyrd soldiers of the Welsh Marches—were unaccustomed to cavalry fighting. The terrain in this region was rough and heavily wooded, and it is natural under these circumstances that local forces would shun cavalry tactics. Moreover, the limitations of a local fyrd tell us nothing of the capabilities of men such as the housecarles. Harold Godwinson was able to acquit himself well when fighting in Duke William's army in Brittany. The art of fighting on horseback, which requires a long period of rigorous training, was by no means unknown to Harold, and if one English earl was familiar with cavalry warfare it would be hazardous to deny that other Englishmen were also familiar with it.

Glover adduces equally forceful arguments for attributing to the Anglo-Saxons a strong force of archers, and explains their virtual absence at Hastings by pointing out that they were, for the most part, unmounted and therefore insufficiently mobile to accompany Harold on his forced march from Stamford Bridge. The absence of English cavalry at Hastings can be attributed to the desperate circumstances of the battle, which obliged Harold to dismount his horsemen and to use them to strengthen his line of defence.

If we accept Glover's theory, even as a mere hypothesis, we must then ask what group in the late-Saxon military

---

[1] *A.S.C.*, A.D. 1016 *bis*.

[2] *Fl. Wig.* i. 221–2 *bis*, 212, 225.

[3] Glover, pp. 15–16. For a recent summary of Old English weapons and warfare, see D. M. Wilson, *The Anglo-Saxons* (New York, 1960), pp. 104–31. The fact that all the English fought as infantry at Hastings does not prove that they always did so. The knights at Northallerton (1138), for example, all dismounted and fought on foot although they were perfectly capable of fighting on horseback.

organization served as cavalry, and what group served as
infantry? In view of the paucity of our evidence, these
questions are difficult to answer. At one point in his article,
Glover states that the housecarles were the cavalry force,[1]
but elsewhere he identifies the cavalry with the Old English
cnihts, and seems to imply that portions of the territorial fyrd
also were capable of fighting on horseback. It is clear that
some members of the select fyrd rode to battle, but whether
they constituted a true fighting cavalry is another matter.
It is so difficult to distinguish between the various components of the late-Saxon army in the battle accounts of the
chroniclers that the question will probably never be answered
definitely. Yet there is one consideration which suggests
that any Anglo-Saxon cavalry must have consisted solely of
housecarles. It will be remembered that members of the
great fyrd and the select fyrd were not bound to an annual
training period and that many years sometimes went by
between summonses. An effective cavalry force, on the other
hand, required a great deal of specialized training. Anglo-
Norman knights were obliged not only to serve two months
in time of war but also to serve forty days a year in peacetime,
evidently for purposes of training.[2] The pre-Conquest housecarles, constituting as they did a professional standing
army, had almost limitless opportunities for such training,
but the warriors of the great fyrd and the select fyrd did not.
These facts suggest that the select fyrd was a well-armed
infantry force which might, on occasion, be supported by
a larger, more amorphous group of foot-soldiers—the great
fyrd—and which often served alongside the housecarles who
may perhaps have fought as cavalry, but who, when fighting
a defensive campaign against unfavourable odds, would be
ordered to dismount.[3] Part of the select fyrd may well have

[1] Glover, p. 16.

[2] Hollister, 'Annual Term of Military Service', *Medievalia et Humanistica*, xiii
(1960), 42. Although he lacked sufficient training to become a good cavalryman,
the warrior-representative was by no means unseasoned, since, as I have shown earlier,
a territorial recruitment unit normally sent the same man on every campaign (see
above, p. 39.)

[3] As at Maldon and Hastings. Glover believes that thegns also fought on horseback, citing as his evidence a passage from the *A.S.C.* (D, A.D. 1079 [1080]) which
describes the English thegn Tokig Wiggodsson saving the Conqueror's life at
Gerberoi by providing him with a new mount when he was unhorsed by his son

served as archers, for archery practice was quite common among Englishmen of the eleventh and twelfth centuries[1] and group training was less essential than for cavalry, but in the absence of further evidence positive conclusions on this point are out of the question.

If, as Mr. Glover maintains, the pre-Conquest army had a body of archers and a cavalry force whose arms and tactics were virtually identical with those of the Normans, are we to conclude that the Saxon and Norman armies were themselves identical? And if not, wherein lay the difference? I would hazard the suggestion that one distinction between the two forces consisted in the considerable superiority of the English infantry. The select fyrd must have been vastly superior to the Norman *arrière-ban*,[2] which was a far less select force. If this were not the case, one would find it impossible to account for the Conqueror's summoning the fyrd in post-Conquest times and transporting it across the Channel to fight in continental campaigns.[3] The Normans apparently did not use the shield wall. Aside from their archers, they had no select infantry. Their heavy emphasis on infantry tactics began only after their conquest of England, and I would suggest that the two things are directly related.

If the Normans were inferior to the English in infantry, were they, on the other hand, superior in cavalry? This is also a difficult question to answer. It must be borne in mind that Duke William's force at Hastings was by no means a typical Norman army. On the contrary, it was a virtually international force of mercenaries and soldiers of fortune from all over north-western Europe, with merely a nucleus of Norman knights. The English cavalry, on the other hand, is so obscure in the sources that little can be said about it. Snorri Sturluson speaks well of it in his account of Stamford

Robert. 'That the particular "Anglus" who provided William with a new horse was the solitary Englishman who went into action mounted seems unlikely' (p. 8 n. 2). But the fact that Tokig provided William with a horse by no means proves that it was Tokig's own horse or that Tokig had been fighting on horseback.

[1] Glover, p. 5.

[2] See Haskins, *Norman Institutions*, pp. 22–23, for a brief treatment of the *arrière-ban*. See also Guilhiermoz, *Essai sur l'origine de la noblesse*, pp. 289–99; Boutaric, *Institutions militaires*, pp. 141–60, 223–39.

[3] e.g. *A.S.C.*, A.D. 1073, 1079.

Bridge, but beyond that we are in almost complete ignorance. Obviously the two military forces differed organizationally. The typical Norman knight was a territorial warrior—a fief holder—whereas the housecarles were mercenaries (as were many of William's cavalrymen at Hastings). Evidently cavalry constituted a larger percentage of the total Norman force, although again precise measurements are impossible. As to the relative quality of the two forces, it is unlikely that Norman knights would be better trained than English housecarles. If anything, the reverse would be true. And if Snorri's description of Stamford Bridge is to be trusted, the two forces ought to be regarded as essentially identical in tactics and in general effectiveness. Neither was comparable in military strength to the feudal cavalry of the later twelfth and thirteenth centuries. Neither was able to charge properly—in close, ordered formation with lances couched beneath their arms. Both, in effect, consisted of mounted javelineers. Glover goes too far in describing their tactics as 'infantile',[1] for all such terms are relative, and what is 'modern' to one generation will seem 'infantile' to a later one. The English shield wall at Hastings lacked pikes or fixed lances and would therefore never have turned back a mounted charge of thirteenth-century knights. But it was perfectly capable of dealing with attacks by eleventh-century Normans, and that, after all, was all that it was required to do.

Can we trust Snorri's account of Stamford Bridge? Although an excellent historian, he was by no means a contemporary observer. And earlier references to English cavalry forces are merely suggestive. Certainly many Englishmen rode to battle and even pursued their enemies on horseback. But aside from the thirteenth-century *Heimskringla* there is no evidence of their using cavalry in pitched battle. Hence we cannot accept Glover's hypothesis as certain. His perceptive criticisms have cast doubt on the accepted view but have not shattered it. The problem remains unsettled.

It should be pointed out, moreover, that the English of pre-Conquest times lacked at least one essential ingredient of the Norman military system: the castle. The issue of

[1] Glover, p. 15.

whether the Anglo-Norman motte-and-bailey castle was a Norman innovation was settled long ago in the affirmative.[1] Not only was the architectural style new; the very concept of a system of fortifications throughout England was a novelty which had not existed in late-Saxon times.[2] Although a discussion of post-Conquest castle building clearly lies outside the purview of this study, perhaps one or two observations should be made. To begin with, the Anglo-Norman castle system was created for two distinct strategic purposes. First, castles were constructed throughout the realm for the purpose of securing it against insurrection and foreign invasion. Second, networks of fortifications were built along the Scottish and Welsh frontiers in order to protect the Marches, and, in the case of certain advance fortresses, to extend Anglo-Norman influence into enemy territory. The marcher castles ought, therefore, to be regarded as distinct from the coastal and interior castles. There is no question but that the former were of considerable military value to the Norman kings. The value of the coastal and interior castles, on the other hand, seems to me debatable. They were doubtless useful during the first four or five years after the Conquest in helping to suppress native uprisings, but their military usefulness in later years is less clear. Professor Beeler remarks that the castles which the Conqueror and his barons constructed 'altered the military geography of England and made another "Norman Conquest" all but impossible'.[3] Doubtless they altered England's military geography, but considering that most of them were in the hands of Norman noblemen, many of whom were strongly addicted to feudal rebellion, and remembering also that after 1087 several of these baronial rebellions were undertaken in support of Duke Robert Curthose of Normandy, the new castle system, if anything, exacerbated the threat of a new Norman Conquest by providing rebellious Anglo-Norman barons with strong bases of operations. Every feudal rebellion of post-Conquest times (and there

[1] See E. S. Armitage, *The Early Norman Castles of the British Isles* (London, 1912).
[2] On the nature of the Conqueror's castle system, see J. H. Beeler's excellent article, 'Castles and Strategy in Norman and Early Angevin England', *Speculum*, xxxi (1960), 581–601.   [3] Ibid., p. 601.

were many) found the rebels protected by their castles, and the monarch could crush a rebellion only by laboriously besieging the alienated fortresses one by one. The problems engendered by the existence of baronial castles during Stephen's reign are generally known, but the same problems existed in the reigns of Henry I, William Rufus, and the Conqueror himself. Often it was the loyalty of the English fyrd that saved the Norman kings from their rebellious nobles, whose strength had been dangerously augmented by the Conqueror's castle policy.[1] When Henry Plantagenet came to the throne in 1154, he undertook an anti-castle policy, destroying many of the baronial castles which had been erected during the previous reign and severely restricting the right to build additional ones.

It is possible, then, to attribute the absence of an interior fortification system in pre-Conquest England to choice rather than ignorance. As for the Anglo-Norman system of marcher castles, this was anticipated, at least in a general sense, by the Anglo-Saxons. The fortification policies of King Alfred and his immediate successors are well known. In their struggle to expand their own territories at the expense of the Danelaw and ultimately to drive the Danish power from England, these kings were constantly engaged in constructing fortifications along the ever-receding frontier.[2] The motte-and-bailey style was unknown to them, just as it was unknown to their contemporaries on the Continent. Professor Lot, who attributes Edward the Elder's success against the Danes to his policy of constructing burghs, points out that the Anglo-Saxon fortress programme is paralleled by a decree of Charles the Bald (869) that cities be fortified, and by the fortress-building policy of Henry the Fowler of Germany in his struggle against the Magyars.[3] Thus, the Anglo-Saxon fortification policies of the ninth and tenth centuries were in tune with concurrent developments on the Continent. The very presence of

---

[1] See the Anglo-Norman narrative sources, especially Ordericus Vitalis, for the years 1075, 1088, 1101, and 1102.

[2] *A.S.C.*, A, A.D. 878, 894, 918, 921 [920], 924 [923], &c. See Jolliffe, *Constitutional History*, pp. 124–5; *Select Documents*, ed. Harmer, pp. 22–23, 106; Asser, cap. 91.

[3] *L'Art mil.* i. 109; Delbrück, iii. 109.

fortress-work among the *trimoda necessitas* illustrates the importance of these policies to the Old English military structure. And there seems to have existed, in addition to this general duty to build and repair burghs, a more specifically military obligation to participate in their defence against the enemy. This latter duty, which is, broadly speaking, analogous to the later Anglo-Norman castle-guard obligation, is somewhat obscure and has been the subject of a great deal of scholarly controversy. The *Anglo-Saxon Chronicle* makes a definite distinction between troops from the fyrd and troops from the forts,[1] and in a very early charter we find the defence of fortresses against enemies listed as a necessary obligation along with bridge-building.[2] This obligation is illuminated to some extent by the Burghal Hidage (A.D. 911–19), an intriguing document which records the districts subject to the burghs of Wessex and to certain Mercian burghs.[3] To each burgh is assigned a particular number of hides. The purpose of these burghal districts is clarified by a closely associated document which describes the system by which the walls were maintained and defended:[4]

> For the maintenance (*wealstillinge*) and defence of an acre's breadth of wall 16 hides are required. If every hide is represented by one man,[5] then every pole of wall can be manned by 4 men. Then for the maintenance of 20 poles of wall 80 hides are required, and for a furlong 160 hides are required. . . .

Many points remain obscure. It is not entirely certain that the above system applies both to warriors and to workmen, and there is every reason to doubt that it continued unchanged

---

[1] *A.S.C.*, A, A.D. 894 [893]. Cf. ibid. 918 [917], reporting that the Danes were opposed by the men of Hereford and Gloucester and from the nearest fortresses, who fought against them and put them to flight.

[2] Birch, *C.S.*, no. 203 (A.D. 770).

[3] The Burghal Hidage is printed in *A.S. Chart.*, p. 246. It has been widely discussed. See Chadwick, *Anglo-Saxon Institutions*, pp. 204–18; Maitland, *D.B.B.*, pp. 502 ff., &c.

[4] *A.S. Chart.*, pp. 246–8. This document follows the Burghal Hidage B.M., Add. MS. 43703, which is a transcript made in 1562 of MS. Cotton Otho B. xi (*c.* 1025), destroyed by fire in 1731.

[5] Cf. D.B. i. 262*b*, in which the reeve of Chester is described as having the authority to summon one man from every hide for the repair of the bridge and city wall.

up to the eve of the Conquest.[1] But however this may be, the system of burghal support is in many ways remarkably analogous to the castleries or *castellaria* of later Anglo-Norman feudalism.[2] The two institutions were in no way connected except in so far as they represented similar responses to a similar need, yet in each, a fortification is surrounded by a definite district which contributes to the support or to the defence of the fortified place.

But gradually the Anglo-Saxon fortress system, which had been so vigorous in the later ninth and earlier tenth centuries, declined in significance. After about the mid-tenth century, references to burghs functioning in a military capacity became rare. The Danish power had been broken in England, the burghs themselves were evolving into centres of commerce and were losing their earlier military character, and the kings were depending on other means to defend the realm—mercenary warriors and a strong fleet, to name but two. Burghers might still man the town walls if their burgh were attacked, but by the eleventh century the burghs could no longer be considered a real part of the military system. When the Normans began to build their castles in England, they were introducing something essentially alien to the English scene. Norman castle organization was anticipated in a general way by the Old English burghal structure,[3] but in no sense was there any real continuity between the two. The castle network established by the Conqueror represented an innovation, and one of very considerable importance. To what extent it actually contributed to the military strength of the post-Conquest state is, as I have suggested, questionable.

The Anglo-Norman military organization was a synthesis of Old English and Norman elements. The Normans contributed the castle and the system of obligations which went

---

[1] Some such system is perhaps suggested by Maitland's 'garrison theory', but that hypothesis has been criticized sharply by several subsequent historians and cannot be accepted today as more than a guess. See Round, *Family Origins*, pp. 252–8.

[2] On these feudal castle districts, see Stenton, *E.F.*, pp. 192–4; Neilson, p. 132; Ellis, i. 180.

[3] There is, however, no clear Anglo-Saxon analogy to the Norman private castle.

along with it.[1] They were also responsible for the development of a feudal military system, although the tactics of the knights which that system produced may possibly have been similar to those of the pre-Conquest housecarles. Indeed, in their remarkable tendency to dismount before battle, the Anglo-Norman feudal warriors were evidently conforming to Anglo-Saxon practices. Nevertheless, the feudal recruitment system was unquestionably Norman rather than English.

On the other hand, the military force of the Norman kings owed to the Anglo-Saxons a powerful navy, a strong select infantry, and a financial system which made possible the hiring of mercenaries in large numbers. A serious and detailed study of the select fyrd's role in post-Conquest English warfare has yet to be made, but it is clear that this force was a crucial factor in the military history of that age, defending the interests of the Norman monarchy against rebellious barons in England and co-operating with the feudal army on continental campaigns.[2] The Anglo-Norman army, therefore, had both Saxon and Norman roots, and yet it very probably did not differ radically in strength from the English army on the eve of the Norman Conquest.[3] This being so, the military force of late-Saxon England was formidable indeed. It was impressive both in organization and in military effectiveness.

But before this appraisal of the late-Saxon army can be accepted, one last problem must be solved. Granted that the Anglo-Saxons fought well under Alfred and his immediate successors and that they fought at least courageously at Hastings, nevertheless the military history of Anglo-Saxon England can by no means be described as a happy or successful story. It has often been pointed out that the Anglo-Saxons were conquered once and almost twice by the Danes and again by the Normans. After 1066 the English were unconquerable, or at least they were never again overrun by a foreign foe. If the Old English army was as effective

---

[1] Yet the Old English fortress-work obligation was retained by the Normans, who applied it to castles.   [2] e.g. the Maine Campaign of 1073.

[3] It differed, in its organizational structure but not in its military effectiveness, as I shall attempt to show presently in an analysis of events surrounding the campaigns of 1066 culminating in the battle of Hastings.

as I have supposed, how does one account for its several spectacular failures?

In the first place, it is unfair to evaluate the late-Saxon military structure prior to the time that it achieved maturity. Only after the process of national unification under the Wessex monarchy had begun was there a military force that was national in character. When, in the mid-tenth century, unification had been fully achieved, the English kings were confronted with an exceptionally precarious and delicate military situation. The Norse menace remained very much alive; the Scandinavians continued to be the chief threat to the security of the realm. Yet as a result of previous invasions and settlements, large areas of England were heavily populated by Danes. This was particularly so in the north and west, where the danger of invasion was most acute. The loyalty of the inhabitants of these exposed areas could never be counted on. Many of the kingdom's leaders—the ealdormen who held positions of command in the army—were Danish or partly Danish. Later in the tenth century there occurred a misfortune which is liable to take place in any monarchy—the accession of a weakling king. In describing the military disasters of Ethelred's reign, the chroniclers allude constantly to these two factors: the weak and indecisive leadership of the monarchy, and the disloyalty of warriors—and particularly commanders—of Danish ancestry. In one famous passage the *Anglo-Saxon Chronicle* laments that when the fyrd should have been out it 'was on its way home. When the enemy was in the east, the fyrd was mustered in the west, and when it was in the south, the fyrd was in the north'.[1] This kind of condemnation of general strategic planning is a theme which recurs throughout the accounts of the warfare during Ethelred's reign, and it is accompanied by the theme of disloyalty. Again and again the ambiguous loyalties of Anglo-Danish leaders are reported to have resulted in disaster on the field. This was the case at Maldon,[2] and in numerous less illustrious engage-

---

[1] *A.S.C.*, E, A.D. 1009.

[2] *Battle of Maldon*, ll. 185 ff. The chief deserters were Godric, Godwin, and Godwig, sons of Odda, the latter name normally betraying a Norse origin: see E. Björkman, *Nordische Personennamen in England* (Halle, 1910), pp. 99–100.

ments of the period. In 1010, for example, during a battle between Ealdorman Ulfkytel of East Anglia and a Danish host, a Danish jarl named Thurkytel the Ant-Head, who was fighting on the English side, fled in the thick of the fight, causing a general panic in the East Anglian ranks.[1] Disloyal ealdormen such as Elfric and Eadric were constantly undermining the military effort. Time after time, the failure of Anglo-Saxon armies in battle during the reign of Ethelred is ascribed to disloyal leadership. Under the circumstances, the Danish successes during these years do not betoken an inadequate organization of the English army or the obsolescence of English tactics. The failure was the result of wretched overall leadership combined with widespread disloyalty resulting from divided allegiance on the part of the Anglo-Danes.

From the accession of Cnut to the death of the Confessor, England faced no overwhelming military challenges. Then came the events of 1066 which have often been taken as the ultimate example of England's military weakness. In this year King Edward died without direct heirs, and Earl Harold came to the throne without a strong claim to the succession. The counter-claims of Duke William and King Harold Hardrada are well known. Equally well known is the dangerous hostility of Tostig, Harold Godwinson's brother, and the rather hesitant support given by Earls Edwin and Morcar, whose family had long been a rival of the Godwin clan. All these factors were working against Harold Godwinson, but one vital thing he had in his favour: unlike the unhappy Ethelred, Harold was a strong and able leader. He was strong, but he was also remarkably unfortunate.

It is unnecessary to review here the military chronology of 1066, for the events of that year have been alluded to throughout this work and are undoubtedly familiar to every reader. The key dates are these: On 20 September the fyrd of the northern counties, led by Edwin of Mercia and Morcar of Northumbria, was defeated after a vigorous struggle by a Norse host led by the great warrior-king, Harold Hardrada of Norway. This defeat occurred at Fulford Gate near York. On 25 September Harold

1 *Fl. Wig.* i. 162.

Godwinson, having arrived in the north with an exceptionally large army recruited from most of the kingdom, annihilated the great Norse host at Stamford Bridge. Nineteen days later, on 14 October, Godwinson lay dead on the battlefield near Hastings. Within one month, the Anglo-Saxons fought three major battles, two of them of epic proportions. Hardrada, who was reputed to be the greatest general in Europe and who led to England a huge force of Scandinavian invaders, was defeated utterly, and had Hastings never occurred, Stamford Bridge would doubtless have gone down in history as one of the most significant and illustrious of English victories.

One point needs to be emphasized. The fighting of three important battles in two widely separated regions within a month would be most unusual in any era. But in the medieval period it was unique, for in this age large-scale pitched battles were quite uncommon. The Conqueror fought only two in his entire lifetime, the other being at Val-ès-dunes in 1047. During the century after Hastings Anglo-Norman armies fought only four major general engagements: at Tinchebrai (1106), Brémule (1119), Northallerton (1138), and Lincoln (1141). None of these battles was remotely comparable in scope to Hastings or Stamford Bridge. None was as long in duration or as heavy in casualties as the two great battles of Harold Godwinson. The military pressures on the last Saxon king defy comparison, and as one studies Harold's activities during September and October of 1066 in greater detail, the unprecedented magnitude of his dilemma becomes ever more evident.

Detailed accounts of Harold's movements during these critical days are available elsewhere and will not be repeated here. Suffice it to say that his army was obliged to march 250 miles from York to Hastings in less than two weeks, that this was the same army which had just emerged victorious from the bloody struggle at Stamford Bridge, and that therefore the military force which supported Harold at Hastings was far weaker than would ordinarily have been the case.[1] Not only does this fact follow logically from the

---

[1] This matter is discussed by Glover, pp. 10–12. See also F. W. Brooks, *The Battle of Stamford Bridge* (York, 1956).

circumstances of the campaign; it is stated explicitly by the chroniclers. The account of Florence of Worcester is particularly illuminating. He reports that the king led his army southward from York by forced marches, and that although he was fully aware that some of England's bravest men had fallen at Fulford and Stamford Bridge and that half his troops were not yet assembled, he proceeded without hesitation to meet the Normans in Sussex.[1] Florence adds that the battle was begun before a third of Harold's army was in fighting order, and that there were many desertions which continued right up to the hour of battle. Nevertheless, Florence remarks, King Harold made a determined resistance from the third hour of the day until nightfall, defending himself with such courage and steadfastness that the enemy almost despaired of taking his life.

William of Malmesbury corroborates this account, disclosing that, aside from his mercenaries, Harold had few of the people with him, and the *Anglo-Saxon Chronicle* reports that the battle of Hastings was fought before all of Harold's host had arrived.[2] Stenton remarks on the terrific strain caused by fighting three battles in one month. Fulford, he observes, destroyed the English army of the north and made aid by Edwin and Morcar at Hastings impossible.[3] Ferdinand Lot states that by the time of Hastings, Harold had little military strength; the north remained hostile and the west did not have time to send its contingent.[4] It should be added that the military strength of the west had probably already been pretty well exploited and exhausted in the struggle against Hardrada. At Hastings, the Anglo-Saxons seem to have been slightly more numerous than the Normans,[5] but their ranks were filled out by untrained peasants of the Sussex great fyrd. There can be no question but that the

---

[1] *Fl. Wig.* i. 227.

[2] Wm. Malm. ii. 282; *A.S.C.*, E, A.D. 1066.

[3] 'English Families and the Norman Conquest', *T.R.H.S.*, 4th ser., xxvi (1944), 2–3. The loyalty of Edwin and Morcar to Harold's cause has also been questioned, as, for example, by Stenton himself, who goes so far as to say that 'delay on Harold's part might only mean that Edwin and Morcar with their forces would have time to come over effectively to William's side': *William the Conqueror*, p. 193.

[4] *L'Art mil.* i. 283.

[5] Ibid. i. 284–5; Delbrück, iii. 153. The Normans probably had slightly less than 7,000 troops; the English, slightly over 8,000.

quality of William's army at Hastings was distinctly superior
to that of Harold's force, but to generalize from this fact
that the military strength of late-Saxon England was
inferior to that of eleventh-century Normandy would be a
serious mistake. The housecarles at Hastings were exhausted
from their previous campaign and their ranks had been
thinned considerably as a result of casualties at Stamford
Bridge. The select fyrd from nearly the entire kingdom had
been committed against Hardrada, and considering that
some of its members probably lacked mounts and were
therefore unable to keep pace on the forced march southward, this important component of the Old English army
must have made a particularly poor showing at Hastings.
It must also be borne in mind that most of the select-fyrd
soldiers had already served their two-month duty period
earlier in the same year and that consequently their recruitment and support system was subjected to an unusually
heavy strain. There remained the local peasants of the great
fyrd, the rudest component of the Anglo-Saxon military
system, fresh and rested, but largely untrained and poorly
armed. It was these men who, contrary to orders, abandoned
the English defensive position to chase the retiring bands of
enemy warriors and who were then cut down as the knights
wheeled and turned against them.[1]

The battle of Hastings therefore tells us virtually nothing

---

[1] The Norman tactic of the feigned flight is one of the most dramatic aspects of
the battle. Round writes: 'There is no feature of the famous battle more familiar
or more certain than that of the feigned retreat. . . . That there was a great feigned
flight, which induced a large portion of the English to break their formation and
pursue their foes, is beyond question' (*F.E.*, p. 380). Nevertheless, Glover has expressed doubt that any of the Norman retreats were actually feigned (p. 14 n. 2).
He adduces several reasons for his scepticism, the most important being that Norman
tactics at Hastings were too infantile to allow of any such sophisticated manœuvre.
As I have said elsewhere, I think that Glover takes an unduly pessimistic view of the
tactics at Hastings. They were, to be sure, more primitive than those of the great
engagements of the later Middle Ages, but I doubt that they were as disorganized
as he suggests. The studies of Verbruggen demonstrate that even in the eleventh
century medieval tactics show considerable sophistication, and that tactics similar to
the Norman feigned flight were used in other battles of the period: *Krijgskunst*, pp.
173–80. Nevertheless, as both Glover and Lemmon (*Field of Hastings*, pp. 47–48)
point out, a feigned flight is both difficult and dangerous, involving the risk of a
general panic and demanding co-ordination of a sort that may well have been beyond
the capabilities of William's army. Lemmon also suggests that the first English
charge may have been planned by Harold: ibid., pp. 46–47.

about the real strength of the late-Saxon army. All too often historians have generalized from the defeat of Harold's force. Round, for example, concluded that 'like Poland, England fell, in large measure, from the want of a strong rule, and from excess of liberty'.[1] And Professor Douglas speaks of 'the civilization which the Saxons produced but which they could no longer defend'.[2] But in fact, if any generalization can be made at all, it is that England's defeat was the result of an almost unbelievable run of bad luck. The society was not to blame, nor was the army.

It is interesting to examine in this connexion the reasons adduced by Professor Verbruggen for the success of the feudal cavalry in the twelfth and thirteenth centuries, and for the success of the Flemish, Scottish, and Swiss infantry in the fourteenth. Verbruggen points out that the feudal cavalrymen enjoyed a significant advantage as a result of their practice of charging in very close formation against an infantry force that was not so closely packed.[3] But how is it possible to imagine a tighter infantry formation than that of the Anglo-Saxon shield wall? Verbruggen also states that the development of a closely packed formation was one of the crucial factors in the successes of the Flemish, Swiss, and Scottish infantry of the later Middle Ages.[4] But again, they were anticipated, at least in a general way, by the Anglo-Saxons. Another factor in these fourteenth-century infantry victories, Verbruggen points out, was the evolution of efficient systems of organization by which foot-soldiers could be adequately provisioned and properly armed. Only in this way could they be expected to fight effectively.[5] But it has been the purpose of this present study to demonstrate that the Anglo-Saxons had exactly such an organization on the eve of the Norman Conquest.

The military structure of late-Saxon England was far from obsolete. It drew from the past, to be sure, but it also

---

[1] *F.E.*, p. 395. The section in which this statement appears (pp. 394–8) seems to me by far the weakest in Round's remarkable book.

[2] *Norman Conquest and British Historians*, p. 33. Such, also, are the opinions of Oman, Stenton, and many others. For the converse, see Glover, p. 18.

[3] 'Le Tactique militaire', *Revue du Nord*, xxix (1947), 177.

[4] *Krijgskunst*, pp. 291 ff., 298 ff.

[5] Ibid., pp. 250 ff., 282–3.

contributed much to the future. Like any other military force, it was less than invincible, but with adequate leadership and under even remotely normal circumstances it could hold its own against any army in Christendom. Its failure at Hastings was both tragic and awesome, but it was a failure that was basically fortuitous. Had Anglo-Saxon England been a highly organized feudal state it could have done no better if, indeed, as well.

BIBLIOGRAPHY

Note. This list includes only materials that have been cited in footnotes or are directly relevant to this study. General reference works are not included.

I. CHARTERS, RECORDS, LAWS, SOURCE COLLECTIONS, AND RELATED MATERIALS

Anglo-Saxon Charters, ed. A. J. Robertson, Cambridge, England, 1939.

Anglo-Saxon Wills, ed. Dorothy Whitelock, Cambridge, England, 1930.

Anglo-Saxon Writs, ed. Florence Elizabeth Harmer, Manchester, 1952.

The Bayeux Tapestry, ed. F. R. Fowke, London, 1898.

Boldon Buke, ed. William Greenwell, Surtees Soc., Durham, 1852.

The Book of Fees (Liber Feodorum), commonly called Testa de Nevill, 3 vols., Public Record Office, London, 1920–31.

Bracton, *De Legibus et Consuetudinibus Angliae*, ed. G. E. Woodbine, 4 vols., New Haven, 1915–42.

Bracton's Note Book, ed. F. W. Maitland, 3 vols., London, 1887.

British Borough Charters 1042–1216, ed. Adolphus Ballard, Cambridge, England, 1913.

Calendar of the Charter Rolls, 6 vols., Public Record Office, London, 1903–27.

Calendar of Inquisitions Post Mortem, Henry III–Edward III, Public Record Office, London, 1904– (in progress).

Calendar of the Patent Rolls, Public Record Office, London, 1891–. Published for every reign from Henry III through the Tudors.

Capitularia Regum Francorum, ed. Alfred Boretius and Victor Krause; *Monumenta Germaniae Historica*, 2 vols., Hanover, 1883–97.

Cartularium Saxonicum, ed. W. de G. Birch, 3 vols., London, 1885–93.

Chartularium Abbathiae de Novo Monasterio Ordinis Cicterciensis (Newminster Cartulary), ed. J. T. Fowler, Surtees Soc., Durham, 1878.

Close Rolls of the Reign of Henry III, 14 vols., Public Record Office, London, 1902–38.

Codex Diplomaticus Aevi Saxonici, ed. J. M. Kemble, 6 vols., London, 1839–48.

The Crawford Collection of Early Charters and Documents, ed. A. S. Napier and W. H. Stevenson, Oxford, 1895.

Diplomatarium Anglicum Aevi Saxonici, ed. Benjamin Thorpe, London, 1865.

Documents Illustrative of the Social and Economic History of the Danelaw (normally cited as *Danelaw Charters*), ed. F. M. Stenton, in *Records of the Social and Economic History of England and Wales*, vol. v, London, 1920.

Domesday Book: Liber Censualis Willelmi Primi, ed. Abraham Furley and Henry Ellis, Record Commission, 4 vols., 1783–1816.

154 BIBLIOGRAPHY

The Domesday Monachorum of Christ Church, Canterbury, ed. D. C. Douglas, Royal Historical Society, London, 1944.

Early Yorkshire Charters, ed. William Farrer and C. T. Clay, Edinburgh and Wakefield, 1914– (in progress).

An Eleventh-Century Inquisition of St. Augustine's, Canterbury, ed. Adolphus Ballard, in *Records of the Social and Economic History of England and Wales*, vol. iv, London, 1920.

English and Norse Documents Relating to the Reign of Ethelred the Unready, ed. Margaret Ashdown, Cambridge, England, 1930.

Facsimilies of Ancient Charters in the British Museum, 4 parts, London, 1873–8.

Facsimilies of Anglo-Saxon Manuscripts, ed. W. B. Sanders, 3 parts, Ordnance Survey Office, Southampton, 1878–84.

Facsimilies of Early Charters from Northamptonshire Collections, ed. F. M. Stenton, in *Publications of the Northamptonshire Record Society*, vol. iv, Lincoln and London, 1930.

Facsimilies of Royal and Other Charters in the British Museum, vol. i, William I–Richard I, ed. George F. Warner and Henry J. Ellis, London, 1903.

Feodarium Prioratus Dunelmensis, ed. W. Greenwell, Surtees Soc., Durham, 1871.

Feudal Documents from the Abbey of Bury St. Edmunds, ed. D. C. Douglas, in *Records of the Social and Economic History of England and Wales*, vol. viii, London, 1932.

Die Gesetze der Angelsachsen, ed. Felix Liebermann, 3 vols., Halle, 1903–16.

Halmota Prioratus Dunelmensis: Extracts from the Halmote Court or Manor Rolls of the Prior and Convent of Durham, 1296–1384, ed. W. H. D. Longstaffe and John Booth, Surtees Soc., Durham, 1889.

A Hand-Book to the Land-Charters and Other Saxonic Documents, ed. John Earle, Oxford, 1888.

Hemingi Chartularium Ecclesiae Wigorniensis, ed. Thomas Hearne, 2 vols., Oxford, 1723.

Inquisitio Comitatus Cantabrigiensis . . . subjicitur Inquisitio Eliensis, ed. N. E. S. A. Hamilton, London, 1876.

The Kalendar of Abbot Samson of Bury St. Edmunds and Related Documents, ed. R. H. C. Davis, Royal Historical Society (Camden Soc., 3rd ser., vol. lxxxiv), London, 1954.

The Laws of the Earliest English Kings, ed. F. L. Attenborough, Cambridge, England, 1922.

The Laws of the Kings of England from Edmund to Henry I, ed. A. J. Robertson, Cambridge, England, 1925.

Liber Niger Scaccarii, ed. Thomas Hearne, 2nd ed., London, 1771.

The Lincolnshire Domesday and the Lindsey Survey, ed. C. W. Foster and Thomas Longley, in *Publications of the Lincolnshire Record Society*, vol. xix, Horncastle, 1924.

Monasticon Anglicanum, new edition, ed. by John Caley, H. Ellis, and B. Bandinell, 6 vols. in 8, London, 1846.

Pipe Roll Society, Publications, London, 1884– (in progress). Includes Pipe Rolls from 5 Henry II onward and other important source materials.

Placita Anglo-Normannica: Law Cases from William I to Richard I preserved in Historical Records, ed. M. M. Bigelow, Boston, 1879.

The Red Book of the Exchequer, ed. Hubert Hall, Rolls Series, 3 vols., London, 1896.

Regesta Regum Anglo-Normannorum, 1066–1154; vol. i, *Regesta Willelmi Conquestoris et Willelmi Rufi, 1066–1100*, ed. H. W. C. Davis, Oxford, 1913; vol. ii, *Regesta Henrici Primi, 1100–1135*, ed. C. Johnson and H. A. Cronne, Oxford, 1956.

Registrum Antiquissimum of the Cathedral Church of Lincoln, ed. C. W. Foster and Kathleen Major, in *Publications of the Lincoln Record Society*, Hereford, 1931– (in progress).

Rotuli Chartarum, 1199–1216, ed. T. D. Hardy, Record Commissioners, London, 1837.

Rotuli Litterarum Clausarum, ed. T. D. Hardy, Record Commissioners, 2 vols., London, 1833–44.

Scriptores Rerum Danicarum Medii Aevi, ed. J. Langebek *et al.*, 9 vols., Copenhagen, 1772–1878.

Select Charters and Other Illustrations of English Constitutional History, ed. William Stubbs, 9th ed., rev. and ed. H. W. C. Davis, Oxford, 1913.

Select English Historical Documents of the Ninth and Tenth Centuries, ed. F. E. Harmer, Cambridge, England, 1914.

Sir Christopher Hatton's Book of Seals, ed. L. C. Loyd and D. M. Stenton, Oxford, 1950.

Transcripts of Charters relating to Gilbertine Houses, ed. F. M. Stenton, in *Publications of the Lincoln Record Society*, vol. xviii, Horncastle, 1922.

Two Chartularies of the Priory of St. Peter at Bath, ed. William Hunt, in *Publications of the Somerset Record Society*, vol. vii, London, 1893.

Wulfric Spot's Will, ed. C. G. O. Bridgeman, in *Collections for a History of Staffordshire* (William Salt Archaeological Soc.), vol. 1916, pp. 1–66, London, 1918.

II. NARRATIVE SOURCES

Ælred of Rievaulx, *Relatio de Standardo*, ed. R. H. Howlett, in *Chronicles of the Reigns of Stephen, Henry II, and Richard I*, Rolls Series, 4 vols., London, 1884–9, vol. iii.

Anglo-Saxon Chronicle: Two of the Saxon Chronicles Parallel, ed. Charles Plummer, 2 vols., Oxford, 1892. Other useful editions: *The Anglo-Saxon Chronicle*, ed. Benjamin Thorpe, Rolls Series, 2 vols., London, 1861; *The Anglo-Saxon Chronicle*, trans. G. N. Garmonsway, London, 1953; *The Peterborough Chronicle*, trans. H. A. Rositzke (see p. 156).

The Battle of Maldon, ed. E. V. Gordon, 2nd ed., London, 1949. Other useful editions in E. D. Laborde, *Byrhtnoth and Maldon*, London, 1936, and *English and Norse Documents*, ed. Margaret Ashdown (see p. 154).

Chronicon Monasterii de Abingdon, ed. J. Stevenson, Rolls Series, 2 vols., London, 1858.

Chronicon Petroburgense, ed. T. Stapleton, Camden Soc., London, 1849. The appendix includes two valuable sources: the Peterborough *Liber Niger* and the *Descriptio Militum de Abbatia de Burgo*. This work is not to be confused with *The Peterborough Chronicle*, ed. Rositzke (see *The Peterborough Chronicle*, below).

Corpus Poeticum Boreale, ed. G. Vigfússon and F. Y. Powell, 2 vols., Oxford, 1883.

Flateyjarbók, ed. C. R. Unger, 3 vols., Christiania, 1860–8.

Florence of Worcester, *Chronicon ex Chronicis*, ed. Benjamin Thorpe, 2 vols., London, 1848–9.

Geoffrey Gaimar, *L'Estorie des Engles*, ed. T. D. Hardy and C. T. Martin, Rolls Series, London, 1888–9.

Guy of Amiens, *Carmen de Bello Hastingensi*, ed. J. A. Giles, in *Scriptores Rerum Gestarum Willelmi Conquestoris*, London, 1845.

Henry of Huntingdon, *Historia Anglorum*, ed. T. Arnold, Rolls Series, London, 1879.

Islandic Sagas and Other Historical Documents Relating to the Settlement of the Northmen in the British Isles, ed. G. Vigfússon and G. Dasent, Rolls Series, 4 vols., London, 1887–94.

Itinerarium Peregrinorum et Gesta Regis Ricardi, ed. William Stubbs, in *Chronicles and Memorials of the Reign of Richard I*, Rolls Series, 2 vols., London, 1864–5, vol. i.

Lives of Edward the Confessor, ed. H. R. Luard, Rolls Series, London, 1858.

Den norskislandske Skjaldedigtning, ed. F. Jónsson, 4 vols., Copenhagen, 1912–15.

Ordericus Vitalis, *Historia Ecclesiastica*, ed. Auguste Le Prévost, Société de l'histoire de France, 5 vols., Paris, 1838–55.

The Peterborough Chronicle, trans. H. A. Rositzke, in *Records of Civilization*, no. xliv, New York, 1951. This is the E manuscript of the *Anglo-Saxon Chronicle*, ending in 1154. It is to be distinguished from later Peterborough Chronicles edited by Stapleton (A.D. 1122–1295, see above), Joseph Sparke, *Historiae Coenobii Burgensis Scriptores Varii*, London, 1723; and W. T. Mellows, *The Chronicle of Hugh Candidus*, London, 1949.

Richard of Hexham, *Historia de Gestis Regis Stephani et de Bello de Standardo*, ed. Richard Howlett, in *Chronicles of the Reigns of Stephen, Henry II, and Richard I*, Rolls Series, 4 vols., London, 1884–9, vol. iii.

The Saga of King Olaf Tryggwason, ed. J. Sephton, London, 1895.

Saxo Grammaticus, *Gesta Danorum*, ed. J. Olrik and H. Raeder, Copenhagen, 1931.

Simeon of Durham, *Opera Omnia*, ed. Thomas Arnold, Rolls Series, 2 vols., London, 1882–5. Includes *Historia Regum*, *Historia Dunelmensis Ecclesiae*, and other important sources.

Snorri Sturluson, *Heimskringla*, ed. Finnur Jónsson, Copenhagen, 1911. Another edition ed. E. Monsen and trans. A. H. Smith, Cambridge, England, 1932.

Suger, *Vie de Louis le Gros*, ed. Auguste Molinier, in *Collection de textes pour servir à l'étude et à l'enseignement de l'histoire*, Paris, 1887.

William of Jumièges, *Gesta Normannorum Ducum*, ed. Jean Marx, Société de l'histoire de Normandie, Paris, 1914.

William of Malmesbury, *Gesta Pontificum Anglorum*, ed. N. E. S. A. Hamilton, Rolls Series, London, 1870.

—— *Gesta Regum Anglorum*, ed. William Stubbs, Rolls Series, 2 vols., 1887–9.

—— *Vita Wulfstani*, ed. R. R. Darlington, Royal Historical Society (Camden Soc., 3rd ser., vol. xl), London, 1928.

William of Poitiers, *Gesta Willelmi Ducis Normannorum et Regis Anglorum*, ed. J. A. Giles, in *Scriptores Rerum Gestarum Willelmi Conquestoris*, London, 1845.

III. SECONDARY WORKS

The Anglo-Saxons: Studies in some Aspects of their History and Culture presented to Bruce Dickins, ed. Peter Clemoes, London, 1959.

Armitage, Ella S., *The Early Norman Castles of the British Isles*, London, 1912.

Ballard, Adolphus, *The Domesday Boroughs*, Oxford, 1904.

—— *The Domesday Inquest*, London, 1906.

Baring, F. H., 'The Hidation of Northamptonshire in 1086', *E.H.R.* xvii (1902), 76–83.

—— 'The Pre-Domesday Hidation of Northamptonshire', ibid., pp. 470–9.

—— *Domesday Tables for the Counties of Surrey, Berkshire, Middlesex, Hertford, Buckingham, and Bedford, and for the New Forest*, London, 1909.

Barlow, Frank, *The Feudal Kingdom of England, 1042–1216*, in *A History of England*, ed. W. N. Medlicott, vol. ii, London, &c., 1955.

Beeler, John H., 'Castles and Strategy in Norman and Early Angevin England', *Speculum*, xxxi (1956), 581–601.

Birch, W. de G., *Domesday Book*, London, 1887.

Björkman, E., *Nordische Personennamen in England in alt- und frühmittelenglischer Zeit*, Halle, 1910.

Blair, Peter Hunter, *An Introduction to Anglo-Saxon England*, Cambridge, England, 1956.

Brooks, F. W., *The English Naval Forces, 1199–1272*, London, [1933].

—— *The Battle of Stamford Bridge*, York, 1956.

Brownbill, J., 'The Tribal Hidage', *E.H.R.* xl (1925), 497–503.

Burne, A. H., *More Battlefields of England*, London, 1952.

Cam, Helen M., *Liberties and Communities in Medieval England*, Cambridge, England, 1944.

Chadwick, H. M., *Studies on Anglo-Saxon Institutions*, Cambridge, England, 1905.

—— *The Origin of the English Nation*, Cambridge, England, 1924.

Chambers, R. W., *England before the Norman Conquest*, London, 1926.

Clapham, J. H., 'The Horsing of the Danes', *E.H.R.* xxv (1910), 287–93.

Corbett, W. J., 'The Tribal Hidage', *T.R.H.S.*, n.s., xiv (1900), 187–230.

Craster, H. H. E., 'The Red Book of Durham', *E.H.R.* xl (1925), 504–32.

Darby, H. C., *The Domesday Geography of Eastern England*, Cambridge, England, 1952.

Darlington, R. R., 'The Last Phase of Anglo-Saxon History', *History*, n.s., xxii (1937), 1–13.

Davis, R. H. C., 'East Anglia and the Danelaw', *T.R.H.S.*, 5th ser., v (1955), 23–39.

Delbrück, H., *Geschichte der Kriegskunst im Rahmen der politischen Geschichte*, 2nd ed., 3 vols., Berlin, 1923.

Demarest, E. B., 'The Firma Unius Noctis', *E.H.R.* xxxv (1920), 78–89.

Dodwell, Barbara, 'East Anglian Commendation', ibid. lxiii (1948), 289–306.

The Domesday Geography of Midland England, ed. H. C. Darby and I. B. Terrett, Cambridge, England, 1954.

Domesday Studies, ed. P. Edward Dove, 2 vols., London, 1888–91.

Douglas, D. C., *The Social Structure of Medieval East Anglia*, in *Oxford Studies in Social and Legal History*, ed. Paul Vinogradoff, vol. ix, Oxford, 1927.

—— 'The Norman Conquest and English Feudalism', *Economic History Review*, ix (1939), 128–43.

—— *The Norman Conquest and British Historians*, Glasgow, 1946.

Drummond, J. D., *Studien zur Kriegsgeschichte Englands im 12. Jahrhundert*, Berlin, 1905.

Ellis, Henry, *A General Introduction to Domesday Book*, Record Commissioners, 2 vols., London, 1833.

Eyton, R. W., *A Key to Domesday, Exemplified by an Analysis and Digest of the Dorset Survey*, London, 1878.

Feilitzen, Olof von, *The Pre-Conquest Personal Names of Domesday Book*, Uppsala, 1937.

Freeman, E. A., *The History of the Norman Conquest of England*, 6 vols., Oxford, 1867–79.

Galbraith, V. H., 'An Episcopal Land-Grant of 1085', *E.H.R.* xliv (1929), 353–72.

Gibbs, Marion, *Feudal Order*, London, 1949.

Glover, Richard, 'English Warfare in 1066', *E.H.R.* lxvii (1952), 1–18.

Grousset, René, *Histoire des croisades et du royaume franc de Jérusalem*, 3 vols., Paris, 1934–6.

Haskins, C. H., *Norman Institutions*, in *Harvard Historical Studies*, vol. xxiv, Cambridge, Mass., 1918.

Hasted, Edward, *The History and Topographical Survey of Kent*, 2nd ed., 12 vols., Canterbury, 1797–1801.

Hodgkin, R. H., *A History of the Anglo-Saxons*, 2 vols., Oxford, 1935.

Hollings, Marjory, 'The Survival of the Five-Hide Unit in the Western Midlands', *E.H.R.* lxiii (1948), 453–87.

Hollister, C. W., 'The Annual Term of Military Service in Medieval England', *Medievalia et Humanistica*, xiii (1960), 40–47.

—— 'The Significance of Scutage Rates in Eleventh- and Twelfth-Century England', *E.H.R.* lxxv (1960), 577–88.

—— 'The Five-Hide Unit and the Old English Military Obligation', *Speculum*, xxxvi (1961), 61–74.

—— 'The Norman Conquest and the Genesis of English Feudalism', *A.H.R.* lxvi (1961), 641–63.

Hoyt, Robert S., *The Royal Demesne in English Constitutional History: 1066–1272*, Ithaca, N.Y., 1950.

Inman, A. H., *Domesday and Feudal Statistics*, London, 1900.

John, Eric, 'The Imposition of the Common Burdens on the Lands of the English Church', *Bulletin of the Institute of Historical Research*, xxxi (1958), 117–29.

—— *Land Tenure in Early England*, Welwyn Garden City, Herts., 1960. (This significant study did not become available to me in time for use in preparing the present book.)

Jolliffe, J. E. A., 'Northumbrian Institutions', *E.H.R.* xli (1926), 1–42.

—— 'The Hidation of Kent', ibid. xliv (1929), 612–18.

—— *Pre-Feudal England: The Jutes*, London, 1933.

—— *The Constitutional History of Medieval England from the English Settlement to 1485*, New York and London, 1937.

Laborde, E. D., *Byrhtnoth and Maldon*, London, 1936.

Lapsley, G. T., 'Cornage and Drengage', *A.H.R.*, ix (1904), 670–95.

—— 'Mr. Jolliffe's Construction of Early Constitutional History', *History*, n.s., xxiii (1938), 1–11.

Larson, Laurence M., *The King's Household in England before the Norman Conquest*, in *Bulletin of the University of Wisconsin*, no. 100, Madison, Wisc., 1904.

Little, A. G., 'Gesiths and Thegns', *E.H.R.* iv (1889), 723–9.

Lot, Ferdinand, 'Le Jugum, le manse et les exploitations agricoles', in *Mélanges d'histoire offerts à Henri Pirenne*, Brussels, &c., 1926.

—— *Les Invasions germaniques. La pénétration mutuelle du monde barbare et du monde romain*, Paris, 1945.

—— *L'Art militaire et les armées au moyen âge en Europe et dans le Proche Orient*, 2 vols., Paris, 1946.

Loyn, H. R., 'The Term *Ealdorman* in the Translations Prepared at the Time of King Alfred', *E.H.R.* lxviii (1953), 513–25.

—— 'Gesiths and Thegns in Anglo-Saxon England from the Seventh to the Tenth Century', *E.H.R.* lxx (1955), 529–49.

Lyon, Bryce, *A Constitutional and Legal History of Medieval England*, New York, 1960.

Madox, Thomas, *The History and Antiquities of the Exchequer in England*, London, 1711.

Maitland, Frederic William, 'Northumbrian Tenures', *E.H.R.* v (1890), 625–32.

—— *Domesday Book and Beyond*, Cambridge, England, 1897.

—— *Township and Borough*, Cambridge, England, 1898.

Mangoldt-Gaudlitz, Hans von, *Die Reiterei in den germanischen und fränkischen Heeren bis zum Ausgang der deutschen Karolinger*, in *Arbeiten zur deutschen Rechts- und Verfassungsgeschichte*, vol. iv, Berlin, 1922.

Mann, James, *An Outline of Arms and Armour in England*, London, 1960.

Mitchell, Sydney Knox, *Taxation in Medieval England*, ed. Sidney Painter, in *Yale Historical Publications, Studies*, vol. xv, New Haven, Conn., 1951.

Morris, William A., 'A Mention of Scutage in 1100', *E.H.R.* xxxvi (1921), 45–46.

—— *The Medieval English Sheriff to 1300*, Manchester, &c., 1927.

—— *A Constitutional History of England to 1216*, New York, 1930.

Murray, K. M. E., *The Constitutional History of the Cinque Ports*, Manchester, 1935.

—— 'Faversham and the Cinque Ports', *T.R.H.S.* 4th ser., xviii (1935), 53–84.

—— 'Dengemarsh and the Cinque Ports', *E.H.R.* liv (1939), 664–73.

Neilson, Nellie, *Customary Rents*, in *Oxford Studies in Social and Legal History*, ed. Paul Vinogradoff, vol. ii, Oxford, 1910 (bound together with Stenton, *Types of Manorial Structure*, see p. 161).

Oleson, T. J., *The Witenagemot in the Reign of Edward the Confessor*, London, 1955.

Oman, Charles, *A History of the Art of War in the Middle Ages*, 2nd ed., 2 vols., London, 1924.

—— *England Before the Norman Conquest*, 9th ed., London, 1949.

—— *The Art of War in the Middle Ages*, rev. and ed. John H. Beeler, Ithaca, N.Y., 1953.

Painter, Sidney, *Studies in the History of the English Feudal Barony*, in *The Johns Hopkins University Studies in Historical and Political Science*, series lxi, no. 3, Baltimore, Md., 1943.

Petit-Dutaillis, Charles, and Georges Lefebvre, *Studies and Notes Supplementary to Stubbs' Constitutional History*, 3 vols., Manchester, 1923–9.

—— *The Feudal Monarchy in France and England from the Tenth to the Thirteenth Century*, trans. E. D. Hunt, London, 1936.

Phillpotts, Bertha S., 'The Battle of Maldon: Some Danish Affinities', *Modern Language Review*, xxiv (1929), 172–90.

Pieri, Piero, 'Alcune quistione sopra la fanteria in Italia nel periodo comunale', *Rivista storica italiana*, l (1933), 533–614.

Pollock, Frederick, and F. W. Maitland, *The History of English Law Before the Time of Edward I*, 2nd ed., 2 vols., Cambridge, England, 1898.

Poole, A. L., *Obligations of Society in the XII and XIII Centuries*, Oxford, 1946.

Prestwich, J. O., 'War and Finance in the Anglo-Norman State', *T.R.H.S.*, 5th ser., iv (1954), 19–43.

Pryce, T. Davies, and Ella S. Armitage, 'The Alleged Norman Origin of "Castles" in England', *E.H.R.* xx (1905), 703–18.

Ramsay, J. H., *The Foundations of England*, 2 vols., London, 1898.

Reid, R. R., 'Baronage and Thanage', *E.H.R.* xxxv (1920), 161–99.

Ritter, H., '*La Parure des Cavaliers* und die Literatur über die ritterlichen Künste', *Der Islam*, xviii (1929), 116–54.

Round, John Horace, *Feudal England*, London, 1895.

—— 'Military Tenure before the Conquest', *E.H.R.* xii (1897), 492–4.

—— *The Commune of London and Other Studies*, Westminster, 1899.

—— 'The Hidation of Northamptonshire', *E.H.R.* xv (1900), 78–86.

—— 'The Domesday Hidation of Essex', *E.H.R.* xxix (1914), 477–9.

—— *Family Origins and Other Studies*, ed. William Page, London, 1930.

—— 'Danegeld and the Finance of Domesday', in *Domesday Studies*, ed. P. E. Dove (see p. 158), i. 77–142.

Rübel, Karl, 'Fränkisches und spätrömisches Kriegswesen', *Bonner Jahrbücher*, cxiv (1906), 134–58.

Sawyer, P. H., 'The Density of the Danish Settlement in England', *University of Birmingham Historical Journal*, vi (1957), 1–18.

Sayles, G. O., *The Medieval Foundations of England*, Philadelphia, 1950.

Seebohm, Frederic, *The English Village Community*, 4th ed., London, 1890.

Smail, R. C., *Crusading Warfare*, Cambridge, England, 1956.

—— 'Art of War', in *Medieval England*, ed. A. L. Poole, 2 vols., Oxford, 1958, i. 128–67.

Smith, Harold R., *Saxon England: A Political History of the English Dark Ages*, London, 1953.

Spatz, W., *Die Schlacht von Hastings*, Berlin, 1896.

Steenstrup, J. C. H. R., *Normannerne*, 4 vols., Copenhagen, 1876–82. Especially vol. iv, *Danelag*.

Stenton, F. M., *William the Conqueror and the Rule of the Normans*, New York and London, 1908.

—— *The Early History of the Abbey of Abingdon*, Reading, 1913.

—— *The Development of the Castle in England and Wales*, Historical Association leaflet no. 22, London, 1910.

—— *Types of Manorial Structure in the Northern Danelaw*, in *Oxford Studies in Social and Legal History*, ed. Paul Vinogradoff, vol. ii, Oxford, 1910 (bound together with Neilson, *Customary Rents*, see above).

Stenton, F. M., *The Danes in England*, in *Proceedings of the British Academy*, vol. xiii, London, 1927.

—— *The First Century of English Feudalism, 1066–1166*, Oxford, 1932 (a new edition of this great study appeared in 1961).

—— 'English Families and the Norman Conquest', *T.R.H.S.*, 4th ser., xxvi (1944), 1–12 (Presidential address, 1943).

—— *Anglo-Saxon England*, in *Oxford History of England*, ed. G. N. Clark, vol. ii, 2nd ed., Oxford, 1947.

—— *Latin Charters of the Anglo-Saxon Period*, Oxford, 1955.

Stephenson, Carl, *Borough and Town*, Cambridge, Mass., 1933.

—— 'The Origin and Significance of Feudalism', *A.H.R.* xlvi (1941), 788–812.

—— 'Feudalism and its Antecedents in England', ibid. xlviii (1943), 245–65.

Stevenson, W. H., 'Burh-geat-setl', *E.H.R.* xii (1897), 489–92.

—— 'Trinoda Necessitas', ibid. xxix (1914), 689–703.

Stewart-Brown, R., ' "Bridge-Work" at Chester', *E.H.R.* liv (1939), 83–87.

Stubbs, William A., *A Constitutional History of England*, 5th ed., 3 vols., Oxford, 1891–6.

Tait, James, 'Large Hides and Small Hides', *E.H.R.* xvii (1902), 280–2.

—— *The Medieval English Borough*, Manchester, 1936.

Taylor, C. S., 'The Origin of the Mercian Shires', in *Gloucestershire Studies*, ed. H. P. R. Finberg, Leicester, 1957, pp. 17–45. Originally printed in *Bristol and Gloucestershire Archaeological Society, Transactions*, xxi [1898], 32–57.

Thompson, A. Hamilton, *Military Architecture in England during the Middle Ages*, London, 1912.

Verbruggen, J. F., 'La Tactique militaire des armées de chevaliers', *Revue du Nord*, xxix (1947), 161–80.

—— *De Krijgskunst in West-Europa in den Middeleeuwen*, Brussels, 1954.

The Victoria History of the Counties of England, Westminster, 1900– (in progress). The Domesday introductions, usually printed in the first volume of each county history, were especially useful.

Vinogradoff, Paul, *Villainage in England*, Oxford, 1892.

—— *English Society in the Eleventh Century*, Oxford, 1908.

—— *The Growth of the Manor*, 2nd ed., London, 1911.

Wedgwood, J. C., 'Early Staffordshire History', in *Collections for a History of Staffordshire* (William Salt Archaeological Society), vol. 1916 pp. 138–208, London, 1918.

Wilkinson, Bertie, 'Freeman and the Crisis of 1051', *Bulletin of the John Rylands Library*, xxii (1938), 368–87.

—— 'Northumbrian Separatism in 1065', *Bulletin of the John Rylands Library*, xxiii (1939), 504–26.

Wilson, D. M., *The Anglo-Saxons*, Ancient Peoples and Places Series, vol. xvi, New York, 1960.

INDEX

acres; number of, in hides, 40; not assessment units, 41; no fixed number in hides or manses, 43.

Ælfgar, Earl, 17, 94, 136.

Ælfhelm of Wratting, 113.

Ælfric, abp. of Canterbury, 108, 110, 111.

Ælfweard, abbot of Evesham, 62.

Æthelmar, tenant of Evesham Abbey, 62.

Æthelric, bp. of Sherborne, 114.

Æthelstan the Fat, tenant of Worcester, 71.

Æthelwold, a *cniht* of Worcester, 82.

Æthelwulf, ealdorman of Berkshire, 93.

aids, assessed by hides, 41, 47.

Alfred, king of Wessex, 85, 103, 142, 145; Dooms of, 81.

Alfwold, bp. of Crediton, 108, 109, 113.

alodarii, 80.

Anglo-Danes, 146–7.

Anglo-Saxon Chronicle, 7, 14, 15, 16, 17, 18, 29, 41, 72, 89, 92, 94, 95, 103, 106, 107, 109, 110, 113, 118, 119, 120, 122, 123, 124, 135, 136, 137, 143, 146, 149.

Ansford, tenant of Peterborough Abbey, 71.

Archenfield (Hereford), 33.

archers, 128, 129, 134, 136, 137, 138–9.

army geld, 50; see also *heregeld*.

arrière-ban, 129, 139.

Arsouf, battle of, 134.

Artois, 28.

Assize of Arms, 27, 57, 58.

Baldwin V, count of Flanders, 126.

Barnstaple, 41, 45, 105.

Bath, hidage of, 46.

Battle, abbot of, 120.

Battle of Maldon, *see* Maldon, battle of.

Bayeux Tapestry, 31, 136.

Beaumont, 90.

Bedford, hidage of, 46.

Beeler, J. H., 141.

Beneficial hidation, 55–57.

Benevento, battle of, 130.

Beorn, Earl, 15.

Beornwulf, thegn of Winchester, 71.

Berkshire, recruitment system in, 38–41, 43–44, 47–49, 64, 69, 73, 79, 80, 86, 88, 90, 104, 107; size of hides in, 40, 41 and n., 47; invulnerability of, 40, 42; royal demesne in, 53, 54; hidation of, 55, 80; neglect of summons in, 66–68; population of, 80; men of, 93; private lordship in, 96.

Bigelow, M. M., 6.

bishops, as military leaders, 93, 110; as leaders of fleet, 124.

Blackwater, river, 115.

Boatswains, 22, 64, 107.

Boldon Buke, 35, 36.

bordarii, 80.

boroughs, *see* burghs.

Bourg Théroulde, battle of, 131.

Bouvines, battle of, 130, 134.

bovates, as recruitment units, 50; in East Anglia, 53.

Bracton, 40.

Brémule, battle of, 130, 131, 148.

Breton mercenaries, 19.

Bridport, 21; hidage of, 46.

bridge repair, 59–63, 70, 71, 72, 82, 99, 101, 143.

Brunanburh, battle of, 132 n.

Buckingham, hidage of, 46 n.

Buckinghamshire, 112.

Burghal Hidage, 72, 143.

burghs, 142–4.

burhwaru, 18.

bur-thegn, 74.

Bury St. Edmunds, abbey of, 72, 97.

butsecarls, 18, 23, 76, 108.

Byrhtnoth, 10–11, 63, 65, 75, 76 n. 93, 127–8, 135 n.

Cam, H. M., 112.

Cambridge, hidage of, 46.

Cambridgeshire, five-hide unit in, 48; men of, 92; 300-hide unit in, 112.

Carolingian kings, 42.

carucates, 40; as recruitment units, 49–52; in East Anglia, 52–53.

castellaria, 144.

castlemen, 36 n.

PRINTED IN GREAT BRITAIN
AT THE UNIVERSITY PRESS, OXFORD
BY VIVIAN RIDLER
PRINTER TO THE UNIVERSITY